Shadows of Realism

Shadows of Realism

*Dramaturgy and the Theories
and Practices of Modernism*

Nancy Kindelan

Westport, Connecticut
London

The Library of Congress has cataloged the hardcover edition as follows:

Kindelan, Nancy Anne.
    Shadows of realism : dramaturgy and the theories and practices of
modernism / Nancy Kindelan.
        p.   cm.—(Contributions in drama and theatre studies, ISSN
0163–3821 ; no. 68)
    Includes bibliographical references and index.
    ISBN 0–313–29736–3 (alk. paper)
    1. Theater—Production and direction.   2. Drama—Technique.
3. Modernism (Literature) I. Title. II. Series.
PN2053.K534   1996
792'.023—dc20   95–20545

British Library Cataloguing in Publication Data is available.

A hardcover edition of *Shadows of Realism* is available
from Greenwood Press, an imprint of Greenwood Publishing
Group, Inc. (Contributions in Drama and Theatre Studies,
Number 68; ISBN 0–313–29736–3).

Library of Congress Catalog Card Number: 95–20545
ISBN: 0–275–95471–4 (pbk.)

First published in 1996

Praeger Publishers, 88 Post Road West, Westport, CT 06881
An imprint of Greenwood Publishing Group, Inc.

Printed in the United States of America

The paper used in this book complies with the
Permanent Paper Standard issued by the National
Information Standards Organization (Z39.48–1984).

10 9 8 7 6 5 4 3 2 1

To

M. M. C.
J. J. K.
F. A. K.

for inspiration, guidance, and encouragement

Contents

Acknowledgments

I owe thanks to many, but especially to those artists whom I interviewed, who allowed me to reap the benefits of their many years of experience bringing the playscript forward to production. Those who influenced this study are Jane Alexander, Robert Brustein, John Conklin, Michael Dixon, Olympia Dukakis, Ben Edwards, Zelda Fichandler, Arden Fingerhut, Jane Greenwood, Tori Haring-Smith, Richard Jenkins, Jon Jory, Shirley Knight, Mark Lamos, Ming Cho Lee, Emily Mann, Robert Morgan, Lester Polakov, Thomas Skelton, Anthony Taccone, Jennifer Tipton, and Douglas Wager.

Many colleagues, friends, and students have helped me bring my manuscript forward. My thanks to Dr. William Elwood and Dr. Stuart Hecht for their helpful suggestions, thoughtful observations, and encouragement. I am especially grateful to William Elwood for the years of mentoring that are reflected in the core of this work. To Dr. Kim Marra, Dr. William Faissler, Meredith Alexander, and the late Jim Moran, I would like to add my gratitude for reading my manuscript, discussing my ideas, and helping me place the finishing touches on the final draft. I would like to thank Lynda St. James for her excellent transcription of my taped interviews. I would also like to acknowledge the support of the Office of the Provost and the College of Arts and Sciences at Northeastern University in awarding me several grants and a research sabbatical. These awards made my early research possible.

Finally, to my husband, Dr. Charles Combs, I express my deepest gratitude for his endless patience and support, as well as his editorial comments and suggestions.

Shadows of Realism

1

Re-experiencing the Playscript

Theatre artists continue to be challenged by the poetic vision of such "modern" playwrights as Ibsen, Chekhov, and Williams. These playwrights, among others, are of particular concern to contemporary actors, directors, and designers who pursue the play's poetry through the creation of a metaphorical mise-en-scène. Because they are not interested in reproducing past productions, these artists explore resonating images, explode the restraints of naturalism, and create productions that speak to the contemporary audience. The theories and practices of modernism have stimulated the twentieth-century actor, director, and designer to ponder the daunting task of "reimaging" the classical playscript.

Artists who prefer to explore the poetry within the playtext rather than to create static works of art on stage have embraced the aesthetic of either modernism or postmodernism, yet many find it difficult to distinguish between the two. Perhaps one way to untangle this maze of controversy is to determine how the cultural climate that informs modernism and postmodernism affects the perceptions of those artists who prepare a play for production. Most contemporary theatre practitioners would agree that the term "modern" applies to the perceptions, movements, and techniques in drama and theatre that emerged in the nineteenth century and developed in the next: naturalism, realism, impressionism, surrealism, expressionism, futurism, and cubism. "Modern" drama first was used in connection with the plays of Ibsen and later with the works of Strindberg, Chekhov, Shaw, and the like. Yet, "modern" theatrical practitioners (such as Saxe-Meiningen, Antoine, Brahm, Stanislavsky, and the other artists of the Moscow Art Theatre and its Studios) found acceptance on the stage only years after the first modern playwrights penned their plays. The traditions established by the modern playwright and theatre artist continue well into the twentieth century. Although the personalities differ as do the techniques, on the whole, "the 'modern' mentality" evolves from the cultural thought that culminated in the nineteenth and twentieth centuries. In his *Romantic Quest and Modern Query*, Tom F. Driver finds three characteristics that illuminate the cultural climate of modern theatre: "The first may be called historicism; the second, a questing for reality, which turns after a time into a query about whether anything is real; and the third, a tendency to regard all experience ironically."[1] In a climate that continually questions current, accepted perceptions, it is not surprising that humanist traditions would also be challenged. "The impulse behind all this modernity to this day is," Martin Esslin argues, "essentially a negative one—a rejection of any closed worldviews, any closed world systems."[2] The postmodernists, in particular, have elected to transcend or dismiss rational thought and the individual's quest for truth. Therefore, artists who perceive reality through the lens of postmodernism disregard much that is associated with modernism's organic, logocentric, wholistic approach.[3] Modernism's organic theories are too limiting and fixed, offering little assistance to a postmodern artist whose vision thrives on dissociation, fragmentation, and a meaningless universe. Responding to the modernist who finds order in the organic infrastructure of the play's parts, the postmodernist is "unable to structure any ordering ideas of reality and so conceives of reality as itself unreal."[4]

Such postmodernists as Robert Wilson, Anne Bogart, Peter Sellars, Robert Israel, and John Conklin challenge the artist's interpretive ability to recreate a truthful representation of a historical period or style. As a result, they have turned to their interpretation of an imagistic/metaphorical theatre to explore with the audience new ways to perceive the play's world. Their metaphorical productions have been criticized by some because their theatrical transformations are so radical or personal that the original work is barely recognizable. The postmodern theatre of the 1970s and 1980s challenged traditional modes of perception and created new styles of performance. Postmodern artists who "deconstruct" the playscript, for example, favor radical interpretive procedures: Their metaphorical productions generally give the impression they have rewritten the play. It is not surprising, then, that their iconoclastic theatre repels those who view the artist's role as being faithful to the author's words. Similarly, the twentieth-century artist who does not alter the playwright's words but renders the production anew has met the same criticism. In *Modern/Postmodern*, Silvio Gaggi offers a distinction between these two elusive ideas: "Postmodernism can be understood as differing from modernism either because it extends modernist principles further than modernists themselves did or because it rejects them."[5] Today's artists who say they have been influenced by postmodernism, but not to the point that they adhere to the rigors of its radical theories and practices, view theatre through the prism of what might be called "contemporary modernism."[6] These artists do not necessarily ignore the imagistic exploration attributed to the postmodernist; instead, I would like to offer that their revelatory interpretations differ insofar as their metaphorical staging tends to "reconceive," not to "deconstruct," the playtext. Essentially, both modernist and postmodernist artists recognize that theatrical interpretation is subject to shifting perceptions and question the logic of an interpretive process that attempts either to determine the playwright's intent or to create an "accurate" reproduction of the play's world. They agree that throughout the twentieth century the interpretation of playscripts has become devoted less to *mimesis* and reflection and more to the roles that subjectivity and informed imagination play in creative thought and practice—especially in how they relate to new ways of seeing the play. Yet, many criticize both contemporary modernists and postmodernists because, as Robert Brustein argues in *Reimagining American Theatre*, their "radical" interpretive process borders on "authoring" the production. The metaphorical approach attributed to the artist who "reimages" or reworks playscripts (especially the classics) has, according to Brustein, a "greater potential for rediscovering the original impulses and energies of the material." The metaphorical director, for example, is an individual whom Brustein perceives to be "more interested in generating provocative theatrical images—visually expressed through physical production, histrionically through character and relationships—that are suggestive rather than specific, reverberant rather than concrete." Brustein concludes: "Naturally, this process is controversial: critics—though somewhat more tolerant of simile directors, who change only the period—invariably accuse metaphorical directors of arrogance and distortion."[7]

Thus, the question of "authorship" is a relevant issue to many artists (contemporary modernists or postmodernists) who seek fresh connections with the world of the play. Although some criticize, Brustein asserts that "most auteur directors genuinely believe they are releasing the original impulses of the plays they direct from the conventions of traditional production, and would vigorously defend their concepts as 'faithful' realizations of a playwright's intention, seen anew through modern eyes."[8]

For obvious reasons, the iconoclastic theories and practices of postmodernism are alarmingly attractive to many young artists who have been born into an imagistic world that all too eagerly dismisses the past and welcomes the new. Because little attention has been paid to how an artist works with a playscript in preparation for production, some artist-teachers find the allure of postmodernism to be a dangerous trend, as it encourages young artists to devalue much of what is associated with the rich tradition of dramatic theory and practice before they have studied and understood it. This raises the following issues:

1. Do we have adequate preparation to help young artists face the complex task of interpreting a playscript?
2. What skills should interpretive artists be developing that address the complexities of twentieth-century aesthetic thought and practice?
3. Before the interpretive practices of postmodernism are addressed, should attention not be paid to the interpretive practices of modernism?

Interviews with some of this country's leading theatre practitioners produced an abundance of specific comments concerning the necessity for the young artist to pursue "dramaturgical literacy." In particular, they stressed the importance of reading history, literature, psychology, philosophy, sociology, and political science. They also suggested that the undergraduate theatre student should be exposed to the rigors of foreign languages, sciences, and math, in addition to being involved with the fine and performing arts. Additionally, many focused on the importance of developing the kind of creative imagination that promotes an interaction between information and intuition, thereby stimulating a personal awareness about the psychology of the play's world.

A liberal arts education coupled with creative thought and practice provides a solid foundation for young directors, designers, and actors who are beginning to think about the complex, synchronous nature of the play's world. The cry is timely, as many universities and colleges are developing interdisciplinary courses and learning clusters that culminate in projects stressing the synthesis of ideas across disciplines. These new methods and programs seem all too pertinent to contemporary aesthetic theories and practices that address the complexities of past and present-day societies. Developing dramaturgical skills and a creative imagination are certainly advantageous to a young artist who needs to appreciate a range of historical artistic perceptions, theories, and practices.

One of the pitfalls for a novice actor, director, or designer is the failure to spend enough time with the playscript prior to production. Instead of quiet study with the playwright's work, there is a temptation to look for quick answers: renting the video to see how someone else did it, running to New York City and attending the play, looking at endless pictures of former productions, or going to the library and reading critical work about the project. Although certain aspects of this type of research can be enlightening, especially in identifying some problems with prior productions, it is more than likely that, if used as a sole means of preparation or without any prior thought, it will result in a production that will be glib, emotionally bankrupt, stale, or dishonest. Additionally, just because a play has been cited as an example of some genre/dramatic form (tragedy, comedy, melodrama, realism, naturalism, expressionism, absurdism), its label should not prescribe what avenues a theatre artist should take when preparing for production. It is unlikely that either duplicating prior productions or rigidly following the guidelines set forth by genre or dramatic form criticism will help the twentieth-century artist when analyzing a script and creating a performance or production that promotes poetic understanding or stimulates new perceptions. Yet, genre/dramatic form criticism is a valuable way of comparing, contrasting, or cataloging plays.[9] For example, one could argue that knowledge of the components of expressionism, surrealism, impressionism, and so on, both enriches the understanding of modernism and stimulates creative thought and artistic imaging.

Dramaturgical skills are valuable in their ability to compare, contrast, or catalogue plays. Knowledge of impressionism, for example, does improve the understanding of dramatic literature and the ability to create various styles of production. However, labeling a play before the artist begins to work not only limits the creative process but also increases the risk of standing back and intellectually observing, thus eliminating the possibility of becoming more emotionally involved with the subtleties, complexities, and ambiguities of the playwright's world. In other words, understanding genre and dramatic form is helpful in expanding the artist's knowledge about literature; however, when it comes to a theatrical interpretation of a playscript, it is more helpful if this discovery is the result of a theatrical analysis.

Though many directors, designers, and actors will mention that there is no "one way" they prepare to direct, design, or perform a play, they agree that dramaturgical literacy guides them into and throughout its world. Yet, none of them embraces a singular methodology; no one theory exists that is applicable to all plays and is *the* technique that assures a successful production. For the twentieth-century artist, limiting interpretive possibilities to what traditionally has been acceptable at best diminishes the chance of creative inspiration and at worst reduces the nature of creativity to nothing more than a good recipe.

The number of regional theatres that not only employ the services of literary departments but also assign dramaturgs to their productions is testament to the respect artists have for any pertinent data that stimulate their perceptions about the world of the play. Theatre artists know that they must develop numerous "literacies" in order to "read" a playscript intelligently and sensitively. My research in this field indicates that respected contemporary theatre artists are well versed in standard dramaturgical analysis. However, reading a play with adroit dramaturgical awareness is possible only after years of training and experience. Like virtuosos who master the elements of musical composition so that the score can touch their souls and they can play or sing with total abandon, theatre artists carefully study the play's parts, paying attention to how they are assembled, to form a "sense of the whole."[10] Thus, rigorous work on the playscript can lead the theatre artist to a competent understanding of the play's world. Such is the effort of actors, directors, and designers as they attempt to satisfy their desire to unearth the playscript's human history so that they can give the play an intelligent reading. However, making a production that is an artful depiction of life means that the artist (like the virtuoso) has found a resounding connection with the playscript's heart or soul.

Although scholarship on this subject falls into several categories (dramatic theory and criticism, play analysis texts, and handbooks that provide the young artist with an introduction to a process that will take a lifetime to comprehend fully), it is Richard Hornby's innovative work, *Script into Performance: A Structural Approach* (1977), that has been most influential for this book, not only in its ability to address how dramatic theory plays a significant role in theatrical practice but also in Hornby's reading of Structuralism and the New Critics. Hornby's book, J. L. Styan's *Elements of Drama* (1960) and *Drama, Stage and Audience* (1975), Bernard Beckerman's *Dynamics of Drama: Theory and Method of Analysis* (1970), Jackson Barry's *Dramatic Structure: The Shaping of Experience* (1970), and Timo Tiusanen's *O'Neill's Scenic Images* (1968) are additional valuable sources for any young artist interested in discovering how to work with a playscript prior to production.

Because artists spend a great deal of time discovering the play's world, they develop the ability to read the play with an eye toward seeing it move and hearing it speak. Therefore, interpreting a playscript is not totally an intellectual pursuit; in fact, an adroit interpretation relies on the artist's informed intuition to spark an imaginative response to the play's poetry. Learning how to read the blueprint, then, has to be the first step in any creative endeavor, which requires judgment, clear thinking, and the ability to participate in the play's imaginative world. There is a learned literacy involved in trying to evoke organic perceptions about its world. For instance, in working with its resources, you see how each thread has contributed to its fabric. Being conscious of how the script comes together at the least provides a better awareness of the playwright's work and at the best might lead to new thoughts, observations, and perceptions. Dissecting the script and discovering its world informs and stimulates the imagination.

Mining the play's theatrical language (images, symbols, metaphors) is another way of handling its resources. By identifying the playwright's use of "scenic image" (for example) and seeing how it poetically embellishes ideas about the story, characters, language, rhythm, and scenic descriptions, the artist may find a way of experiencing the internal life of the script. Words inspire images; dramatic rhythms create atmospheres; characters and situations jog memories; and leitmotifs tease the artist's imagination. The ability to weave words, characters, situations, and atmospheres into theatrical images helps the artist experience the play's heartbeat and sense further poetic possibilities. Therefore, entering the internal world of the play should be foremost in the preliminary work of an actor, a director, and a designer.

The goal of an artist's journey into the playscript is to emerge with an artistic vision that makes a poetically resonant statement. Many agree how important it is, upon a first reading, to have an immediate emotional response to the play as a whole. Some artists value the initial response for its ability to ignite primitive, uncensored connections and spontaneous fragmented images. No matter how inspirational, uncluttered, or resounding a first response (image) might be, it should be scrutinized thoroughly to determine if it is compelling enough to illuminate something new about the play's psychology. The remaining process in preparing a playscript for production is more analytical and less emotional; however, an equal amount of time should be devoted to synthesizing knowledge and imagination so that perceptions not only are aesthetically sound but also are filled with provocative and accessible theatrical images that help an audience participate in the play's interpretive vitality.

Therefore, at the root of analysis is the desire to perceive the play's world poetically. A modernistic reading of the play is always filtered through a subjective understanding and emotional response to the playwright's manipulation of time and space. Allowing for the possibility that perceptions differ, continually change, and evolve permits diverse artistic views. Seemingly, it is one of the reasons that productions of the same play differ from artist to artist; it is also why a contemporary production of a play from another time and place will not only be different from the original production but will also bring forth new, hitherto-undiscovered thoughts about old material. Consequently, it is specious to assume that there is only one way to approach a playscript or that the production of a play is only perceivable in one particular way.

Artists view the playwright's use of time and space the only way they can—relativistically. Einstein's work with relativity (especially his thoughts on time and space) not only inspired numerous twentieth-century playwrights but also influenced current performance theory. Additionally, twentieth-century performance theory pertinent to production might do well to consider how prior critical methods (notably Aristotelian, Platonic, Structuralist, and Psychological) may serve as a materialistic infrastructure supporting a metaphorical inspiration. Thus, the interpretive task of rediscovering the playscript evolves through a dramaturgical analysis that is both objective and subjective, both extrinsic and intrinsic.

An analysis of a playscript that produces a series of poetic images or a metaphorical production involves reinterpreting or "reimaging" the playwright's original ideas. Successful metaphorical productions are the result of how well individual artists can collaborate and combine their disparate perceptions to make a unified production that is poetically stimulating and not diffuse. Therefore, theatre artists (from the dramaturg, to the director, to the designer, to the actor) must develop certain skills:

- receptivity to multiple perceptions
- literacies that help them in sensing, collecting, and synthesizing images that are capable of evoking human history
- imaginations that are adept at processing the play's time and space "metacognitively"
- techniques to transfer an artful perception of the play's psychology to the stage

Because theatre artists develop the skill to synthesize information with imagination, they can reinterpret the play's world in disciplined fashion.

An analysis of a playscript through the prism of modernism requires that the theatre artist has developed the skills to render a metaphorical production, thereby addressing one of Peter Brook's concerns—"deadly theatre." Today, theatre artists accept Brook's challenge and enter the world of the play anticipating that they will be intellectually mining and emotionally responding to its resources. However bifurcated this approach might appear, the mix can inspire creative impulses, such as a series of images, a commanding image, or a metaphorical response.

The purpose of this book is to consider how the artistic perceptions and interpretive methods of twentieth-century artists evoke new readings of classical playscripts. Chapter 2, therefore, historically traces the development of modernism's imagistic metaphorical theatre. Chapter 3 is a dialogue with a sampling of leading professional actors, directors, designers, and dramaturgs who work in the American theatre, concerning the ways they prepare a playscript for production. (The artists who contributed to this study are Jane Alexander, Robert Brustein, John Conklin, Michael Dixon, Olympia Dukakis, Ben Edwards, Zelda Fichandler, Arden Fingerhut, Jane Greenwood, Tori Haring-Smith, Richard Jenkins, Jon Jory, Shirley Knight, Mark Lamos, Ming Cho Lee, Emily Mann, Robert Morgan, Lester Polakov, Thomas Skelton, Anthony Taccone, Jennifer Tipton, and Douglas Wager.) The remaining chapters illustrate my speculation concerning their process. Chapter 4 pursues how the theories and practices of modernism have contributed to a dramaturgy that centers on imagistic cognition. Chapter 5 illustrates how imagistic readings of *The Seagull* produce metaphorical productions, and to conclude, Chapter 6 considers how current interpretive trends have stimulated thought concerning the artist as auteur.

Metaphorical productions are the result of contemporaneous connections to the world of the play. In particular, these new readings often explode the playwright's naturalistic scenic descriptions by disturbing the play's causally based reality. Moreover, they draw attention to the arbitrary nature of interpretation. Like others who write about the complicated issue of analysis and the performance potential of playscripts, I too recognize how difficult it is to cover all the approaches, perceptions, and issues related to this topic. By taking into consideration the theories and practices that lead artists to view playscripts through the prism of modernism, I hope this book may help students of theatre continue to ponder the complex and stimulating journey into the world of the play.

2

The Theories and Practices of Modernism

Twentieth-century modern artists have become so increasingly aware of the communicative power of the image that they have developed not only an ability to elicit an imagistic response to the playscript but also the creative skill of transferring images to, and manipulating images on, the stage. Imagistic theatre explodes mundane reality into a never-ending collection of metaphorical moments producing multiple perceptions. It surpasses the limitations of an earlier realism that often is associated with those artists (e.g., Stanislavsky and Antoine) who attempted to present on stage a static, more finite representation of life. Concluding that the traditional views and practices of realism are far too restrictive (often denying access to the play's poetry), many artists have opted to look beyond the obvious and materialistic characteristics of the play's world by putting into practice ideas associated with modernism. For example, the artistic director of the American Repertory Theatre, Robert Brustein, emphatically rejects the limited superficiality that often defines realism's dramatic form and restricts its production techniques. He feels, for example, that Ibsen is misunderstood by many because on the surface he seems "to be a realistic dramatist, but underneath (as he continually says) he is a poet.... I have directed two of Ibsen's plays, *Ghosts* and *The Wild Duck,* and in each case I've looked for the poetic image that Ibsen buried in them."[1]

Perhaps it is useful to ask why artists find images to be a tantalizing way to experience and capture their perception of the playwright's world. Most contemporary actors, directors, and designers have moved away from reproducing the literal, linear, tangible world of the realists and have become more interested in ways to elicit potential, not absolute, realities on stage. The journey is similar to what Henri Bergson suggested in his *Creative Evolution* (1907):

He who installs himself in becoming sees in duration the very life of things, the fundamental reality. The Forms, which the mind isolates and stores up in concepts, are then only snapshots of the changing reality. They are moments gathered along the course of time; and, just because we have cut the thread that binds them to time, they no longer endure. They tend to withdraw into their own definition, that is to say, into the artificial reconstruction and symbolical expression which is their intellectual equivalent. They enter into eternity, if you will; but what is eternal in them is just what is unreal. On the contrary, if we treat becoming by the cinematographical method, the Forms are no longer snapshots taken of the change, they are its constitutive elements, they represent all that is positive in Becoming.[2]

Modernists are fond of images for a number of reasons: images provoke subjective responses; they act as storehouses; they convey thoughts and feelings (some of which are of a timeless nature); they are the soul of imaginative thought. Additionally, the play's images, singularly and collectively, tell us something about how its author perceives time and place, characters, and dramatic action. The artist's immediate imagistic response to the play's world sometimes lingers, becoming visual and/or aural parts of the production. Therefore, physical images can be the materialistic representations of a particular time and place; however, they also can be powerful metaphorical communicators —fleeting instantaneous subjective responses *defying* the logic of a causal reality. Eventually the theatrical image seduces the play's audience into participating in its ephemeral and ambiguous nature. (Implications and examples will be elaborated at a later point.) Imagistic theatre and, to a somewhat lesser extent, its forerunner, the theatrical form of poetic realism, rely on the power of the transitory image to convey, on stage, twentieth-century impressions of reality that surpass the reductive nature of materialism.

The process of imaging a play, therefore, is really one of "reimaging" the playwright's original images. It is driven by a desire to experience more fully or participate in the play's world. Therefore, theatre practitioners talk about seeing *and* hearing the play in their imaginations. When these fleeting images (inspired by the script's poetry) find their way to the stage, the artist has become a significant player in the play's world.

Images are, in part, responsible for creating the psychology (theatrical style) of the production. The poetic transmogrification of the playscript's images to the stage contributes to the creation of the production's unique identity or personality. In his article "Postmodern Design," Arnold Aronson suggests, "Modern design functions by visually and metaphorically placing the specific world of the play within some sort of broader context of the world of the audience; it is a kind of metanarrative that attempts to encompass the world within a unified image."[3]

The artist who perceives reality through the prism of modernism produces an imagistic style of theatre that is a poetic extension of the play's world— organically evolved yet subject to the interpreter's subjective point of view. Modernism produces a particular "private style," which the postmodernist theoretician Fredric Jameson says is "as unmistakable as your fingerprint" and "can be expected to generate its own unique vision of the world and to forge its own unique, unmistakable style."[4]

Production style is often a maligned topic because in the past it has been difficult to pinpoint its relationship to the script or its function on stage. For example, a glib or "stylized" production may occur when a playscript has been given a hasty interpretation, when there is a lack of understanding of the play, or when artists feel the production will not be successful without a gimmick. A production that has been "stylized" may contain characters, movements, gestures, costumes, and designs that generally are larger than life, one-dimensional, and lacking in depth and cohesiveness. This type of production is often the result of a quick general analysis of the playscript, where there has been little or no attempt organically to mine the play's ideas, dramatic rhythms, and leitmotifs, the characters' psychology, or the subtle intricacies of mood and atmosphere. Surface treatments of a playscript not only are devoid of substance and intelligence but suffer further abuse by being called "stylized." When this occurs, the concept of theatrical style has been misunderstood and misused.[5]

However, when style is understood to be the psychology of production, it would be short-sighted not to consider its relationship to an analysis of a playscript. Michel Saint-Denis, in his *Theatre: The Rediscovery of Style* (1960), finds that theatrical style transforms a deep understanding of the play's reality from the page to the stage and goes beyond duplicating or recording the external details of a particular historical period. He suggests, "Psychological, social, emotional reality must be called upon to give substance to the form" [play and production]. He implies that uncovering the reality of the play's style means that the practitioner goes into the play and discovers its organic integrity. He cautions that if we use only our subjective resources we are likely to bring a contemporary interpretation to a play whose reality will then be separate, inorganic, and jarring. He quickly adds that although such an interpretation might be interesting, it would "create a conflict between reality and style. We have seen that if the form is destroyed or altered, the sense is also destroyed, and the right sort of revelation will not be produced.... It won't be the reality which the poet tried to express in his text."[6]

Most theatre artists who are influenced by modernism agree that the production style emerges from the depths of the play's world: it is revealed on stage physically (gestures and movements), audibly (rhythmical words, phrases, or sounds), and through scenic diction (images, metaphors and symbols). If one can look at particular individuals and be aware of their "sense of style," then one can attend a production that has been influenced by modernism and identify that the psychology informing its style is a response to synthetic thought and a collection of images that are the product of an informed imagination. However, because modernism invites reinterpretation (its theatrical style is subjective and unique, encouraging additional reinterpretation by the audience), the contemporary artist would question Saint-Denis's position concerning the author's intention.

The modern or postmodern artist continues to explore the role interpretation plays in theatre. Recently, postmodern artists have suggested an even further departure from realism and modernism by dismissing most, if not all, prior analytical methods as far too reductive, logocentric, and organic. This century's recent interest in postmodern deconstructive interpretations champions the role of the artist as auteur; therefore, many are questioning the traditional methods of interpretation as well as the more recent approach of Structuralism. Theatrical style has become an even more complicated question for postmodernists who celebrate incongruity and depend on semiotics to codify meaning. Postmodern theatre practices, however, are not the focus of this book, not because they do not offer a great deal to consider in terms of interpretation but because we have yet to come to terms with the ways in which modernism has influenced performance theories and practices.

Innovative performance practice occurs decades after revolutionary aesthetic thought or playwriting. Modern theatre essentially maintained an allegiance to late-nineteenth-century thought and practice. The following reflected the aesthetics of an expanding vision of reality: the "isms" associated with the turn of the twentieth century; Appia and Craig's new stagecraft movement; Meyerhold's grotesque theatre; the performance theories of the Moscow Art Theatre, its First and Third Studios, and the other laboratory theatres throughout Europe; and the plays of (for example) Chekhov, Strindberg, Yeats, and Pirandello. American theatre in the 1960s produced some experimentation (the Happenings, The Living Theatre, The Open Theatre) that along with the theories and practices of Artaud, Brecht, Grotowski, Cage, and Eastern European theatre have continued to influence most of modernism and a great deal of postmodern thought and practice.

A contemporary production that transcends the dullness of a literal statement often is the product of an analysis that has been informed by modernism. Its interpretive method relies on an informed imagination, stimulated by creative/subjective imaging, which often produces a metaphorical reinterpretation of the world of the play. This chapter is a historical examination of the evolution of play analysis, specifically as it relates to modernism. It addresses how an artist's preparation of a playscript, perceived through the prism of modernism, contributes to the imagistic metaphorical rediscovery of a play. Such a study is advantageous to those actors, directors, and designers who are stimulated by such controversial issues as subjectivity, imagistic theatre, "reconceiving," and the artist as auteur.

SEEDS OF MODERNISM

Late-nineteenth- and early-twentieth-century examples of the genre/dramatic form of realism were a departure from the dramatic theories, literature, and theatrical practices of romanticism in the early nineteenth century. Unlike romanticism's subjective and nonrational view of life, the realists boldly depicted a more reasoned treatment of the ills that plague society. Scientific knowledge had opened new vistas for the arts. European culture found validity in recording life in an empirically verifiable manner. It was thought that if playwrights, actors, directors, and designers observed the lives of men and women and carefully detailed how their actions and/or their environments caused their problems and if the audience could see the effects of their actions, then this causal relationship would provide the scientific foundation to depict on stage a truthful representation of life. The visual artists were first in finding a new way of depicting life. One such artist, Gustave Courbet (1819-1877), was in the vanguard of those who first worked with realism. His work was described as being "concerned with the present, not the past; with the momentary, not the permanent; with bodies, not souls; with materiality, not spirituality."[7]

Realism's logical and systematic approach seemed an appropriate technique to those artists who wanted to depict the problems of an ailing society whose very existence was being challenged. With broad strokes they painted an 1850 society responding to

- the rise of the middle class brought about by the American Revolution (1776) and the French Revolution (1789)
- the Industrial Revolution
- the demographic adjustment as men and women left the farms for the new factories in the cities

While urban relocation signaled the need for the expansion of educational resources, such as land-grant colleges and institutions, it also meant that the harsh day-to-day realities of city life were compelling enough to call for new social welfare programs and hospitals. Although the problems of urbanization seemed to be more dramatic than those found in life on most farms, the rapid change from living in the country to life in the city was met with strength and courage. The rising middle class was comforted by thinking its problems could be addressed, or even solved, by the very methods that advanced technology. The scientific method (the observation and recording of data followed by causal analysis) was used by natural scientists and later by social scientists (psychologists, anthropologists, and sociologists) as the correct approach to chronicle and study society's problems. The scientific method would eventually empower the nineteenth-century middle class by giving the impression that facts and logic could unravel life's complexities, help people solve their problems, and change their lives.

In theatre the playwrights embraced the nineteenth-century genre/dramatic form of realism. They tended to write carefully crafted domestic plays that recorded "life as it is." Like the scientists, it seemed that they too were studying humanity under a microscope and detailing their observations in a logical, objective manner. It has been reported that late-nineteenth-century playwrights like Emile Zola (1840-1902), Gerhart Hauptmann (1862-1946), and Henrik Ibsen (1828-1906) sometimes wrote like social workers recording a case history.

Detailed recording of domestic life enabled the artist to uncover the characters' inner turmoil and depict more than surface or predictable dramatic action. Prior to realism, the early-nineteenth-century romantic dramatists wrote sentimental plays, with no attention paid to the so-called unities of time and place and little attention paid to the subtle psychological development of characters (at least in the context of emerging psychological thought), conversational dialogue, or a set that looked like an actual physical environment (as defined by realism). But by the mid-nineteenth century this dramatic form was replaced by the "well-made plays" of Eugène Scribe (1791-1861) and Victorien Sardou (1831-1908). In keeping with the scientific tradition, their plays—for examples Scribe's *Glass of Water* (1840) and Sardou's *Scrap of Paper* (1860)—were constructed in a formulaic manner: careful exposition, causal development, scenes that built to a logical climax, letters and mistaken identities that caused reversals, surprises, and suspense. Because this systematic construction carefully detailed the causes of certain effects, the nineteenth-century audience could follow the origin of an action. The plays of Scribe, Sardou, Alexandre Dumas *fils* (1824-1895), and Emile Augier (1820-1889) are early examples of what later would become what we recognize today as realism. However primitive their work may seem, they successfully planted the seeds of modern realism in their attempt to write about the attitudes and problems of the middle class in much the same way that a scientist records the findings that are the outcome of an experiment.

As the leader of the *école de bon sens*, François Ponsard (1814-1867) would stress in his writings, for example, rational thought, simplicity, and truth when conveying the social concerns of the middle-class family and society. By 1850, Dumas *fils* and Augier perceived that the purpose of playwriting should be to show members of society who they are and how they can become better. Professing that playwrights should capture truth diminished prior interest in the emotion of the romantic school and signaled the arrival of Zola's theories on Naturalism. Zola's dramaturgy championed

no romantic yearnings, no poetic outpourings. Man would be analyzed scientifically and placed in his true environment, which should be staged just as minutely as it is described in the novel.... Plays were put together just like the parts of a watch, and the dramatist was nothing but a clever watchmaker. Zola was for abolishing every convention previously known to the drama. Exposition, intrigue, dénouement were entirely unnecessary. For the drama of invention and imagination, he would substitute a drama of observation and scientific fact. To write a play, a dramatist need only reproduce on the stage the story of a person or a group of persons taken from real life.[8]

Zola's notion of a "fragment of existence" would later be paraphrased by one of Antoine's dramatists, Jean Jullien, as "*tranche de vie*," "a slice of life." The careful study of humanity requires returning to nature, the observation of objective phenomena, and the recording of what exists. However, the "mathematical and scientific imagery" that Marvin Carlson asserts is often associated with Zola's naturalism "can be misleading unless we recognize that Zola never forgot the contribution of the artist's personality." Positivism and Hippolyte Taine's (1828-1893) work on determinism served to inform Zola's naturalism, but not to the extent that Zola proposed "mere photography." He accepted the artist's role in perceiving and transferring "nature into art"; however, Zola does caution that, when transferring "nature into art," an artist should be careful not to "distort or falsify to suit either his own concerns, the conventions of the form, or the tastes of his public."[9]

Perceiving a work of art as an example of a unique, organic whole links Taine with G. W. F Hegel's (1770-1831) ideas about content and form. Significant to this study is Taine's "triad: *race, moment* and *milieu*," which illustrates how "*race*" (hereditary disposition, related to human physiology) combines with "*milieu*" (our environmental surroundings, such as climate, geography, and social and cultural assumptions) and one's historical "*moment*" in time to produce individual and social behavior.[10] Taine's triad shows how the forces of society create a particular period that is reflected in its literature. In particular, Zola's form of naturalism applied Taine's scientific determinism to demonstrate the causes and effects of human action. Zola pays homage to determinism when he states,

I want to explain how a family, a small group of beings, conducts itself in a given society, giving birth to ten, to twenty individuals who seem, at first glance, profoundly dissimilar, but whom analysis reveals to be intimately linked to one another. Heredity has its laws like the phenomenon of weight.

I will try to find and follow the thread that leads mathematically from one man to another, by resolving the dual question of temperament and environment. And when I hold all threads, when I have an entire social group in my hands, I will depict this group at work as an actor in a given historical period; I will show it acting in the full complexity of its efforts; I will analyze at once the sum of the individual wills of each of its members and the general thrust of the whole.[11]

Consequently, Zola disliked the theatrical conventions of nonspecific painted wings and backdrops and the theatricality of footlights (he prophesied their abandonment), as well as stereotyped acting and costume for the actor rather than the character.

André Antoine

Zola's theories are far more celebrated than his playwriting. His most illustrious attempt, *Thérèse Raquin* (1873), was criticized for being "too cold, too naked, too matter-of-fact" and lacking "poetic inspiration."[12] Yet, André Antoine (1858-1943) admired Zola, other naturalists (Taine, Becque, Balzac, Goncourt, Daudet), and the classics, as well as the ultrarealists' plays that had been refused production. His Théâtre-Libre (1887) became a laboratory for new playwrights and artists interested in experimenting with the techniques that would create the new forms of drama and theatre. Because the modern artist was faced with plays filled with unconventional types based on astute observations of life, Antoine felt, actors should become "keen," "quick-witted," "subtle," and "intelligent." He continues, "The art of acting, will not rest, as at present, on physical qualities and on natural gifts, but on truth, observation, and direct study of nature."[13] He offers that modern designs should represent reality; for example, real wood should replace a canvas painted to look like wood. If environmental conditions have become a major factor in the development of realism and naturalism, "Is not," as Antoine writes to the French theatre critic, Francisque Sarcey, "the setting the indispensable complement of the work?... Is it not a sort of exposition of the subject?"[14] Carlson describes Zola's active interest in determinism: "people act as they do in real life in part *because* of the clothing they wear and the surroundings in which they live."[15] Similarly, Antoine felt that his actors, when placed in a more naturalistic environment, would have to adjust (as we do in life) their gestures and vocal intonations to conform to their surroundings.

New forms of drama necessitate new methods of interpretation. But the laboratory theatres, in their early stages, perceived interpretation to be little more than recording the external details of life. For example, it is reported that from 9:00 A.M. to midnight Antoine's actors would rehearse their monologues. Surrounded by contemporary realistic paintings, the actors would search for true gestures and physicalizations that would convey the reality the playwright intended. In a response to the actor Le Bargy, who requested the playwright make textual changes, Antoine instructed his actors to interpret, not modify: "[Actors] are in reality manikins, marionettes, more or less perfected in proportion to their talents, whom the author dresses and moves about at will." In Antoine's theatre, the playwright's word is sacrosanct: Actors should make themselves "a keyboard, an instrument, marvelously tuned, on which the author may play at will." Technique is not enough; the actor should also have "an intellectual training that will permit him to understand simply what the author would have him express."[16]

Georg II, Duke of Saxe-Meiningen

The material realization of the playwright's text was the product of evolving creative visions. Antoine saw the Duke of Saxe-Meiningen's (1826-1914) troupe perform in 1888 and was inspired by his ability to capture, through ensemble, composition, gesture, props, and costumes, a more truthful representation of the world of the play. For many, it was the vision of Meiningen (aided by his associates Ludwig Chronegk and Ellen Franz, who provided assistance in artistic, dramaturgical, and managerial areas) that signaled the emergence of the modern-day director. However, his contribution was in part indebted to Johann Wolfgang von Goethe's (1749-1832) interest in a rehearsal process that would result in harmonious stage pictures, detailed composition, and mood; Karl Immermann's (1796-1840) return to the text as the source for the director's (not actor's) interpretation; Heinrich Laube's (1806-1884) attention to detail, unity, and illusion of reality; Franz Dingelstedt's (1814-1881) creation of historical realism that often resembled pageantry; and Richard Wagner's (1813-1883) ideas on unity and synthesis.[17]

The Duke placed primary emphasis on eliminating the theatricality of an earlier age interested more in idealized historicism than verisimilitude. Georg II was first a visual artist; his pencil-and-ink drawings favored those images that historically documented a particular place. Therefore, it was not surprising that his scenery, props, and costumes were researched assiduously and rendered anew. When preparing to design Ibsen's *Ghosts*, his concern for authenticity prompted a letter to the playwright. Ibsen replied, sending a detailed description of "a characteristic interior in a middle-class Norwegian home." Meiningen's preliminary designs are found on the back of Ibsen's letter.[18] In the case of the Berlin production of *Julius Caesar*, Georg II asked an eminent Roman historian, Hermann Köchly, to verify his design.[19] While many found the Duke's attention to detail and archaeological research pedantic and performed at the expense of the script and character development, others saw Meiningen's process of creating historical pageantry as responding to a society affected by "the advances of ethnography and history of civilization."[20]

In anticipation of the naturalist and realist movements, Meiningen's process created "an easy and natural relationship between the actor and the most immediate elements in his environment."[21] He abandoned stock sets for original designs that historically detailed specific places. Three-dimensional units, steps, ramps, platforms, and floor and ceiling treatments were carefully integrated with elaborately painted illusionistic drops. Every attempt was made to create the illusion of reality for both the actor and the audience. Georg II's renderings are not unlike the paintings of this period: in both, a dynamic quality and openness illustrate "the relationship between foreground and background, between what is seen clearly and what is implied, between the individual figure and her environment." Often he would design scenery that had openings, "such as windows, arches, doorways, and gateways, which afford a (complete or partial) view into the depths beyond."[22]

In addition to his detailed authentic scenery and props, there were historically accurate costumes, which, like the sets and props, were more than likely available for the first day of rehearsal. Actors were instructed how to wear their costumes and handle their props. Meiningen's intent was to control every moment, thereby creating a mise-en-scène that was artistically stimulating and historically accurate.

A new production would be rehearsed twenty to thirty times, for five to six hours daily. This increase in rehearsal time allowed attention to be paid to supernumeraries; they (for the first time) were assigned specific identities, lines, and business. As there were no stars in the Duke of Saxe-Meiningen's company, actors were expected to take minor roles as well as to work on creating characters from the very beginning of rehearsal. There is little evidence to indicate that Meiningen constructed any specific theories or procedures to aid the actor in developing the intellectual or emotional core of character.[23] There is, however, an anecdote that illustrates how his carefully executed external world of the play may lead an actor to discover something about the character's psychology. Ludwig Barnay was to perform the role of Petruchio in *The Taming of the Shrew*. He knew the production was to be in Renaissance dress; however, despite the company's rules, he thought he would be allowed to wear his thigh-high leather boots and spurs. The footwear, reminiscent of "the military dress of the Thirty Years War," helped to create the traditional outlines of the masculine Petruchio. However, Georg II's design offered little that suggested previously accepted interpretations; Petruchio's doublet and hose required that Barnay create the character with more subtlety, adroitness, and self-awareness. The actor attributes his new insights to being inspired by Meiningen's design: "Thanks to this purely external element the style of my interpretation imperceptibly underwent a transformation, and came, perhaps, to correspond more closely to the dramatist's intentions."[24]

It seems unlikely, given his drive to recreate historical representations, that the Duke's fidelity to the text would be questioned. However, in his book *The Meiningen Court Theatre*, John Osborne works on two of Meiningen's playscripts (*Julius Caesar* and *Prinz Friedrich von Homburg*). There, he reveals alterations; he summarizes the Duke's approach as making changes "designed to improve the historical accuracy of the drama according to external criteria; dramaturgical amendments which serve, directly or indirectly, the predominantly visual style of the production; and changes which affect the substance or tendency of the drama."[25]

When a director changes "the substance or tendency of the drama" by omitting or transposing scenes to eliminate sets and shorten production time; when lines are cut because they impede the action and "offset the reduction of pace caused by the more static, visual character of the *mise-en-scène*"; or when the director rearranges the scenes in *The Merchant of Venice* to enhance visual imagery over "Shakespeare's more extended and more subtle scene-by-scene comparison," the issue of textual integrity is called to question. Osborne cites many examples that illustrate how and why Meiningen adjusted the play when creating the performance-text; he concurs with Wolfgang Iser's opinion that these changes were intelligent, carefully selected choices that supported the director's point of view.[26]

Throughout Europe and America other theatre practitioners—Otto Brahm (1856-1912), Augustin Daly (1836-1899), Henry Irving (1838-1905), and David Belasco (ca.1854-1931)—continued to expand late-nineteenth-century ideas concerning the principles of realistic staging. Experimentation continued; however, theatre artists generally created a style of theatre that attempted to represent life on stage by authentically reproducing rooms, selecting authentic props, and observing the "fourth wall." Their productions emphasized how the physical environment was a distinct part of their assumptions concerning reality.

Constantin Stanislavsky and the Moscow Art Theatre

It is not hard to understand why Constantin Stanislavsky (1863-1938) and his Moscow Art Theatre (1898) would be intrigued and influenced by scientific thought when, for centuries, acting had been a craft maligned for its ephemeral, highly subjective nature. When Stanislavsky developed a process that aided the actor in systematically and logically developing characterizations, he positioned the actor and director as interpretive artists capable of perceiving, organizing, and physically projecting the complex psychological nature of the human condition.

Acting became more than the beautiful expression of sounds often attributed to the declamatory style of romanticism; instead, those who were working on realism invested their attention on the emotion or feeling that occurs before words are produced. Gone was the ego-oriented actor who was interested primarily in projecting on stage the self rather than the psychology of a character. The foundational goals of the Moscow Art Theatre indicate how emphasis shifted from romanticism (in which the actor used exaggerated gestures to match the play's exotic images and free-flowing action) to simplicity, directness, and "truth." Oliver M. Sayler offers in *The Russian Theatre* that Chekhov's dramas gave Stanislavsky the opportunity to develop his theories and practices, especially those that explored the play's hidden reality and mood. He continues, "The motives of Tchehoff [Chekhov], although they have not been applied blindly to all other productions at the Art Theatre, give a clue to the aim of Stanislavsky in the theatre." Vladimir Nemirovich-Danchenko (1858-1943) outlines Chekhov's goals as follows:

To free the stage from routine and literary stereotypes.
To give back to the stage a living psychology and simple speech.
To examine life not through rising heights and falling abysses, but through the every-day life surrounding us.
To seek "theatricality" of dramatic productions not in exceptional staging, which has given over the theatre for many years to a special kind of masters and has turned away from it the contemporary literary talents, but in the hidden inner psychologic life.
The art of Tchehoff [Chekhov] is the art of artistic freedom and artistic truth.[27]

Stanislavsky felt that when actors became interested in a simple and direct approach to acting, they were far more capable of creating the character's inner psychology. "The quieter and more restrained my body felt on the stage," Stanislavsky recounts in *My Life in Art*, "the more there arose in me the necessity to supplant gesture with mimetics, intonation of the voice, and look of the eye. "[28]

The Moscow Art Theatre's theories and practices were an obvious outgrowth of the predominant scientific thought at the end of the nineteenth century: cause and effect. The cause was the actor's feeling, desire, or emotion that had been evident in man from the beginning of time, and the effect was the action or speech of such an emotion. Much later, in *An Actor Prepares* (1936), the first of several books, Stanislavsky maintained the position that the actor's work should be logical, truthful, and systematic: every bit of imagination must be carefully thought out. The actor must be able to answer "when, where, why, [and] how."[29] His famous, often misunderstood, method would eventually entail imagination, concentration, relaxation, units and objectives, faith, communion, adaptation, and the super-objective. His late-nineteenth-century thoughts on creativity did consider how to combine organic and inorganic elements to create a rich depiction of humanity; therefore, an appraisal of Stanislavsky's early process hints at the development of a structural approach to artistic synthesis.

The early work of the Moscow Art Theatre initiated new ideas about acting, developed appropriate rehearsal techniques that physically embellished the actor's work, and placed significant emphasis on a realistic mise-en-scène. There are numerous historical accounts that illustrate how Stanislavsky approached verisimilitude. The 1898 production of *Tsar Fyodor*, for example, was remembered for years for its attention to realistic detail, especially within the garden scene, in which decorations were placed along the footlights, creating a fourth wall.[30] Attention to detail, organized rehearsals, the psychological development of character, and the physical depiction of the play's time and place reveal an early attempt in creating a representation of reality on stage. Several months later, however, when Stanislavsky was working on Chekhov's *The Seagull*, he began to question and consider changing his original thoughts concerning what constituted a truthful depiction of reality. (A more in-depth treatment of *The Seagull* appears in Chapter 5.)

Impressionism and Symbolism

No book on modernism and its relationship to artistic interpretation would be complete unless it was clear that the development of impressionism and symbolism at the end of the nineteenth century had a significant impact on artistic perception. Whereas scientific evaluation froze the object in order to study it, impressionism freed the object by permitting it to be, to change, and to develop. Although it was first thought that the scientific method could bring order to a disordered universe, work with unconscious thought (images, imagination, feelings, or emotions) uncovered other viable areas that needed attention. These issues were more difficult to study because they were ephemeral, illogical, or irrational. However, because the unconscious lies deep within one's self and contains elements that are unfathomable and uncensorable by the intellect, many felt that its spontaneous eruptions could be a more truthful source for revealing human nature.

The symbolists, for example, thought the reality of the moment, which passed so quickly, could be preserved forever in the memory or imagination: "The art of the symbolist was one of the fleeting moment; everything rushes past in an accelerated panorama. With the metaphor as a starting point, a symbolist prose poem flows by in a sequence of images that sweeps the reader along on a swift current of words with a minimum of slowing down to ponder on their meaning."[31] The potential of images, not fixed reality, was an exciting proposition to those artists who valued imagination and memory as a rich warehouse, a never-ending resource that stores and releases fragments of truth. Symbolism and impressionism were ways in which we could capture materially that which was part of a more metaphysical world. Philosophers like Arthur Schopenhauer (1788-1860) and Henri Bergson (1859-1941) or visual artists like Claude Monet (1840-1926) and Paul Cézanne (1839-1906) saw that we are unable to control time; we cannot freeze time within space and represent it as a full depiction of reality. No longer was it appropriate to accept what appeared on the surface as a complete representation of reality. Subjective exploration of unconscious thought signaled the possibilities of multiple realities. The philosophy behind these new movements neither embraced causal reality nor insisted on duplicating the outward physical image of reality. Reality included subjective images envisioned and created by artistic intuition and imagination.

The vision of such poets as Edgar Allan Poe (1809-1849) and John Keats (1795-1821) was stimulated by the possibility of the artistic symbol evoking the release of unconscious thoughts/ideas. In theatre the material symbol, either the end product of a series of momentary images or the catalyst in the awakening of the unconscious, became a fruitful way to express an artistic idea. The synthesis of words, images, ideas, and symbols developed in a manner similar to that of a musician creating a leitmotif. They could be orchestrated individually or collectively to create a scenic image representative of the play's poetic ideas. Impressionism and symbolism were followed by an interest in mysticism and religion in the late 1890s—further distinguishing the disillusionment with scientific thought and a search for other means of determining the poetic nature of reality.

Maurice Maeterlinck (1862-1949), Hugo von Hofmannsthal (1874-1929), August Strindberg (1849-1912), and William Butler Yeats (1865-1939) often are cited as symbolist playwrights whose iconoclastic vision far surpassed the limitations of realism. Their lyrical work is filled with images and symbols that are capable of depicting on stage multiple levels of reality. For example, they explored certain metaphysical issues (such as death) by selecting visual and aural images powerful enough to elicit perceptions beyond a material reality. However, playwrights like Ibsen, Chekhov, and Strindberg—the accepted forebears of realism—also were influenced by the symbolists. Many of Ibsen's plays (*A Doll House, Ghosts, When We Dead Awaken*), as well as Chekhov's (*The Seagull, The Cherry Orchard*) and Strindberg's (*A Dream Play, The Ghost*

Sonata, The Dance of Death), exemplify poetic perceptions of reality.

Ibsen's *Ghosts* (1881) often is cited as the play that signals the arrival of modern drama. His modernity can be attributed to his ability to speak directly and poetically to his audience. For example, *Ghosts* is a socially relevant play, in which heredity and environment are linked to society's development. Yet, while truth is preferred over beauty, Ibsen is able to suggest the characters' psychology, the play's inner life, without diminishing the external appearance of contemporary life. For two decades experimental theatres all over Europe produced *Ghosts* (as well as other symbolic plays), but most found Ibsen's world difficult to assimilate, primarily because a gross form of naturalism prevailed as the predominant performance theory and practice.

By the end of the nineteenth century, impressionism and symbolism had affected artistic thought. Europe's experimental theatres were struggling to find new interpretive methods that would support the creative process and the evolution of truth, evoke impressions of the character's inner psychology, and encourage the validity of subjective perceptions. When modern drama shifted from creating the external materialistic trappings of a surface reality to situations, characters, dialogue, and a mise-en-scène that suggested the inner world of the play, artists began to consider how contrast, ambiguity, and synthesis create an idealized form of naturalism. The continual evolution of truth was soon to be preferred over the frozen consistency of causal thought, but not at the total expense of keen observation and attention to detail.

Aurélien-Marie Lugné-Poë and the Théâtre de l'Oeuvre

Expanding artistic visions were attractive to Aurélien-Marie Lugné-Poë (1869-1940) and to others. European experimental theatres were presented with plays that stretched the limits of naturalism or totally rejected verisimilitude. At the height of naturalism, Strindberg's *Miss Julie* (1888) and Hauptmann's *Weavers* (1892) used tableux vivants and sound-evoked images that suggested the transitory nature of time and place. Hauptmann's play, perceived to be an exemplary illustration of naturalism, de-emphasized the cohesiveness of an Ibsen-like plot and the tradition of dramatic structure, and used a collection of scenes that slowly built to the weavers' revolution. Further, it focused on "the psychology of the mass" over the development of an individual's psychology.[32] The playwrights who interspersed naturalistic detail with periodic fantasy presented further problems for interpretive artists who were barely competent in the management of realistic detail, let alone unity, contrast, and ambiguity. At the Théâtre de l'Oeuvre (1893), Lugné-Poë found suggestion, not imitation, preferable when his theatre staged the symbolic and social masterpieces of Ibsen or the primitive grotesque world of Alfred Jarry's *Ubu Roi* (1896). The philosophy that informed the theatre of French symbolism was devoted to projecting what they found to be the essence of drama, the poetic world of universal images. However, evocative images tested not only the audience's patience but also the interpretive abilities of most artists. Lugné-Poë, for example, found actors too subjective, their gestures too conventional, and the set too detailed and illusionistic to create a heightened reality suggestive of the play's poetry.

Theatrical Idealism

It is not surprising that many directors and designers favored replacing the actor with a puppet or marionette. Like the mask, both of these theatrical devices have the ability to condense and capture the play's poetic archetypal ideas as well as the essential nature or emotion of a character. Edward Gordon Craig (1872-1966) proposed the Über Marionette: an "inanimate figure" who, unlike the living actor, is not prone to arbitrary, subjective, and emotional states but reliably projects the idea behind the character. He would later adjust his position by conceding that the actor might not need to be eliminated if physical imitation and representation were replaced with more artful forms of presentation, the symbolic gesture or the mask. The mask, Craig maintained, signaled the theatre of the future, for only it could portray "the expressions of the soul."[33]

Some late-nineteenth-century French Idealists (Stéphane Mallarmé, Teodor de Wyzewa, Théodore de Banville) would continue to reject or at least to diminish the role of actor and scenery. To their minds, current theories and practices of naturalism took their toll on the expansive possibilities of the written word. Removing the actor from the stage and eliminating all elements of the mise-en-scène essentially suggest that drama is not meant to be performed; however, the antirealist was not prepared to abolish theatre. Perhaps their animosity stimulated the endangered theatre artist to consider finding new ways to interpret and present plays that would elicit the play's spiritual reality.

However, at the end of the nineteenth century, the metaphysical idealism of the early nineteenth century reappeared and merged with naturalism to form a poetic view of reality. The term *poetic realism* was offered by Otto Ludwig some fifty years earlier; however, Ludwig was speaking about the evolution of modern tragedy, in the sense of characters' internal struggles as opposed to their struggle against fate or society. Marvin Carlson summarizes Ludwig's position in *Theories of the Theatre*: "The tragedy Ludwig champions he calls poetic realism, which he sees as a synthesis of the partial perspectives offered by naturalism and idealism. From naturalism, it takes the elements of the real world; from idealism, the artistic unity arising from harmony and contrast. Naturalism gives it material; idealism, form."[34]

Anton Chekhov and Poetic Realism

By the turn of the twentieth century, playwrights like Anton Chekhov (1860-1904) returned to poetic realism, finding its form to be a highly desirable way to suggest the subtle, volatile nature of the human condition. For example, the well-placed Chekhovian pause or silence and, more specifically, his development of what David Magarshack calls "indirect action" are some of the dramaturgical techniques that Chekhov used to explore and project what was being felt or said silently (the play's internal actions).[35]

It was during the famous production of *The Seagull* (1898) that Chekhov challenged Stanislavsky to consider the difference between depicting "life as it is" and a more imaginative (imagistic) perception of life. Although he was in ill health, Chekhov, who had been attending some of Stanislavsky's rehearsals, made it clear to the director that he did not want this production to repeat the same rehearsal methods (melodramatic style of acting and a short rehearsal period) that had caused its disastrous premiere a year before in St. Petersburg. Nemirovich-Danchenko reports in *My Life in the Russian Theatre* that, after watching for a period of time, Chekhov responded with: "They act too much. It would be better if they acted a little more as in life."[36] On a similar note, when Stanislavsky was defending his use of realistic detail on stage (the sound effects of a rural locale—dogs barking, frogs croaking, crickets chirping), Chekhov retaliated with, "The theater has its own conventions. There is no fourth wall. Besides, the theater is art and reflects the quintessence of life; it wants nothing superfluous."[37] Chekhov's position was clear; he was in relentless pursuit of a new form of theatre, one that was more suited to suggesting the hidden poetry of his play. (For further clarification, and to appreciate the significance of this production as a turning point, see Chapter 5.)

At first glance, *The Seagull*'s dramatic form appears to be a good example of realism. Not only are its plot, characters, and language all logically developed, but Chekhov also wrote specific stage directions that called for the smell of sulfur, music across the lake, a raging storm, and the like.

But the world of *The Seagull* is not that straightforward. Its reality lies in its subtle tones and references. For example, in *The Seagull* the characters speak of wanting to go to town, but they never go; or they talk about wanting to get married, but they never get around to it; sometimes they even cry out passionately about wanting to become writers, but when told how they can improve their work, they turn a deaf ear:

> *Dorn:*   ...Oh, you're so high-strung. Look—tears in your eyes. Now what was it I wanted to say? You've taken your plot from the realm of the abstract, and rightly so: a work of art needs a great idea behind it. Nothing can be beautiful without being serious. You look so pale.
>
> *Treplev:*   So you think I should keep at it?
>
> *Dorn:*   Yes...But stick to what's important, what's eternal. You know, I've had a decent life, full of variety. I'm satisfied. But if I'd ever had the chance to feel the exaltation an artist must feel during the

process of creation, I'd have spurned my material self and all that
goes with it and taken wing, soared into the heights.

Treplev: Excuse me, but where's Nina?[38]

Because it appears that there is little dramatic action in Chekhov's plays,
many find his dramas dry and monotonous. It has been suggested that Chekhov
is writing about late-nineteenth-century middle-class Russians, whose lives are
dull and frustrating because they have little, if any, clear-cut direction. The
dramatic action appears to be either uneventful (most of the characters simply
are not capable of solving their problems so that they can move on with their
lives) or even morbid (one commits suicide). Yet, in 1895, Chekhov describes
his work as a "comedy [with] three female roles, six male roles, four acts, a
landscape (a view of the lake), much conversation about literature, little action
and five tons of love."[39] Chekhov's world appears to be filled with
contradictions. One would hardly find it surprising if today's actors were as
frustrated and confused as Stanislavsky's were in 1898.

However, *The Seagull*'s static structure is not unlike Chekhov's image of
the "magic lake." What appears to be one way soon changes when the reader
disturbs the surface to discover what lies below. If you look at the characters
carefully, you discover that they are the victims of their own indecision and
inertia: they want to move forward and solve their problems, but they simply do
not know how to achieve their goals. In fact, one of the keys to unlocking
Chekhov's reality is found deep in the characters' world of indecision as well
as in the play's comic rhythms. Chekhov's dramatic action, therefore, is found
not on the surface of things but deep within the characters' psyches: in their
feelings, desires, and emotions. Therefore, the dramatic action in Chekhov's play
is not necessarily apparent from what the characters are *doing* (external physical
action), but instead can be found within what the characters are *experiencing*
(internal psychological development).

Stanislavsky and his company were the first to explore the psychological
development of Chekhov's characters; what they found was action that was
anything but dull. When Stanislavsky urged his actors to find the characters'
"inner feelings," or the play that lay beneath the text or between the lines,[40] as
well as "to be" the character "by 'getting under the skin' of the Chekhov
character by penetrating into the most secret places of his heart,"[41] he left
surface reality and *mimesis* behind and began to search for a more comprehensive
understanding of the inner meaning of Chekhov's plays.

None of these attributes is noticeable on a first reading; they are the result of
an imagistic exploration of the play's internal resources. Chekhov's work with
the play's internal dramatic action, with his lyrical vision of realism, is
significant inasmuch as it helped to provoke Stanislavsky's search. Later, it
would become part of the foundation of his system. Eventually he offered two
concepts, objective and subtext, both of which have become instrumental

and acceptable ways to discover and illustrate the play's poetic reality. The psychology of Chekhov's characters is but one facet in his complex world; his ability to weave moods and atmospheres with characters and ideas illustrates the lyrical density of his poetic realism. Certainly, Stanislavsky was helped by the comments of the playwright who, to a degree, worked beside him and told him to search deep in the play's structure for its reality. When he did, he not only found another layer of the play, but he also recognized the need to continue the pursuit, especially in an effort to capture an ever-richer vision of a character's psychology and to discover new methods to enhance new perceptions.

The importance of the actor's imagination as the essential catalyst in achieving the creative state challenged Stanislavsky; eventually it would be the topic of conversation between Stanislavsky and Mikhail Chekhov (1891-1955), Anton's nephew. Although the younger Chekhov was a student of Stanislavsky, he differed from his mentor in one area: the power of imaginative thought. Stanislavsky at first disagreed with Chekhov concerning the emphasis imagination plays in creating character, but he later embraced much associated with Chekhov's bias. In an eight-hour conversation at a Berlin cafe in 1928, they discussed the relevance of including the actor's personal imagination in the creation of a character. In "Life and Encounters," Chekhov recounts that Stanislavsky held fast to his theory that the actor's "affective memories" lead to "living, creative feelings, which are necessary for the actor on stage." Chekhov countered with the argument that "truly creative feelings [were] achieved through the imagination. According to my ideas the less an actor touches his own personal experiences the more he creates. In this he employs creative feelings which have been purified from everything personal. His soul forgets the personal experiences, reworks them in its subconscious depths, and transforms them into artistic feelings. Stanislavsky's device of 'affective memories,' on the other hand, does not allow the soul to forget personal experiences." They continued to disagree about how an actor should employ imagination. Chekhov felt strongly that the actor should be encouraged to "reimage" the play. If, for example, the actor observes a character, such as Othello, "(and not himself) in his imagination...the actor will feel what Othello feels, and his feelings in this case will be pure, changed, and will not involve him in his personality."[42] Obviously Chekhov was countering Stanislavsky's concept of the "magic if," in which an actor pays more attention to filtering the character through his personal emotional reality than to relying on creative inspiration.

Throughout Stanislavsky's career he endeavored to find ways to interpret the play's inner truth. Christine Edwards's comprehensive study, *The Stanislavsky Heritage: Its Contribution to the Russian and American Theatre*, divides his search into two periods of thought:

In the beginning, when the Moscow Art Theatre presented the plays of Chekhov, Stanislavsky found the right technique for their performance. Commencing with the atmosphere, the environment, he worked to make the everyday objects which surrounded the actors reflect the external truth of everyday life and disclose the inner life of the characters as well. Later, he was able to reverse this approach and start with an intuitive idea of the character, and after a complete understanding of his inner life, his motives, and the "trunkline" of his psychological actions, to discover the externals of the character. This led him to see the bond between the inner psychological actions and the external physical actions, and finally to evolve his method of physical actions.[43]

Stanislavsky's system continued to evolve throughout his career; eventually his views on the power of the actor's imagination would alter. Nevertheless, he continued to believe that an artful representation of life on the stage was created by the careful manipulation of the artist's imagination. In *The Stanislavsky System*, Sonia Moore offers a solid summary of Stanislavsky's thoughts on imagination: "Everything you imagine must be precise and logical. Always know who you are, when your imaginary scene is happening, where, how, and what for. All this will help you to have a definite picture of an imaginary life. Creative imagination will help an actor to execute actions naturally and spontaneously—this is the key to his emotions."[44] Although his procedures changed, Stanislavsky essentially believed in an artful representation of life on the stage—not actuality, not theatricality, but a psychophysical representation of life created by the careful manipulation of the artist's imagination.

Early Imagistic Designers

Adolphe Appia's (1862-1928) nonillusionistic designs resolve some of the controversy surrounding whether the physical stage was capable of suggesting the play's hidden poetry. Enriched by Wagner's vision that the total performed work of art (if unified by music) can be a mystic expression of life far beyond the secular concerns of naturalism, Appia suggests that by diminishing or rejecting representational scenery the theatre would be provoked to "look elsewhere for a valid principle to measure the degree of realism that can be brought to the stage through plastic media."[45] In *Music and the Art of the Theatre* (1899), Appia reveals how a harmonious unification of the play's external images (the synthesis of light and shadow, music, the symbolic rhythmic movement of a "word-tone" actor, a three-dimensional setting) can express the play's internal ideas.

Gordon Craig's approach to scene design was not unlike Appia's; it too was based on an imagistic response to the world of the play. Craig mentions in "The Artists of the Theatre of the Future" that the design of a play should help in creating "a place which harmonizes with the thoughts of the poet."[46] (Consider, for example, Craig's design of *Hamlet*.) The modern designer, then, works to echo the essence of the play, in ways that suggest, not describe, and provoke, not illustrate. In his article "Postmodern Design," Arnold Aronson summarizes this point when he characterizes "the new, modern décor" as "the spiritual essence of an object—scenery as Platonic shadows." This is, of course, in contrast to naturalistic design, which he perceives to be "a physical representation of psychological or sociological theory."[47] The scenic metaphor became one way in which modern designers could address their need to present the play's inner life in a way that echoes, enhances, or animates the drama.

The Potential of Subconscious Thought

The turn of the twentieth century brought new views of reality that included not only the power of the subconscious but also Einstein's theory on relativity (especially his thoughts regarding time and space) and the publication of the quantum theory. Previous perceptions about truth and its depiction were now met with skepticism. No longer did the scientific or artistic world rely solely on causal development or objective material delineation of time and space to illustrate truth and reality. Much of naturalism and realism's reliance on logic was replaced by an interest in re-evaluating the importance of subconscious thought. Yet the dreamlike world of subliminal images, which attempted to project the mythic subconscious state, was thought to be too vague, abstract, and decadent to elicit substantial communication. Often the impact was less than desirable because the theatrical execution of subjective thought and feeling was too amateurish or still caught in the "too, too solid flesh" of materialism to create a stimulating vision of the poetic world of symbolism. Innovative playwrights and experimental theatres, however, continued to explore neoromanticism, irrationality, and subjective thought. As perceptions enlarged, formula plays were replaced by those that explored the psychological development of individuals by showing how different levels of consciousness affect the human condition.

The theories of both Sigmund Freud (1856-1939) and Carl Jung (1875-1961) introduced the idea that multiple levels of reality—Freud's superego, ego, and id as well as Jung's collective unconscious—uncover uncensored, therefore more truthful, revelations about human needs and relationships. It was during this time that Freud completed *Interpretation of Dreams* (1900), in which he studied unconscious passions, instincts, and dreams. Later, in *Psychology of the Unconscious* (1912), Jung refuted Freud's substructuring of the mind, calling it incomplete; as well, he found Freud's theories on sexuality, aggression, and symbology too limiting. Friedrich Nietzsche (1844-1900), the cultural anthropologists, and Jung championed an art form that accessed the collective unconscious through symbol, myth, archetype, or primitive social structures.

Freud's and Jung's contributions to psychological realism are immense. Free association, a psychotherapeutic technique used to access the unconscious, produces a collection of images and symbols. These uncensored thoughts, pictures, feelings, and emotions surpass logical reasoning. Therefore, when these thinkers elected to explore the unconscious scientifically, they validated irrationality, subjectivity, and spontaneity, thereby presenting a more multifaceted truth behind human actions, needs, and desires.

Additionally, Freud's and Jung's theories have helped to clarify and inspire artistic thought and practice. In his book *Man and His Symbols*, Carl Jung offers, "A word or an image is symbolic when it implies something more than its obvious and immediate meaning. It has a wider 'unconscious' aspect that is never precisely defined or fully explained. Nor can one hope to define or explain it. As the mind explores the symbol, it is led to ideas that lie beyond the grasp of reason."[48]

Symbolists began to ponder dreams for symbols thought to be the keys that help to unlock a more spontaneous, primitive, or purer way of communicating. The free association that you might attribute to a dreamlike state produces symbols that elicit uncensored thoughts, feelings, and emotions that surpass logical reasoning.

The role of the image and symbol, especially when they are used to spark the audience's imagination or to suggest meaning and feeling that reach beyond traditional logical discourse, attracted the attention of artists who, like Appia and Craig, were interested in artful ways of saying something significant about the play's ideas, environment, mood, and atmosphere or in reaching the psychology behind a character's actions and relationships. The power of the visual symbol is invaluable for artists whose interest is either in creating a design on stage or in using physical gesture and movement to communicate the play's poetic ideas to the audience. At the turn of the twentieth century, the evolution of the theatrical form of poetic realism functions in several ways: It both depicts the outward appearance of reality on the stage and is a fertile source for revealing the play's subtle internal world. Thus Freud's and Jung's work helped to expand our understanding of reality through a combination of the rational and the nonrational, the objective and the subjective, the conscious and the unconscious.

The theories of Freud and Jung, Strindberg's plays, symbolism, and the impact of World War I influenced the expressionists and surrealists. The fragile nature of expressionism began in Germany as a literary movement with such writers as Ernst Toller (1893-1939), Walter Hasenclever (1890-1940), Reinhard Sorge (1892-1916), and Georg Kaiser (1878-1945). Perceiving reality to be neither finite nor causal, their plays exhibit exaggerated, rhapsodic images and symbols illustrating the nightmarish existence of a protagonist's internal state.

Like other nineteenth- and twentieth-century artistic movements, surrealism focused on the unconscious state for a more truthful depiction of reality; however, its founder, the theorist and playwright, André Bréton (1896-1966), felt the need to come to terms with the "absolute truth." For Bréton, surrealism became a means to attain a superreality through a system he labeled "automatic writing." Rooted in fantasy, imagination, and intuition, this technique is similar to improvisational drama and music, as it encourages the artist to work with the spontaneity of unconscious thought.

The development of a nonillusionary theatre certainly helped to capture the transitory nature of the dramatic form of poetic realism. Yet expanding perceptions created new problems for theatre artists. What interpretive techniques would help the artist explore the poetry within the play? How could current performance theories and techniques continue to address the challenges of modernism: contemporaneous subjective interpretations, imagistic thought, metaphorical staging, and synthetic practice?

THE FLEDGLING IMAGISTIC THEATRE AND THE METAPHORICAL ARTIST

The seminal practices of Goethe, Meiningen, Wagner, Antoine, Stanislavsky, Nemirovich-Danchenko, Appia, Craig, and others eventually elevated the director to a position where the *regisseur* could contemplate the wholistic nature of theatre. "I have many times written," Craig explains in *On the Art of the Theatre* (1911), "that there is only one way to obtain unity in the Art of the Theatre."[49] This way, Craig asserts, is the preeminence of the stage director, who should take responsibility for controlling and unifying each aspect of the performance, even though not creating every element of the production. Craig's stand was aided by the position of the "New Critics," who, by 1910, were advocating an end to genre criticism and a rejection of all rules, thereby suggesting that each work of art has its own integrity. The virtuoso director replaced the virtuoso actor, who had earlier relinquished the predominant position in response to the demands of ensemble acting. The director was given the power to control and therefore attain, as Appia suggested in *Music and the Art of the Theatre*, "a harmonious relationship between feeling and form, a perfect balance between the idea which the artist wishes to express and the means he uses to express it." The notion of aesthetic pleasure, then, is dependent upon not only a harmonious balance but also clarity. Appia continues, "If one of the means seems to us clearly unnecessary to the expression of the idea, or if the artist's idea—the object of his expression—is only imperfectly communicated to us by the means he employs, our aesthetic pleasure is weakened, if not destroyed."[50] Again the artist turned to the laboratory, the Studios of established theatres, this time to ponder modernism and its relationship to mise-en-scène.

Russia's cultural revolution was influenced by European artistic movements (reported and illustrated in Diaghilev's *World of Art* in 1898) and a newfound interest in Russian iconography and eighteenth-century painting. The Ballets Russes and their designers (among them Leon Bakst and Alexandre Benois) advanced the acceptance of symbolism by developing a form of sensual stylization through astonishing color combinations, the illusion of false perspective, or the avoidance of perspective altogether. Deliberate flatness created designs reminiscent of primitive paintings, icons, and folk art. Additionally, artistic collaboration, not unlike Wagner's *Gesamtkunstwerk*, promised the possibility of unity between thought and practice.

At the turn of the twentieth century, the pillars of Russian society (the autocracy of the Czar, Russian religion, and the structure of the family) crumbled under the weight of Marxism. As the foundation of Russian culture dissolved, its society reflected the ill effects of a country that ultimately had lost direction. Many felt that the theories of impressionism, symbolism, and cubism and, later of expressionism and surrealism, rather than the ordered principles of naturalism and realism, illuminated the complex nature of Russia's social and political unrest brought about by World War I.

Vsevolod Meyerhold

Provoked by the artistic vision of Chekhov, Maeterlinck, and other nonrealistic playwrights as well as that of the Russian symbolists, Stanislavsky turned to a respected member of the Moscow Art Theatre, Vsevolod Meyerhold (1874-1940), to explore nonconventional methods of production. In 1905, Meyerhold was invited to join the Moscow Art Theatre Studio on Povarskaya Street; promptly, he began working on two productions, Maeterlinck's *The Death of Tintagiles* (1894) and Hauptmann's *Schluck and Jau* (1900). Meyerhold's experimentations, however, concerned Stanislavsky; he felt, "The talented stage director tried to hide the actors with his work, for in his hands they were only clay for the molding of his interesting groups and *mises en scène*, with the help of which he was realizing his ideas."[51] Stanislavsky immediately postponed the Studio's premiere production. (Meyerhold and Stanislavsky amicably parted company, not to work together again until the end of their careers.) Meyerhold realized that a new form of theatre necessitated a complete break from Stanislavsky's naturalism and the illusionary concept of the fourth wall. Too much attention to detail was obfuscating the mystery and ritual of the theatrical event. Meyerhold elaborates, "The naturalistic theatre teaches the actor to express himself in a finished, clearly defined manner; there is no room for the play of allusion or for conscious understatement."[52] By removing the footlights and act curtain, extending the stage into the auditorium, leaving the lights on during the performance, his new *theatre of masks* made the audience aware that the actor was a craftsman playing a role, thereby welcoming the audience to participate "in the corporate creative act of the performance."[53]

In his pre-Bolshevik years, Meyerhold preferred the stark simplicity of suggestive scenic pieces. He felt that the setting, like the characters, should create the impression of the play's essence. In a 1906 production of *Hedda Gabler* at the Komissarzhevskaya Theatre, Meyerhold staged an "impressionistic" production of Ibsen's play. In defense of his nonillusionistic production, he offered, "Life is not like this, and it is not what Ibsen wrote.... Its aim is to reveal Ibsen's play to the spectator by employing new unfamiliar means of scenic presentation, to create an impression (but only an *impression*) of a vast, cold blue, receding expanse.... The theatre is attempting to give primitive, purified expression to what it senses behind Ibsen's play: a cold, regal, autumnal Hedda."[54]

Inspired by the theatrical conventions of the *commedia dell'arte*, the Greek, medieval, and oriental theatre, and marionettes, Meyerhold's "stylized" theatre trained actors to present rational, functional, utilitarian gestures that theatricalized a moment within the script. Whereas Wagner and Appia employed music and lights to create the inner dialogue or the soul of a work of art, Meyerhold orchestrated the actor's plastic movements ("gestures, mimes, poses, glances, and silences") into compositional patterns and pictures eliciting a series of scored images that communicated something about the play's essence to the audience. After discovering the playwright's pervading thought or significant idea, artists would translate "the *jeu*" into a theatrical style appropriate to the piece.[55] The actor's plastic movements, the accentuation of momentary image over naturalistic details, therefore helped in creating the play's inner dialogue.

What is meant by Meyerhold's "stylized" theatre? During the period when he was searching for a new theatre (1902-1907), he offered the following definition: "To 'stylize' a given period or phenomenon means to employ every possible means of expression in order to reveal the inner synthesis of that period or phenomenon, to bring out those hidden features which are to be found deeply embedded in the style of any work of art."[56] An early interest in impressionism, symbolism, and cubism influenced his ideas on style, later to be identified as Meyerhold's "theatre of the grotesque." For this artist, grotesque is

a deliberate exaggeration and reconstruction (distortion) of nature and the unification of objects that are not united by either nature or the customs of our daily life. The theater, being a combination of natural, temporal, spatial, and numerical phenomena, is itself outside of nature. It finds that these phenomena invariably contradict our everyday experience and that the theater itself is essentially an example of the grotesque. Arising from the grotesque of a ritual masquerade, the theater inevitably is destroyed by any given attempt to remove the grotesque—the basis of its existence— from it.[57]

In order to effect Meyerhold's "grotesque theatre," no attention would be paid to naturalistic details; originality would serve to appropriate "everything that corresponds to its *joie de vivre* and to its capricious and scoffing attitude toward life."[58] "What is basic in the grotesque," Meyerhold writes, "is that the audience is continually led from the plane that it has guessed to another one that it does not expect."[59] Nikolai Gorchakov adds, "If the method of stylization is analytical, then the method of the grotesque is synthetic."[60]

Unlike Stanislavsky and Nemirovich-Danchenko, Meyerhold was not attracted to the literary nature of theatre. Although he consistently considered the playwright's intentions, he wrote in 1912 that he was less interested in reproducing the playwright's words: "Words in the theatre are only a design on the canvas of motion."[61] Neither did he find the playwright's dramatic form (its linear causal progressions) or references to time and place beneficial. Instead, he thought the playscript was a springboard from which one could create the "stylized" version of the playwright's ideas. For example, in *Meyerhold's Theatre of the Grotesque* (a study of his postrevolutionary productions), James M. Symons describes how Meyerhold's 1924 reinterpretation of Ostrovsky's *Forest* is suggestive of his early interest in theatrical montage as well as satirical stylization. Symons offers: "By reordering the sequence of some scenes, by playing some episodes simultaneously in different areas of the stage, and by changing the locale of some episodes, Meyerhold sought to sharpen the satire of *The Forest*. The result was a contrapuntal effect of contrasting manners, morals, motives, actions, and reactions."[62]

Although many traditionalists criticized the presumptuous nature of a director who would alter the intent of a playwright, others argued that Meyerhold's production only sharpened the social satire intended in Ostrovsky's play.[63] It is not possible to know the intentions of a playwright (especially Ostrovsky, for he died in 1886); however, during Meyerhold's search for new forms, part of his preproduction work often included exploring everything the author had written that corresponded to the mood of the play, as well as reading everything written on the subject.[64] At the time of this writing, no performance-text is available that might offer whether he continued to research the work of the playwright or to survey correlated material. What we do know is that the production of this play illustrated Meyerhold's avant-garde position: "A play is simply the excuse for the revelation of its theme on the level at which that revelation may appear vital today."[65] In light of his stylized interpretation, which ridiculed the position of the government, it seems reasonable to suggest that Meyerhold was aware that Ostrovsky rewrote *The Forest* to emphasize that it was a social, *not* a domestic, comedy, whereupon his job as director was to theatricalize that idea on stage. As Meyerhold's vision evolved, his work appeared to be far less arrogant than biased toward theatricality. Materially duplicating the surface reality of a playscript was not part of Meyerhold's aesthetic; finding ways to inspire "the actors with his devotion to the work" by infusing them "with the spirit of the author and with his own interpretation" was. Meyerhold continues: "In this way the spectator is made to comprehend the author and the director through the prism of the actor's art. *Above all, drama is the art of the actor.*"[66]

Throughout the 1920s, Meyerhold all but abandoned the stylistic extremes of "biomechanics" and scenic constructivism.[67] A modified or "refined" version of both appeared in the production of *The Forest*, but the set for this production, as Symons describes, "did not consist of a multileveled 'machine for acting' or a series of such constructions. Instead, the flat stage floor and the broad, curving stairway...comprised the playing area."[68] A compromised form of "biomechanics" also appeared in the Ostrovsky production. When the virtuoso actors modified their acrobatics and more attention was paid to how they used props to present the play's ideas theatrically, the characterizations (albeit grotesque types) appeared to be less mechanized and more or less a metaphorical device. In *The Theatre in Soviet Russia*, Gorchakov provides several examples that illustrate how Meyerhold creates metaphorical physical action on stage: "A single phrase in Ostrovsky's text recalls that Neschastlivtsev had once performed some tricks, so a good number of them were shown on the stage. Aksiusha recalls, 'Day and night, since I was six, I have helped my mother work,' and so Meyerhold had her constantly working on the stage. When the merchant declares, 'I shall give up everything,' a flood of furs, shoes, and hats drops down on the stage from above."[69]

Meyerhold's approach contributed much to contemporary theatre; in particular, one of the contentions of this study is that most of Meyerhold's work anticipated modern metaphorical auteur-directing. Meyerhold's position concerning the role of the playwright is clear: "The director's art is the author's art, and not the performer's. But you must have [earned] a right to it."[70] Moreover, when the director assumes the role of the auteur, that does not mean that the *regisseur* has carte blanche to tamper frivolously or glibly with the architectonic structure of the play's inner world; in fact, Symons offers, "he was severely critical of directors who changed scripts just to be different or to create a hubbub."[71] The challenge was to expose boldly the play, highlighting its social, not its psychological, content.[72] Like the playwright's, the director's work stimulates subjective perceptions concerning human emotions and motives; however, the director brings them to life on the stage. In fact, Meyerhold sees the potential of a playwright in a good director: "You see, once these were one profession; only afterwards did they separate.... This is not a division in principle, but it is technically necessary, for the art of the theatre has become complicated, and one would have to be a second Leonardo da Vinci in order both to write dialogue with sparkle, and to cope with the world (I am, of course, simplifying a bit)."[73]

Meyerhold's highly acclaimed 1926 production of *The Inspector General* best exemplifies how this director "reimaged" Gogol's ideas, rendering a more timely social satire. Meyerhold's stylized version depicts what Gogol cloaked in subtlety. From eyewitness reports, Symons reconstructs Meyerhold's adaptation: "Not only did he go back to Gogol's original 1836 script, but he took the action out of its provincial setting, plopped it down in the midst of Petersburg-like aristocracy, and promoted the minor civil servants to high-ranking authorities in Tsarist officialdom. As a result, the 'distancing' of the tale which Gogol had found necessary and which allowed even the Tsar himself to enjoy the play's satire was eliminated and the ridicule fell on the heads of the most authoritative and 'respectable' persons in nineteenth-century Russia."[74]

The staging of the last moment boldly depicts a society of puppets. After hearing that Khlestakov was an impostor, the townspeople freeze in a collection of distorted, shocked physicalizations. The lights go out and come up again; this time the actors have been replaced by mannequins who duplicate the same shocked poses. Gorchakov describes the effect: "Meyerhold for the first time revealed his secret to the audience. For him, the world still possessed the young passions of symbolism. Even in the 'proletarian dictatorship' the world struck him as merely an exhibit, a collection of benumbed puppets who were the playthings and victims of Fate."[75] Fifteen episodes and a series of tableaux vivants, a continual musical orchestration of the play's leitmotif ("a stage symphony on Gogolian themes"), stark lighting, simplified setting, and the evolution of a new actor illustrate how Meyerhold creates the playscript's inner dialogue by accentuating momentary images over naturalistic details.[76] Some twenty-five years later, Meyerhold had begun to address Anton Chekhov's cry, "Theatre should be the quintessence of life."

The Studios of the Moscow Art Theatre

Leopold Sullerzhitsky's (1872-1916) work at the Moscow Art Theatre's First Studio (1911) had a profound impact on Yevgeny Vakhtangov, Mikhail Chekhov, and Richard Boleslavsky. While these artists experimented with Stanislavsky's system, Sullerzhitsky in particular encouraged his directors to experience passionately the play's images. He favored spontaneity over too much intellectual analysis; however, he recognized that not everyone is a creative genius with a never-ending stream of artistic images. Sullerzhitsky offered that the development of the informed intuition provided a possible solution: "Not all are endowed with the power of intuition in an equal measure; and besides, with the help of the mind the intuition itself can be aroused and stirred up 'to consciousness via the subconscious,' as Stanislavsky used to say. I always hated reason when it became the master of the soul—but it can be an excellent servant and one ought to know how to use it."[77]

A neoromantic who tempered vulgarity with beauty, spirituality, and a love of humanity, Sullerzhitsky suggested that the play's world be entered through the heart of the playwright. While Dickens's *Cricket on the Hearth* (1914) was in rehearsal at the First Studio of the Moscow Art Theatre, Sullerzhitsky is reported to have said: "Go to the very heart of Dickens, reveal it and the heart of the audience will open up to you."[78] Although the production (which was adapted and directed by Boris M. Sushkevich) came close to Sullerzhitsky's vision of theatre, P. A. Markov remarked in his manuscript *First Studio: Sullerzhitsky, Vakhtangov, and Chekhov* that in actuality the part where Sullerzhitsky suggested the actor should try "to come nearer to the author" was never realized; apparently, because "the *theme* of the story was at this time of greater importance for the Studio than the reconstruction of the Dickens style, the Christmas story prevailed over the Dickens humor."[79]

When Sullerzhitsky died, Vakhtangov (1883-1922) took over the leadership of the First Studio. There, and later at the Third Studio, he developed his "fantastic realism," a combination of Stanislavsky's "psychological realism" and Meyerhold's "theatricality." He favored Nemirovich-Danchenko's ideas on the through line of action but rejected the limited nature of verisimilitude: "We found an amazing way of making the theatre function as a substitute for life, and not copy life."[80] Unlike Meyerhold's "theatre of the mask," Vakhtangov preferred thought fused with feeling: "He demanded a 'forceful scenic diction,' he aroused within the actor the elemental subconscious feelings and a certain keenness of thought."[81] While minimalism, theatrical gesture, and Appia-like lighting were attractive, sterile aesthetic form or art-for-art's-sake were not. Vakhtangov never demonstrated what he wanted to his actors; instead, he relied on the power of suggestion by utilizing pictures or images. He preferred the harmony of content, form, and material and the generalized images of characters that better emphasized internal contradictions over creating theatricalized types. Yet, physical gesture was important to Vakhtangov; the actor's graphic movements created the sparse outlines of characters that were "the condensed signs of hidden feelings and perceptions."[82]

Vakhtangov's 1921 production of Strindberg's *Erik XIV* stressed the fate of a king who longs to live the simple proletariat life. Erik's character is woven out of contrasts and sooner or later must self-destruct. Vakhtangov's interpretation of one of Strindberg's later history plays focused less on the historicalization of the king of Sweden and more on the spirit of the Revolution and contemporaneous aesthetic innovations: "The dead world" (the aristocracy) depicted by "the massive quality of the stone-like figures was emphasized by their corpulence, heavy clothes, [and] laconic words" and was contrasted with "the living world" (or the proletariat), "the full-bloodedness and humanness of the living figures" depicted by more realistic characterizations and naturalistic makeup.[83] Ignaty Nivinsky's scenic design followed Vakhtangov's metaphorical depiction of Strindberg's play. Markov described the throne room as symbolically depicting the internal stress and disintegration of Erik's world: "The twisted columns of the palace, the spots of gold, the rust-spotted bronzes, gave an impression of Erik's decline and impending death. There were huge columns of straight lines, broken off here and there; these were fragments not of a palace, but of a prison—a prison for Erik."[84] The stylized doom of Erik's world was in sharp contrast to the realistically detailed setting for the commoners. Markov provides an eloquent illustration of how Vakhtangov's staging both reveals the script's inner meaning and supports an aesthetic based on stylistic unity:

The troops are coming near. Soon they will envelop the palace. An ominous hum is heard from afar. There is alarm in the palace. Eric with his chancellor stands in the middle of the stage.... They must strike the alarm. Then a courtier appears. He does not halt when the king calls him.... This in itself constitutes rebellion.... The system of platforms, arranged in the form of steps, gives the impression of flowing movements, of lifts, turns. Only three courtiers whispering on the central platform, while the fourth one hurriedly crosses the stage—convey the impression of alarm. A minute later and they leave in diagonal directions. The palace becomes deserted. Vakhtangov conveyed to it the feeling of alarm with the help of four side scenes, four courtiers, a system of ingratiating, leisurely movements; he transversed it with the lines of people dashing about, and by having set up small groups of people (who whisper to each other), by having one of the courtiers dashing by such a group (everyone for himself, save your own skin first) and then having everyone leave in diagonal directions into various corners (the rats scurried away)—he created in two minutes' time the impression of a deserted palace.[85]

Mikhail Chekhov, who played Erik XIV, began his innovative work with his association at the Moscow Art Theatre's Studios. Chekhov's aesthetic sought a balance between Stanislavsky's naturalism and Meyerhold's "theatricality." However, Nemirovich-Danchenko's careful approach to script analysis, Sullerzhitsky's search for the kernel of the play, and Vakhtangov's disposition toward contrasts and creating stylistic unity also contributed much to Chekhov's aesthetic. It was Mikhail Chekhov's initial work with images, feelings, and responses that created not only his well-known concept of *psychological gesture* but also a theatre whose style continued to test the limitations of naturalism.

When approaching a playscript, Chekhov championed ways to create a "psychology of style" by synthesizing information with imagination.[86] Chekhov favored improvisational acting and, generally, saw the role as a scenario, but not at the expense of ignoring theatre history or script analysis.[87] Becoming dramaturgically literate was perceived by this artist to be a springboard to imaginative thought, design, and action. Working with the play's images, scenic language, and rhythmical motifs, then, "not only lessens the probability of sterility, but also gives feeling to form."[88] Authenticity, for Mikhail Chekhov, existed only in the artist's imagination; therefore, it is not surprising that this actor's version of Malvolio at the Second Moscow Art Theatre appeared to be cocreated by Chekhov and Shakespeare.[89]

Mikhail Chekhov's early work with the playscript now sounds remarkably similar to how a contemporary artist engages in "reimaging" the play. An interview with two of his former students, Deirdre Hurst du Prey and Beatrice Straight, reveals something about early reliance on the actor's ability to reinterpret imagistically the playscript. Chekhov would take the playscript or scene and read it to his student actors. Deirdre Hurst du Prey continues, "We sat there and listened as [the play] was read very slowly, our eyes would be closed, and you began to immediately see the images that you heard, and it would be read more than once with this very slow and definite approach.... And then we would begin to improvise on the themes."[90]

Chekhov insists that the actor's work on character be in harmony with the play's dramatic form, composition, and rhythm. His work on the playscript mirrors his concept of the "anticipatory feeling of the whole," in which he suggests that the artist must first see the whole and then the parts. The 1942 version of "To the Actor" illustrates his position: "Each attempt to find the true composition of all parts, by means of the intellect, leads to false conclusions. The artistic intuition must first pronounce its judgment, and then the intellect can verify.... The intellect must help but it must not lead."[91] He later suggests that the twentieth-century artist must learn to use intellect in a different way, turning it into "a vivid imagination."[92] Chekhov's informed "reimaging" anticipated what will later be seen as a significant factor in interpretive cognition.

After the actor has experienced the "anticipatory feeling of the whole" in relationship to his character and the play's idea, Chekhov suggests, a thorough study of the playscript is in order. Chekhov perceives the complex organization of the script as similar to the laws that govern nature. He maintains that every play has a "compository gesture" consisting of the following parts: unity (the beginning and the end), the polarities of the beginning and the end (based on similarity), metamorphosis, climaxes (main, auxiliary, and accents), repetitions, and waves. The higher the art form, the more important the work of internal rhythm and composition in creating oneness. The artistic idea will emerge in wavelike repetitious patterns, similar to the rhythms of life, whereas the dramatic structure will be "complete, enclosed within itself, in a sense a unique world, with beings that belong to it and no other."[93]

Bertolt Brecht

Bertolt Brecht (1898-1956) has been cited by Robert Brustein in his *Reimagining the American Theatre* (1991) as an excellent example of a metaphorical auteur-director. Brecht's virtuosity is due, in part, to his ability to rework a play's images (either adapting an existing playscript or changing his own work) until its physical reality showed historically the condition of humanity. The intent of this auteur-director was to manipulate the production's visual and aural images continually, thereby encouraging the audience to question, ponder, and find possible solutions to contemporaneous moral problems. Physical gestures and the scenic images were used to distance the participant from making an emotional connection to the characters or the events on the stage. The images of Brecht's Epic Theatre, particularly those that achieve *Verfremdung* (estrangement), are in their own way seductive, but not in the sense of the poetic metaphor; they tantalize by stimulating the intellect, by turning everyday events "into something peculiar, striking and unexpected." Brecht's visual metaphors illustrated his Marxist politics; his didactic arrangement of images, however, was not without humor and artistry. Artistic ambiguity is part of the Epic Theatre: "What is obvious is in a certain sense made incomprehensible, but this is only in order that it may then be made all the easier to comprehend."[94]

Perceiving the world as constantly changing and changeable, Brecht challenged the static nature of Aristotle's *mimesis* and unity of time and place, as well as the passivity engendered by his interpretation of empathy. He was equally disinterested in a veristic theatre that, he felt, trivialized reality in its depiction of a linear arrangement of "culinary" objects. He also was suspicious of the illusionary hypnotic effect in Wagner's and Appia's theatre. After *Baal* (1918), *Drums in the Night* (1922), and *In the Jungle of Cities* (1923), he dismissed the symbolism of expressionism as self-indulgent and effete. He suggested instead that the complacency of voyeurism and the murky process associated with subconscious images should be replaced by a more vigorous theatre that would encourage social awareness, rational thought, and change.

The function of Brecht's concept of *Gestus* (interpreted by Willett to mean both the gist and gesture) tracked audience perception and made them aware of the social implications of each imagistic moment.[95] Carlson points out in *The Theories of Theatre* that Brecht is clearer about estrangement than *Gestus*; however, Brecht does distinguish between *Gestus* and traditional gesture, that is, gesture and *Gestus* both "make external something otherwise hidden, but gesture reveals subjective personal states, while *Gestus* is always social—it makes corporeal and visible the relationship between persons."[96]

Brecht's scenic images exposed the play's social history. Whereas the dramatic experience of the Aristotelian theatre supported collective participation in the play's world (from Sophocles to modern drama), Brecht found collective participation and universality illogical and unhistorical and actively sought ways to tell the play's story, showing the character's relationship to a given situation. Historification was achieved through the technique of alienation (*Verfremdungseffekt*), a device used to surprise or arouse the audience's curiosity. Whereas the bourgeois theatre's poetic images "emphasized the timelessness of its objects," the universality of its situations, and the unalterable nature of it all, Brecht's theatre historicizes events and characters.[97] The Brechtian device of halting emotional connection and dismissing theatrical mysticism, therefore, is intended not "to help the spectator but to block him."[98] By seeing a depiction of the play's social history, the audience understands how the world has changed, and, because change has occurred, additional alterations can take place.

Seemingly this theatre is nonillusionistic; its images are neither completely "lifelike" nor random. Brecht favored the impact of moral tableaux, songs, speeches, placards, projections, film, the turntable, specially stylized props, nonillusionistic scenery, and lights to reinforce the social implications of each moment of the play. The perception that any playscript needed to be treated in special theatricalized ways and that "almost everything was stylized to make it more expressive" continued to be practiced at the Berliner Ensemble long after Brecht's death.[99]

Following the tradition of Brecht's Epic Theatre, scenic designers create unique theatrical worlds that are functional and metaphorical. Often beginning with a storyboard, Brecht's designer, Caspar Neher, carefully would outline the important moments, particularly those that illustrate how the characters relate to a specific situation. Historical research is part of the design process, but only to the degree that the set functions as a space with only those architectural details that help the actor tell a story. What is far more important is the clarity with which the scenic design, if left by itself, tells the audience "the play's story and conflicts, its period, social relations, etc."[100] As with the set, props were carefully researched but not restricted to period; both were functional and artistic. In particular, props served as an expressive, albeit intellectual, metaphorical image of the play's historical/social reality. For example, the swords used in a production of *Coriolanus* that premiered at the Berliner Ensemble Theatre in 1964 after Brecht's death were worn horizontally on the front of the soldiers; the position was described as "practical" and pleasing to the eye. The short sword—more like a butcher's knife than a sword—was chosen because it was "an implement for crude stabbing rather than elegant piercing."[101] But even more provocative was the ensemble's use of Brecht's famous revolving stage. Prior productions had already featured Coriolanus as a fascist, but their new reading of Shakespeare's play showed a connection to Stalin and the cult who followed his powerful personality. According to one of the production's directors, Manfred Wekwerth, the revolving stage made it easier to illustrate that war is not chaotic but carefully choreographed. Further, it helped to show Coriolanus as not merely a fascist bully but also, at the beginning, a capable soldier, "an expert in all the technical skills of war...much needed by his countrymen."[102] Only later he "exploits his usefulness for purposes of blackmail." Because it was necessary to show the protagonist's "extraordinary gifts as a soldier and general," the battle scenes, Wekwerth explains, carried a great deal of weight and were carefully executed. He continues, "They also show the differences between the two elements necessary to make a cult: those who worship and those who are worshiped, the people and Coriolanus."[103]

The polemical intent of Brecht's performance theories and practices is clear: The dialectics of the play and production change according to its social context. His performance theories and techniques, however, are often complex and contradictory. Actors are trained to show both their attitude toward their character and their awareness of participating in a social/historical event; they are to be observed standing between the events on stage and the audience. Therefore, it is not hard to understand why the standardized movements and gestures of the traditional Chinese theatre would interest Brecht: "The Chinese performer is in no trance. He can be interrupted at any moment.... After an interruption he will go on with his exposition from that point."[104] Like the Asian actor who masters technique and shuns the spontaneity of individual creativity, the Brechtian actor assiduously rehearses each gesture. Clarity, communication, and beauty are significant to both; however, Brecht's perception of gesture is from a social point of view—as a way to illustrate how an individual's "work forms his habits, his attitudes, his physical behavior down to the smallest movement." He is interested in how, for example, Grusha (the kitchenmaid in *The Caucasian Chalk Circle*) would pick up a baby.[105] Because the actors master the nature of the character, they are freed from unpredictable emotions and relaxed enough to stand back and show how they feel about the character and encourage the audience to do likewise. Yet with all this emphasis on curtailing the actor's subjective emotions, psychological motivations are not totally abandoned. Ekkehard Schall, the actor who played Coriolanus, offers, "I like to add psychological touches—virtues and vices—to the roles I play, but they are not useful in making basic judgments about the characters." He adds that work in this area is part of the early dramaturgical stage of rehearsal, when there is discussion about the play's fable, what is going on in the play, and what must be shown by the characterizations, but it is not part of the on-stage rehearsal process. He continues, "Although the actor may indulge him self by providing the villain with many virtues, the important thing is that nevertheless the character behaves badl y."[106] Likewise, to keep the audience entertained, the Brechtian form of theatre doesn't completely abandon empathic responses; in fact, part of the complex nature of his theatre is his understanding of artistic ambiguity, the contradiction between feeling and thought. The combination of opposites (empathy and alienation) stimulates thought and was, according to Richard Hornby, "respectable for Brecht because, as a Marxist, he was dedicated to the Hegelian 'dialectical' form of thinking, which makes a virtue of contradiction. For Hegel and Marx, the truth is never to be found in a single viewpoint, but always in a combination of opposites."[107]

In the ten to twelve months that it often took to bring the play to production, each moment was carefully examined "for the characters' situation, for the story's situation, [and] for the actions going on around the character."[108] In preproduction, or before the actors started to work on stage, they would spend months exploring their characters' social relationships, subsequent behavioral patterns, attitudes, and human weaknesses. After the blocking (which Brecht considered "the backbone of the production") was completed and the actors knew their lines, attention was paid to refining gesture.[109] To do this, Brecht encouraged his actors to explore images derived from characters in photos and the paintings of both Breughel and Bosch. Brecht favored these paintings for their storytelling ability, not in the linear fashion of naturalism and early realism but because "their people were stamped by their lives and occupations, their vices and beliefs."[110]

Prior to Brecht's theatre, the metaphorical capacity of the scenic image or the actor's gesture was—with the exception of Meyerhold—relegated to revealing something about the play's metaphysical dimensions. Brecht's intellectually based metaphors were the result of fresh interpretations of plays that address current, not past, realities. The "metanarrative" in Brecht's theatre provoked thought, not feelings, about the relationship between subjects (humanity) and objects (events). In essence, Brecht's work as a metaphorical auteur-director with the Berliner Ensemble consisted of reworking a playscript until its gist and gesture gave the participants a clear literal picture ("no gold plated images of false heroes") of social conflict seen through modern eyes.

Antonin Artaud

Much has been written about Antonin Artaud (1896-1948), his theories, and his impact on contemporary theatre. What is significant to this study, however, is his insistence that theatre must seek ways "to express objectively certain secret truths, to bring into the light of day by means of active gestures certain aspects of truth that have been buried under forms in their encounters with Becoming."[111] Artaud wrote a series of essays and manifestos illustrating his theories, some of which are found in his book *The Theatre and Its Double*

(1938). Essentially the object of Artaud's "pure theatre" is not to perpetuate surface understanding by recording the external details of reality on stage, nor is it to resolve "social or psychological conflicts, [or] to serve as a battlefield for moral passions."[112] Instead, Artaud championed a theatre that would recover life's mysteries, free humanity from life's atrocities, and renew the human spirit. He altered plays, replacing much of the verbiage with an enhanced mise-en-scène. Artaud envisioned a ritualized theatre whose modern-day myths would exorcise the shadows in a collective unconscious imbued with the real problems of contemporary society. He would therefore question many traditional Western theatre theories and practices: "the playwright as god," the ability of discursive language to communicate effectively, the acceptability of merely reproducing a play on stage, the traditional relationship between the stage and the audience, the illusionary depiction of time and space, and the personalized psychological development of character. Influenced by Asian theatre, especially the Balinese dancers, Artaud elevated the significance of the mise-en-scène to a position of preeminence by suggesting that theatrical images should link the physical to the metaphysical world.

Western theatre's reliance on language, adherence to text, and rational thought were far too limiting for an artist whose prior association was with the surrealist movement. However, whereas the surrealist founder, André Bréton, would favor "automatic writing" as a technique to release the uncensored world of the unconscious, Artaud would rather abolish words altogether. His theatre never completely abandoned language, yet he continued to seek ways to communicate nondiscursively. Thus, Artaud's theatre consisted of symbolic gestures, archetypal characters, and other images of depersonalization (masks, ritualistic costumes, nonverbal and grotesquely exaggerated intonations). Artaud preferred the eloquence of the Balinese dancer over the Western actor, whose personality often obfuscated any possibilities of poetic resonance. The carefully articulated gestures/movements and modulated sounds of the Balinese formed a collection of "animated hieroglyphs"[113] that liberated uncensored attitudes unavailable to rational thought.

Artaud's theatre was constructed to evoke an immediate emotional response from his audience; it was not an intellectual theatre of ideas. He decried the development of psychological realism and determinism and professed that too much attention was paid to producing the masterpieces and preserving the culture of societies that no longer existed. If interest in the theatre was declining, Artaud surmised, it was because masterpieces were too literary and "fixed in forms that no longer respond to the needs of the time."[114] Theatre had lost its immediacy because it had become too safe and common. Therefore he proposed that the efficacy of the theatre could be restored if the poetry within the text were ritualized on stage; if poetic images collectively evoked painful revelations concerning our repressed fears and anxieties; if we rejected the great myths of the past and embraced the myths of a new world order; and if the theatrical event became like the plague (a crisis that collectively cleanses society either by death or cure). Only then would there be the possibility of revelation. Artaud continues,

the action of theater, like that of plague, is beneficial, for, impelling men to see themselves as they are, it causes the mask to fall, reveals the lie, the slackness, baseness, and hypocrisy of our world; it shakes off the asphyxiating inertia of matter which invades even the clearest testimony of the senses; and in revealing to collectivities of men their dark power, their hidden force, it invites them to take, in the face of destiny, a superior and heroic attitude they would never have assumed without it.[115]

Artaud values the liberating power of the symbolic gesture to free the unconscious to discover "allusions to secret attitudes inaccessible to thought."[116] He also trusts the symbolic gesture to convey simultaneously its material form and the mystical nature of its metaphysical shadow: "The plague takes images that are dormant, a latent disorder, and suddenly extends them into the most extreme gestures; the theater also takes gestures and pushes them as far as they will go: like the plague it reforges the chain between what is and what is not, between the virtuality of the possible and what already exists in materialized nature."[117] In his essay "The Theatre and the Plague," Artaud makes a compelling, albeit not scientific, case concerning the extrarational suggestive nature of images. He suggests that the fear of the plague (its images) has the power to affect humanity when physically nothing actually has occurred. Artaud's rendition of the plague causes (among other things) swollen tongues, fever, blisters, discharges, and eventually death. But when subsequent autopsy produces no scientific cause of death, Artaud finds a correlation between the individual who is psychosomatically affected by a fear of the plague and the actor who is transmogrified by the suggestive power of poetic images. Artaud summarizes his position as follows:

The state of the victim who dies without material destruction, with all the stigmata of an absolute and almost abstract disease upon him, is identical with the state of an actor entirely penetrated by feelings that do not benefit or even relate to his real condition. Everything in the physical aspect of the actor, as in that of the victim of the plague, shows that life has reacted to the paroxysm, and yet nothing has happened.[118]

If images are so powerful, then why are they often subordinate to language in the theatre? Stating that "dialogue—a thing written and spoken—does not belong specifically to the stage," Artaud offers

that the stage is a concrete physical place which asks to be filled, and to be given its own concrete language to speak.

I say that this concrete language, intended for the senses and independent of speech, has first to satisfy the senses, that there is a poetry of the senses as there is a poetry of language, and that this concrete physical language to which I refer is truly theatrical only to the degree that the thoughts it expresses are beyond the reach of the spoken language.[119]

Theatrical gesture, movement, and scenic diction can create a language for the senses that surpasses the logic of traditional discursive forms of communication.

If Meyerhold can be accepted as the first metaphorical director, it was Tyrone Guthrie (1900-1971) and Peter Brook (b. 1925) who followed suit and set their eyes on a theatre that rejected the duplication of accepted interpretations of playscripts and the impulse to recapture the author's "intent" and "message." The printed play, instead, was perceived, as Guthrie put it, as "not the end of the matter [but] the beginning."[120] Rumanian directors Liviu Ciulei (b. 1923), Andrei Serban (b. 1943), and Lucian Pintilie (b. 1933) were influenced by the evolution of modernism, the theories and practices of the Russian theatre, Brecht, and Artaud; Serban also spent a number of years working with Peter Brook in Paris. Like their predecessors they found preparatory work on a playscript or the style of a production pedestrian if one merely traced the outlines of a play. Often controversial, their liberties with the text and their stunning metaphorical tableaux, movements, gestures, and overall production design elements released a new vision and provided further insight into the play.

For Peter Brook, the preparation of a playscript and the eventual production are subject to multiple shifting perceptions. He enters the play's world imagistically: His first response is a "deep, formless hunch," which could be "a smell, a color, a shadow."[121] All conceptual images are left open and remain responsive to the subjective perceptions of his collaborators. Rehearsals begin with no set speeches or definitive ideas about the play's meaning, let alone a fixed directorial approach. Some twenty years later, Brook continues to be challenged by many of the ideas on contemporary directing he originally set forth in his first book, *The Empty Space* (1968). The play's poetic possibilities, as outlined in his "holy theatre," play a significant part in his next book, *The Shifting Point* (1987); however, his imagistic exploration appears to be clearly influenced by rediscovery, or the continual evolution of momentary events, and the subjective perceptions of the artistic collaborative. Yet, multiple perceptions can be accomplished on stage only if facts, dates, places, and set interpretations are freed from the logic of a rigid construct of materialism and an overzealous need to recover the author's intent. The work of the contemporary theatre artist continues to demand a willingness to accept and the skills to perceive and metaphorically project what Brook calls the *density* of the playscript.

Brook's theatre evokes a series of subjective theatrical images that both present and suggest something about the playscript's contemporaneous nature. Believing that the play's fabric—especially in poetically dense plays (Shakespeare, Chekhov, or Weiss's *Marat/Sade*)—evokes a series of impulses, not fixed messages, to its audience, Brook seeks comparable ways to echo the playscript's latent imagery on the stage. Yet, his is not an example of a formalist aesthete theatre whose heavy symbolism ("grotesque masks, heightened make-ups, hieratic costumes, declamation, [and] balletic movement") existed for their own sake.[122] Everything on stage—sounds to silence, theatricalized gesture to simple movement, material objects to an empty space—is accepted both as a recognizable aspect of reality (albeit limited) as well as a metaphorical but transitory perception of truth. Brook encourages simplicity: One stick suggests an entire forest; a simplified gesture/movement or the broad outline of a characterization offers a provocative fragment of a complete personality. (It is important, however, to point out that these results are the products of substantial discussion, searching, improvisation, and experimentation, as well as years of theatrical experience and the resultant skill.) Ironically, Brook discovers that his nonillusionary metaphorical theatre is, in some ways, more illusionary: its simplicity encourages the audience to fill in with their imagination.

Not wanting to choose the "fire" of Artaud's theatre over the "clear vision" of Brecht's or the "humanity" of Stanislavsky's, Brook selects and imaginatively combines those techniques that aid his effort to make the playscript's content speak simultaneously to the emotions and intellect of his audience.[123] Influenced by modern theatre artists, Brook's vision of theatre ultimately discourages the complacency associated with determinism and voyeurism and encourages action. He champions a theatre whose images elicit immediate responses from its participants (artists and the audience), thereby stimulating subjective "reimaging" and participation. Moreover, one could argue that this dynamic exchange continues throughout the run of a production, thereby exemplifying the momentary nature of his theatre. The role of theatre, Brook concludes, "is to give this microcosm a burning and fleeting taste of another world, in which our present world is integrated and transformed."[124]

At roughly the same time that Guthrie and Brook were exploring a theatre that reached beyond the reproduction of accepted interpretations, the regional theatre movement (for example, the Guthrie Theatre in Minneapolis) began to affect the way American artists perceived and practiced theatre. Broadway's star system and the realities of commercial theatre had eliminated much that is associated with the rich history of the European laboratory theatres. Although many artists who worked in the United States (such as Robert Edmond Jones, Mordecai Gorelik, Jo Mielziner, O'Neill, Wilder, Williams) and its theatres (Provincetown Players, Theatre Guild, Group Theatre, Federal Theatre Project) had been influenced by the theories and practices of modernism, the harsh realities associated with survival and competition discouraged significant long-term synthesis of artistic thought and practice. The emergence of this country's regional theatres in the early 1960s fostered experimentation and artistic collaboration without the trappings of commercial expediency and conservatism. The development of an imagistic theatre and the evolution of a metaphorical mise-en-scène not only produced a theatrical style whose temperament was as volatile as twentieth-century perceptions, but it also brought theatre back to the people when it continued to rediscover the mysteries of the human condition buried deep within the poetry of the playscript.

3

Dialogues with Professional Artists: Contemporary Perceptions of Play Analysis

As the years went on, I became convinced that more is better. The more you do before, the better off you are. Because a number of times I refused certain plays that turned out to be very good, very successful. Some other times I took plays and did them, and they turned out to be terrible. Looking back, I should have been able to anticipate that. I believe that you can really analyze and discover what is in the script. And there are a lot of people who do not believe that at all. They will say, "Well, we will find out." At that point it is often too late. Or certain directors put the play into rehearsal before they really understand it. They just sit and listen to the actors and get something from that. Usually they do not know what the script's structure is, and you cannot get that from listening to a rehearsal. You only understand that after all the rehearsals are over, and the thing has taken shape. Then it is too late.[1]

— Lester Polakov

I never sit down and say, "This is the way I am going to do this play." The whole thing just seems to evolve. And that means I come in with a clean slate. I do not have a set design. I do not want a set designed; I do not want costumes designed; I do not want any decisions made before the rehearsal period starts. I think that one of the greatest things about the theatre is that you have the time to find the play. And if you have made your mind up before it begins...once you make a decision, your options are gone. So I think you have to keep your options open as long as you can. The rehearsal period is just that for me. And it is that not only for me, but also the designers, the prop people.... You know, things evolve and productions evolve. That's the way I approach the production as a director and an actor too.[2]

— Richard Jenkins

Artists who are interested in the play's hidden poetic reality, in fresh and perhaps more relevant insights about its world, and in metaphorical productions pursue the playscript's imagistic infrastructure. Nonliteral artists do not like illusionistic theatre because they know that the audience, more than likely, will get involved with the decorations instead of what is happening in the play. Artists who work imagistically might or might not do a substantial amount of preplanning. As stated in the previous quote, the director Richard Jenkins likes to trust his subconscious, the rehearsal process, and working in collaboration over conscious planning, whereas other artists do specific kinds of research prior to the beginning of rehearsal. Consensus is not at issue here. What artists do see eye-to-eye on, however, especially those who are interested in experiencing the play imagistically by responding to the play's hidden poetry, is how they can make the playscript come alive today. This is one of the reasons that director Zelda Fichandler attempts to read the playscript prior to production (even though she might have read it many times before) as if she were encountering the playwright's words for the first time. For the professional, the task is a daunting one. Consider that these practitioners are well read; yet, this artist, in particular, makes a compelling case for learning how to read the play as if "you had never met it before, not studied it in class, not seen it at auditions a thousand times, not witnessed a dozen productions at the regional theatres; but read it, encounter the experience of the play totally freshly."[3]

Participating in the process of dropping into or rediscovering the world of the play is an exhausting endeavor even for established artists, and experiencing a play "for the first time" especially is difficult if they are working on a classical play. For example, even though artists might not remember in detail the plot or characters of Chekhov's *Cherry Orchard*, for instance, they more than likely have read one of his plays or perhaps have worked on or seen his plays; worse yet, they might recall, with some trepidation, that this playwright is remembered for his dry, listless, and uneventful work. If artists hold on to past, generalized notions about the playwright's work, their readings and subsequent productions will be tainted with yesterday's feelings or, even more deadly, a warmed-over version of someone else's interpretation. Even if Chekhov is one of the artist's favorite playwrights, that does not guarantee that the resulting production will not be stale. How refreshing and important it is, then, to make an attempt to read the playwright's words with virgin eyes and ears. When artists suppress preconceived thoughts and feelings about the play they are preparing and meet the author's work anew, there is the distinct possibility they will discover something more about the world of the play.

THE TASK OF ARTFULLY READING THE PLAY

When one asks prominent contemporary artists how they begin the process of preparing for production, many immediately answer how important it is to learn to read the playscript. Although this comment might appear to be elementary and simple, it is important to bear in mind that artists do not view this part of preparation lightly. The most accomplished artists talk about reading the playscript over and over again without any interruptions. Zelda Fichandler remarks, "If the phone rings or someone comes to the door, I put the play away. I don't go on with it after I'm interrupted." Lighting designer Thomas Skelton also relishes those early encounters with a play: "If someone wants to talk to me about a production of a play, I organize a period when I can read the script in one sitting, when I can be fairly assured of no phone calls and no headaches. I really indulge myself." He views this time as one of his few creative opportunities to work with the script, because this is the only time he approaches the play as an audience member. Skelton continues,

I try to read the script without reading the stage directions. I simply keep track of the characters' names. But otherwise, I try to just read the play in one sitting and allow myself to react to it on an emotional level without identifying where the scenes are taking place or making any notes of any kind, so if there are lanterns or fireplaces that are referred to, I don't write it down at that point because I'm really working with the words.

I try to find out where the play takes me and what I am thinking. Or I think through the characters and how I am responding to them and if they are sympathetic and if so, why? Or, if they are not sympathetic, why? So that I begin to figure out, without doing a detailed script analysis, who the antagonists and protagonists are and how I feel about it. Maybe I will produce some doodles or something else physical or pictorial that I can hang on to later.[4]

The actress Shirley Knight prepares by reading the play every day (prior to rehearsal, during rehearsal, and in production) in order to discover it word-for-word, much like a pianist discovers a concerto note-by-note: "Theatre is like playing the piano; it's a very technical thing. Playing notes over, over, and over again until the player is at one with the notes, and they no longer have to think about which notes they are playing. And when they reach that place, artistic instinct takes over and the music flows."[5]

Continually rereading the play is one avenue that takes the artist into the world of the play. It is a rigorous process; however, artists find that through close reading the words, phrases, monologues, and dialogue become catalysts that expand the play's reality from the logic of the text to a series of explosive poetic images. They are well aware that a good playscript is filled with images waiting to be found, mined, or rediscovered. The director Mark Lamos remarks that when he begins working on a play, he crawls "through the script like a caterpillar—word-by-word." He continues,

I speak [the play] out loud. I find connections between words. I take it apart to see how it's put together as a piece of poetry. I do not try to impose a sound. I believe the structure of the play is musical. There are quarter notes, and there are half notes, and there's a metronome marking. Poetry is structure. You can't just pick up an Emily Dickinson poem and say: "Oh, right, I get it." It takes a minute. It's the same with every speech written in iambic pentameter. You cannot take it for granted. Ibsen, on the other hand, writes characters who speak straightforwardly, but underneath, their subtext is refuting them. It says a lot about our age that plays that actually have a great deal of subtext are easier for us to read than plays like Shakespeare, for instance, which don't.[6]

Needless to say, a careful rereading of the play is an essential component when preparing a playscript for production. Whereas the solitary first reading provokes unbiased, purely emotional responses that unite the reader with the material, subsequent readings allow artists to focus on the play word-by-word, concentrating on how the play's language contributes to its overall structure, internal rhythms, leitmotifs, colors, tones, and textures.

Many artists remark how important it is for them to hear and see the play in their imaginations. However, artists cannot engage in a play on a metacognitive level unless they have indulged in the luxury of taking time with its language. Some artists, in particular Robert Morgan, spoke about how they enjoyed having the play read out loud to them by the director. This costume designer engages in the play's world by playing all the roles. He recalls,

I go back and read very slowly in the privacy of whatever space I can manage, and pretend that I am each of the actors, and I act the scenes out. And I am a terrible actor. But what I'm after is the impulse of the actor in every scene of the play because it tells me what is delicious about the material. I like to experience the play not from an analytical point of view, but, instead, from the instinct of the actor on stage who is trying to make a moment happen, to make a character flower, to make a difference in the audience's life, to be seen, to be thought beautiful or clever or powerful dramatically—because that's where the blood of the piece is.[7]

Taking the Time to Reflect

Careful readings are essential, but time away from the play can be inspirational. Because artists trust the possibility of what can happen when the play simmers in their imagination, many find it productive to take the time to simply sit and daydream about the script. During this reflective period, artists provoke unconscious connections with the material by listening to music or looking at some form of visual art. They feel that free spontaneous association with other stimuli conjures additional images—some of which are far more provocative than their original impressions.

PREPARING NEW ADAPTATIONS AND TRANSLATIONS

Artistic directors such as Robert Brustein and Mark Lamos value the process of working firsthand with *new* translations. Often the goal of becoming intimately aware of the nuance in words and phrasing can be hindered by the translation. The translation can become, as Mark Lamos states, "[a] barrier between you and the play.... And yet it is paradoxically the only thing that makes the play available to you." On translation as a way of effectively reading a play and as an early form of analysis, Robert Brustein offers,

One of the ways I have found to read a play is to adapt it from an early translation if I do not know the language. When you are putting a play in modern language and getting underneath those words, you are doing a form of analysis. It creates a stronger emotional connection to the dialogue than a literary approach. As a matter of fact, most of the productions done recently at the American Repertory Theatre have been my adaptations. The productions I did at Yale were adapted by others, and I was often not satisfied with the translations. So I thought maybe I can make this more actable if I can put it into language more available to actors. Less literary and more actable. But it had a very important side-effect for me. I would generally do my adaptation in the summer before production started, revising, and rerevising, following the nub of what this author had to say. It helped me understand the play a lot more through this process of translation and adaptation than any other form of preparation.[8]

When appropriate, Mark Lamos works with two translators: someone who knows the language and another individual who does not know the language but who knows how the language effectively translates to the stage. He explains:

When we produce Ibsen we have two translators: one who is a Norwegian, and one who is not and does not understand Norwegian at all but is an actor. So between those two people and the transliterations and three or four other texts—I slowly begin to understand what the meaning of each word might have meant to Ibsen a century ago in Norway—or what it might hold in terms of meaning for us now. But, I only work with translations which we commission—it serves as a learning technique for me. It's really an essential way for me to understand what the play means word-by-word.

When Tori Haring-Smith translated Chekhov's *Seagull* for a production at the Trinity Repertory Theatre (1992), her goal was to provide the director, Richard Jenkins, with what he wanted, namely, "an American translation that wouldn't be jarring to American ears any more than the original script would have been to Russian ears." Her meticulous work on the script produced not only a new translation but also some helpful observations concerning the subtle nature of Chekhov's humor. For example, she finds his comic spirit is due, in part, to the ways in which this playwright "paces his writing" and in the repetition of certain words. She explains,

Chekhov uses ellipses in the original script quite a bit. However, in Trigorin's Act Two speech to Nina, where he talks about hating his life as a writer, there are almost no ellipses. The rapid colloquial speech, repeated words, and the lack of ellipses suggest that he just wanted Trigorin's lines to burrrr. It became important for me to make the language run like that.

I found in other translations there was a tendency both to muddle syntax and to vary words more often than Chekhov did. Chekhov would use the same word over and over again like "charming, charming, charming, charming." In another translation, you would find "charming" translated as "genteel" and then "warm" and then "pleasant" or something like that. And I said, "No! There is a reason why Chekhov kept repeating that word. The character keeps getting caught." Repetition becomes a key to the character. For example, I spent a tremendous amount of time going back to the first act when Sorin says, "What do you think about Trigorin's novel?" Treplev responds, "I don't know, what can you say about it? It's very clever and charming. But after reading Tolstoy, you don't want to read Trigorin's stuff." The words "clever and charming" are exactly the same words that Trigorin later uses when talking about his own writing. We found humor in that connection—a retrospective humor.[9]

THE IMPORTANCE OF DRAMATIC ACTION

While many of the artists who contributed to this study saw the importance of making an initial emotional connection with the playscript, they also made it clear that their subjective, initial responses had to correlate with the play's dramatic action. Identifying and tracing dramatic action from the beginning to the end of each scene helps the actor, director, and designer clarify what is happening *in* the play's world. Zelda Fichandler remarks that her early training involved watching the director Alan Schneider's rehearsals and hearing him say to the actors, "What's going on here? I don't know what's going on." Although she says it took her a long time to understand what she called a psychophysical action, she finds that asking a direct question can uncover dramatic action. She explains, "If you want something then you do something to get it. A psychophysical action could be my reaching for this glass, or it could be my killing a king. But it is still a psychological action. Motion is the result of emotion. And emotion is the result of thought. Thought is the result of needing and wanting. And wanting and needing is the result of the central conflict at the heart of the play."

To this day, when preparing a play for production, Fichandler finds it valuable to ask, "What's the event? What's the hunger? What's the need?" And because characters' needs are rarely met, it is equally beneficial in the development of dramatic action also to locate who or what keeps them from obtaining their desires. Rhythmical patterns are created from characters' actions as they continue to face and challenge those obstacles that keep them from getting what they need. When action becomes repetitious, the playwright is telling the artist something more about how the emotional world of the character drives the play's dramatic action.

CREATING THE PORTRAIT GALLERY AND STORYBOARDS

The scene designer Ming Cho Lee and the lighting designer Arden Fingerhut present compelling cases concerning the importance of creating a "portrait gallery" or "storyboard" as a means by which the artist can find out more about the play's characters and its world. Ming Cho Lee insists that the designers and directors he trains do a portrait gallery as part of their early preparation. He explains,

The most concrete way of grabbing hold of the play is to make its characters as vivid as possible. And when those characters are vivid and events are vivid and it grabs you, then there is passion. There is a need to do that play. If you don't do it you lose something. And so the portrait gallery is paintings or portraits of people. Although I tend to insist that they should not bring [to class] great paintings, that they really should be photographs of people. They can be actors; they can be living; they can be anything we can look at and say: "That is Amanda, Laura, Treplev, Arkadina, and on and on." *In the case of the previous characters I insist that these photographs are unrelated to the historical period.* However, if you are doing *Buried Child* you would look for the landscape of central Illinois. What kind of openness, or how dry it is, or what kind of weather, or what kind of light? It is important to pick up a picture and say, "This is great! I think that is what the play looks like. That's the heat!"[10] (italics added)

Arden Fingerhut's journey into the playscript often included what she termed a "storyboard":

I do a lot of sketching. I sketch. I draw. I do a lot of schematic drawing. I always do that before I do colors. I do a specific scene-by-scene, cue-by-cue drawing. I rarely use color; I do black and white sketches. If I am really into mood, I will use black paper and use pastels so that it really comes out. These drawings are so the images can come out. It has to do with the images being specific. Lighting is very specific; each moment has to specifically relate to the play. If you do a general light plot, then you get a general design that does not have very much to do with images.[11]

Portrait galleries and storyboards are rigorous, time-consuming, and complex projects. Yet, Ming Cho Lee feels that "meaning, theme, and subject are revealed through action" and that action can come alive through the portrait gallery and/or storyboards. But most would agree that before an artist can select a meaningful collection of individuals who might inhabit the play's world or can detail with any kind of precision the moment-to-moment images that illustrate the play's "virtual reality," it is advantageous to undertake some form of dramatic analysis.

CREATING THE DRAMATIC SCORE

A form of analysis that involves working word-by-word or image-by-image is called "scoring the play." Some artists talked about breaking the play down into what commonly are referred to as "beats" or "French scenes." Scoring permits artists to work with the play moment-to-moment, revealing both its shape and structure as well as any hidden potential in the play's dramatic structure, character development, or "scenic diction." Costume designer Robert Morgan made it clear that he begins his work on the play by making a "French-scene chart." He explains,

I put all the characters' names down on one side and all the scenes across the top, and I start checking off the structure of the play so that I can understand how the play works as a mechanism—like a watch. And then I go through scene-by-scene and try to understand each scene in relation to the larger structure of the play: how long it is, what happens in it, who's in the scene, and what I understand at the beginning of the scene and then at the end of the scene. Every scene has to move the play forward somehow, and I need to understand just how that happens.

Olympia Dukakis mentions that there are a number of skills an actor should develop, one of which should be the ability "to break down a scene." She adds, "The actor should take a look at the structure of a scene and see the beats, transitions, needs, and obstacles that create the dramatic conflict." She likens this part of an actor's work to finding the "bone of the scene." When young actors do not take the time to discover how the story is advancing, she feels, they run the risk of interpreting far too soon.[12]

More than likely, playscript analysis that is influenced by the theories and practices of modernism will in some way include a reference to Aristotle's elements, namely, plot, character, thought, diction, song (dramatic rhythm), and spectacle. Breaking the play into parts and recognizing how they come together to form a "sense of the whole" is an excellent way to test early spontaneous impressions. If the score supports the artists' early imagistic response, enhances understanding, or points to interpretive problems or weaknesses, it has been beneficial.

Many artists have developed their own unique ways of applying Aristotle's elements when scoring a play. For the director Jon Jory, scoring begins with finding an overall thematic statement that is evident in each scene of the play. He applies Stanislavsky's ideas about the super-objective and objective when he looks at each scene and defines what he calls "the arc of the characters—where they start and where they finish." He then heads a piece of paper with what he perceives to be the play's theme. He tests his thematic idea by breaking the play down into three columns: "the psychological, visual, and aural." Using those columns, he says, "I try to theatricalize the theme and my knowledge of the theme in those three areas." He feels he is ready to go into rehearsal only if his ideas about the play's theme work throughout the entire structure of the play.[13]

Thomas Skelton spoke about how his early work, under the tutelage of the designer, visual artist, and teacher Lester Polakov, included work on scoring the playscript. Throughout the years, Mr. Skelton developed his own approach to scoring the play; however, he credited his early training with Polakov as being a necessary and inspirational introduction to how the process of scoring can lead to artistic thought.

Indeed, many designers spoke about Polakov's insightful skill in dissecting a playscript. His unique process is detailed and complex. For example, he begins with finding a "graphic image" that metaphorically expresses the play. (In his preparatory notes for the Broadway production of *The Member of the Wedding*, he has written, "This play is like a green jungle under glass.") He suggests that the designer follow his initial imagistic impression by creating a "non-objective representation [an abstracted form, shape, or sculpture] of the feeling of the play." He explains his process of scoring a play as follows:

The script is broken down into beats and that is the story in the script, that is the physical action. I number those in this column. These beats are then grouped into episodes, French scenes [which are numbered in a column down one side of the paper]. You now begin to discover the texture of the play and the rhythm. This [next] column details the meaning of each beat, the subtext. They read like titles of beats.

It is here that your designing takes place. Because here is where you begin to relate to the Graphic Image, your Central Idea, and the meaning of the play. The last column is for the play's physical needs: kitchen, morning, large table, etc. Sometimes when I put something down, I put the initials of the author after it. He said those are necessary; I may have a better way of doing it.

Then I identify the attack (where the chief dramatic question is asked), crisis, and the resolution. I'd say these three moments are the main things to design. What is it going to look like in the attack, crisis, and resolution? Now you are ready to write a concept that is like the play's central idea. When writing the concept it should include the central idea, what your Graphic Image is, a brief paragraph about the style or form of the play, and, in *very general terms* another paragraph about how you intend to design it. Now you are ready to discuss the play with the director. (italics added)

Polakov's former student Thomas Skelton did not completely adhere to his teacher's method of scoring. He tended not to use Polakov's method of "breaking down the play into a beat every time a new idea is introduced." Skelton does, however, score the playscript.

I'd like very much to try to break down everything that we have been taught about playwriting. What is the dramatic question? When is it asked? Who asks it? What is the answer? Where is the climax of the play? Who is the antagonist... the protagonist? Sometimes I go through that in a very difficult play, or in a play that I do not understand very well, [or] that's hard to read. And sometimes I do not go through the process at all. But [when I do] I am making myself very familiar with the script and very familiar with the reason why each character is there so that I will be able to have an intelligent conversation with the director.

His abbreviated method of scoring a playscript (Skelton said he breaks the play into a series of "lumps") not only helped him become more intimately involved with the play's world but also (when he is in rehearsal) served as an expedient reminder about a particular moment within the script. He explained, "Since I don't follow the script when I am lighting, I don't have time to follow the words. Sometimes I title the scenes—that is enough to trigger me to know what the scene is about."

As a moment-to-moment schematization, the score becomes a way in which the artist can map

- the play's dramatic action, by following each character's objectives and noting where obstacles occur
- how each beat furthers the story (What type of French scene—expository, conflict, denouement, atmosphere—has the playwright created?)
- where the playwright attacks the question
- the development of scenic images (props, visual design elements, and sounds), noting their relationship to the development of the character's psychology or the play's dramatic action
- progressions, leitmotifs, and rhythms

It is obvious that scoring a playscript can be an effective way in which artists can organize their thoughts and test their immediate impressions. But what makes this analytic process approach something more than just an overly pedantic and highly technical exercise? The answer lies in the artist's ability to recognize how scoring can be an effective way to mine a play. At this early stage of analysis, generally the artist is concentrating on how the dramatic structure validates or negates early imagistic perceptions. Studying the dramatic frame of a script from the inside out and discovering how its landscapes, foundation, framing, fixtures, decor, color, and texture reveal more about its architectonic structure is one way the artist can feel less like an alien and more like a participant in recreating the play's world.

FACTORING IN RESEARCH

The theatre artist also engages in more traditional forms of research. Reviewing pertinent information (visual, aural, and written) often can uncover enlightening material about the play's human history. Research material is reviewed by the director, designer, and actors working either alone, in a group, or with a dramaturg. Factual information, the play's production history, and literary criticism can be used to clarify ideas and answer questions about the play's characters, the nature of its time, environment, and dramatic structure, as well as thoughts about the play's thematic ideas, issues, or politics. Some directors, actors, and designers (especially those in regional theatres) have the opportunity of working with literary departments, which compile much of the preliminary research. Artists use this material (scholarly articles, biographies of the playwright, reviews of other productions, historical/political/philosophical/aesthetic information about the period) only as it applies to their needs, addresses their questions, and, perhaps most significantly, inspires further creative thought. In the introductory stage of preparing a playscript for production, Jon Jory, for example, asks his literary department to compile reviews of that play covering the last seventy-five years. Jory remarks: "I find that this is wildly helpful because you have a tremendous sense of what the problem may be with specific characters. You really get a carpenter's view of the work, hopefully avoiding the very problems that were apparent by reading some of those reviews."

The ability to tell a good story is the goal of many artists. They realize, however, that telling a good story involves more than repeating the playwright's words, getting the facts in the right order, establishing place and atmosphere, collecting pieces of clothing, or making objects. A good storyteller attempts (at least imaginatively) to walk in the characters' shoes and face those events that have caused and shaped their destinies. Good research skills can both inform and inspire the artist's creative impulses, leading to effective, if not inspirational, storytelling. It was not surprising to hear dramaturg Tori Haring-Smith, recount how in the true collaborative spirit, the cast artfully used an actor's research in rehearsal for Richard Jenkins's production of *The Glass Menagerie* (1991-1992). She recalls,

Jonathan Fried [the actor who played Tom] had taken a train to St. Louis in preparation for the production. And he had taken photographs of the house—the tenement—that Tennessee Williams had lived in, that was the basis for *The Glass Menagerie*. So we looked at that and said "Oh my God, people really lived cramped together. What can we do with that notion of being cramped and having no privacy?" Then we just started putting things on the set.

Interestingly, in preparing to design the setting for *Hedda Gabler*, Ming Cho Lee insists his students speculate on similar factors without making a connection with a specific model.

What kind of house is it? How close are the neighbors? Which part of town is it in? Then I want to see what kind of interior feels right for that house. Before you draw the ground plan of the set, you must draw the ground plan of the house. There has to be discussion [research] about how big or small the town is; whether it is a house or an apartment building. If it's an apartment building, is it three or four stories? Which part of town do they live in? Is it off the main street? All of this has to be done before you get to the next step—designing.

Mark Lamos also finds that research can function to kindle the creative fires.

I think about the [historical] period that gave birth to the play. Essentially, I am seeking advice from the dead that I can take into the production. Then if the play seems very much a part of its period, I work very hard to think of it in an extremely personal context. I stay in touch with what I call the play's "subconscious." I actively work to disengage the play from its roots, its source. If it is still "walks," I believe it will speak anew in a vibrant, truthful way. Once I have absorbed the text, I allow designers and actors to influence my "reading."

The function of research is not recreation but insight that informs the play's actions or intentions. Certainly, information has its place in planning a play for an audience, but experienced practitioners are quick to point out how important it is not to make production choices too early or to become too intellectual about research, too rigid about your initial ideas. In particular, Mark Lamos feels, "It is still more important for the actor to be truthful moment-by-moment than to know what sort of teacups one drank from in the nineteenth century." He then adds, "There is a lot of interesting information that you can learn about a period if you are doing a period play. But you must not allow the information to give a false sense of aesthetic self-confidence. The actors' goal is to make a performance available to an audience extremely unfamiliar with a play's previous life." Additionally, Jon Jory is "suspicious" and "edgy" about "the dangers of producing a play based on research that is not inspired by the text." He only "scans" the documents that his dramaturg has placed before him, saying, "I am fairly cavalier about history. I tend to be more interested in creating, on stage, my own Restoration rather than doing a lot of research on the actual period. (I say this to you so I can be attacked from all quarters.)" Jory continues, "I particularly like visual support in terms of research, because I find that extremely stimulating. So I love looking at artifacts. We tend, when we are doing a play that has a history, to go over the history with the dramaturg and actors. All with the disclaimer that we are only going to use the pieces of it that support thematically what we are trying to do."

Effective preparation should not be concerned with how much the artist knows about some particular dramaturgical detail. Research should stimulate additional artistic perceptions (images) about the play's world. Analysis-research-reflection should stimulate the creative imagination, help inform subjective reactions, and clarify original impulses and images. Essentially, the type of research preparation that designers, directors, and actors value the most is that which does not diminish the humanistic values that permit the production or performance to communicate with the audience on the level of the collective unconscious. For example, director Douglas Wager uses his research to find synchronistical connections with the play's "human history."

I try to go back and take a comprehensive view of the world as it was when the material was written. Not just in terms of who the writer was and what the writer's background was, but what was happening in art and science and literature to look at what point in human history this act of imagination actually took place, and to find out if there are any points of contact that are common to my own emotional response to the material. Then, usually, that provides me with a research framework because I may not find it directly in the background of the writer or in the history of the production of that particular play; but I might find it in something that was happening in music or in art or in history or in politics or in theology. That is a humanistic approach that I go through in order to uncover my own impulses; because very often my feeling is that my job is to be a storyteller.[14]

On the Art of Creative Research

In 1991, Douglas Wager directed *The Seagull* for the Arena Stage. His preparation included a journal, museum work, dramaturgical articles, and some reading on contemporary psychoanalysis. The following remarks indicate some of the ways Wager traveled into the world of Chekhov's play:

I keep a notebook, sort of a stream-of-consciousness notebook, whenever I am working on something. In preparing for *The Seagull*, I went to England to see an exhibit at the Hayward Gallery called "Twilight of the Czars" that was about the shift from the late-nineteenth-century romanticism into the *Style-Moderne* and symbolist period; the shift between 1890 and 1915 in art, literature, and architecture. It had common objects used in everyday life: book covers, magazine covers, candy wrappers, cigarette wrappers, photography. One of the big things in the exhibit when you first walked in was that famous picture of Chekhov sitting with the cast of the Moscow Art production of *The Seagull*. And on the opposite wall was a series of paintings that were not really in the symbolist mode, but they were just prior to that period, that kind of almost nouveau style, but not quite—nouveau impressionism, I guess. The exhibit was a sort of fabulous stimuli for me because it helped to break into the world that Chekhov was experiencing. Another thing that helped me was material compiled by Larry Maslon, such as: [Laurence] Senelick's articles on Chekhov and *The Seagull* and the Danchenko/Stanislavsky casebook that was published in 1952 that detailed what Stanislavsky wanted the Moscow Art Theatre production to be like (which of course it was not). Then there was Irvin Yalom's *Love's Executioner* that really gave me the emotional authority for my production of *The Seagull.*

On her initial preparation for the Arena Stage production of *A Doll House* (1990), Zelda Fichandler comments on how prop research can produce pertinent information and relevant revelations about the human history within Ibsen's play. She talks about transferring information into psychological insight:

I thought *A Doll House* was about leaving home. Right after Christmas, leaving home at Christmas. And the next thing Doug Stein [the designer] did was bring in some old things he had wrapped up, Christmas ornaments from Germany that belonged to his, I think, grandparents. Because I was talking about Christmas. The wonder of the holiday, the warmth. So he came in with the ornaments, and they mattered a lot to me. They were exquisite. And I said something about warmth and hearth. I said somewhere there has to be warmth and hearth. And he got me a book called *The Origin of the Home* or *The Evolution of the Home*, and we dealt with how the home was formed in bourgeois society, and how it evolved from a mercantile point of view. And how it affects family structure and relationships and individuation, and how those things affect the structure of the home. So we did a home study in which we discussed everything possible about how Nora lived. How the family lived. What rooms there were in the house. What the economic structure was. What it meant when she left home. How she was going to earn a living. What the clothes were. How many servants she had. What the expectations of marriage were at the time, and how were they different from now. What accommodations they were making to each other and to society. What the disharmonies and harmonies were as compared to now. What the area of malfunctioning was in the family. What the role of children was. What the nannies did. Why the nanny in the play had to give up her child.

Zelda Fichandler is a director who values uncovering everything she can about the play and playwright. She also finds "how the action of the play is connected to the action beyond the play: how [it] connects to the Gestalt of the moment—politically, socially, and emotionally." The archives at the Arena Stage in Washington, D.C., document her systematic and meticulous directorial mining of playscripts. In preparation for her production of *A Doll House*, for example, she recorded the conversations she had with her dramaturg Laurence Maslon and Fritz Brun, a dramaturgical consultant who specializes in Scandinavian studies. This tape and transcription describe how they selected, researched, and synthesized certain areas that, they felt, had a direct relationship to Ibsen's play as produced by the Arena Stage. Their dramaturgical mining included both speculative and actual explorations of those areas pertaining to historical style and function. The following regimented social attitudes of a bourgeois Victorian society in late-nineteenth-century Norway were thoroughly discussed.

- *Art, Music, Dance, Drama*
  Appropriate music for the party
  Music of the historical period
  The Tarantella—the music and its significance
- *Architecture*
  The layout of a typical middle-class apartment
  Norwegian construction and architecture
  The play's setting
- *Furnishings*
  Furniture and china
  The stove (its style and function)
  Household articles: tubs, toilets, sewage
- *Transportation*
- *Clothing*
  The dress of the period
  Tarantella costume
- *Law*
  Divorce
  Bankruptcy
  Illegitimacy
  Forgery
- *Customs and Rituals*
  Victorian Christmas
- *Religion*
  Lutheranism

- *The Role of Men*
  Helmer and Krogstad's jobs
  Financial situation
  Career tracks
  Nora/Helmer
  Narrowness of Norwegian society and Helmer
  Helmer and shame
  Parents and children—heredity and guilt
  Children/Pregnancy/Birth Control
  Dr. Rank's disease
  Family without a mother/career women
- *The Role of Women*
  Nora's household duties/cleaning/labor
  Nora's background
  Nora's relationship to men
  Children/pregnancy/birth control
  Family without a mother/career women
  Nora/Helmer
- *Household Issues*
  Division of labor
  Cleaning
  Servants
  Food
  Nora's responsibilities
- *Education*
  Nora's education
- *Economics*
  Economy and immigration
  Currency
  Salaries
  Winter/economic development/politics
  Economic situation in *A Doll House*
- *Geography*
  Weather
  Natural resources
- *Language*
  Pronunciation of names
  Translation (title of the play)
  Irene B. Berman/Gerry Bamman's new translation
- *Playwright*
  Ibsen and language
  Ibsen's views: on freedom, unconventionality, and Freud
  Laura Kieler (the "real" Nora)
- *Production History*
  Ingmar Bergman's reconception
  Danish sequels
  Modern interpretations
- *Dramatic form*
  Symbolism

Nora's self-discovery
Play's questions
Freudian aspects
"the most wonderful thing"
* *Mise-en-scène*
Costumes
Setting of the last scene
Creativity

When deemed appropriate, Fichandler researches the play through study of the playwright. Archival research at the Arena Stage revealed that her ensemble for Chekhov's *Three Sisters* (1984) devoted time to reading about Chekhov's life, his relationship with the Moscow Art Theatre, and his responses to the productions of his plays. Apparently, the company continued to study the playwright because the archives show additional attention was paid to uncovering what he thought, who influenced him, his personality, his writing style, his education, and his life before he was a writer. Fichandler comments on how she uses what some would call external research on the playwright to find out more about the play's internal reality:

I like to know where the play came in the playwright's life. I am, of course, not so naive as to think there is a direct correspondence between life and the artwork. But there is some correspondence because the artwork came out of the man. It is not a blueprint, nor can you make automatic connections. There is, however, some meditative correlation between the person and the artwork. It may even be contradictory. The person could be very depressed and write a capricious piece of work. But that depression, as it transmogrifies, may have a manic quality that turns into something capricious. I like to know who the playwright is as a character in his own world, and I study the playwright as a character in that world.

She encouraged her company not to approach their research in a manner that would invite "intellectual anxiety"; instead, they were reminded of what she has said about the meaning behind research and how it can affect production: "[Research] is not about scholarship, but [about] discovering a universe that the characters live within." Fichandler values the process of research, but what is perhaps more revealing is how she adroitly applies her information to awaken her creative imagination:

I had a hard time with Ibsen in the beginning. I kept saying to my friend: "I don't know, if I had him to dinner, I wouldn't know who to ask along with him. I don't know who he'd be good with. What would I serve? Is he stuffy? I think he is stuffy. I think he is a little pompous. I think he is a little righteous. And I think he is passionate. And I think he is tormented." I had to understand him as a character.

Sometimes directors, designers, and actors have the distinct advantage of actually working with the playwright on a project. Not only can questions about the playscript be at least addressed, if not immediately resolved, but also an awareness of the playwright's personality can provide some insightful information about the play's characters or even the rhythm of the dialogue. Shirley Knight, for example, knew Tennessee Williams, and she refers to his sensitivity in a way most of us can only imagine from (perhaps) assiduously studying his plays, reading his biographies or autobiography, talking to the people who knew him, or doing other research. Knight used her firsthand observations of the playwright when she prepared to play Amanda in the McCarter Theatre's production of *The Glass Menagerie* (1991):

Tennessee could not bear it if anyone was unkind. I mean he would say, "Nothing upsets me more than deliberate cruelty." But he accepted that people were cruel, and that he, himself, was cruel. It is an element of his character that's in all of his plays. I mean Amanda is an incredible case in point. She is very cruel, but never intentionally, never deliberately. Her cruelty comes out of her wanting so much for her children out of love.

Ming Cho Lee concedes that he understands why artists read about the playwright or the circumstances under which the work is written; but for him, "it can get in the way. If the play does not hit home and you cannot hear it then sometimes it helps; but sometimes it really doesn't." Ming Cho Lee finds pictures to be his primary resource; he recalls how the images from an illustrated magazine article made certain qualities of Sam Shepard's *Buried Child* more accessible for the Adrian Hall-directed and student-designed production.

The costume designer brought in a *Life* magazine article about a grandfather who had Alzheimer's disease and his grandchildren. The article went through the stages of the disease: from the time he was healthy to a picture of him wearing a baseball cap, sitting on the couch, looking at television. Then, of course, the end was the two grandsons actually holding the grandfather like a baby in their arms. It was the most remarkable piece of research because it brings *Buried Child* alive.

Selecting the right visual material does not preclude other preliminary homework on the play. Identifying provocative images (the ones that say, this could be the place; those are the people; these are the colors; that is the light) means you have engaged in some prior dramatic analysis, or you would not be able to recognize what images have the potential of suggesting the play's world. One might engage in imagistic research not only to compile factual evidence but also to be creatively inspired by the characters in a portrait gallery or the moments that can be captured in a storyboard. Each exercise provokes associative imagistic responses. Even Robert Brustein, when directing, finds he tends to work more with visual images and less with literary material because, as an accomplished scholar, he has already done a great deal of the reading. What stimulates him are "visual images." Brustein continues: "I want images having to do with the flesh and the blood of drama to begin to impinge on my consciousness. And that happens in a variety of ways. I have in the past looked in books of paintings, and I have looked at architecture. I sit in quiet places and contemplate—I look for places that have a particularly beautiful quality to them to help me think."

Research does not lead to immediate answers or foregone conclusions concerning how a play should look in production. In fact, sometimes museum or library research might not reveal anything at all about the people in the play's world. As a costume designer, Jane Greenwood finds that period research might only scratch at surface reality: "You know, when you are doing research that takes you way back you can always find wonderful pictures of the kings, queens, and rich people. But you always have to look in the corners of the paintings for the poorer folk. Very often that is what your playwright is dealing with, and that is much more difficult research."[15]

Research can stimulate ideas about the play, clarify thoughts, and spark imaginative associations, but research alone does not give you access to the world of the play. The professional artist is quick to point out that research should not begin and end with the project; it is an ongoing endeavor. Directors, designers, and actors all spoke about how important it is to be well read, versed in the visual arts, music, opera, languages, architecture, philosophy, psychology, poetry, history, dance, and politics. Research as a theatre practitioner should go on every day so that you become increasingly aware of how life's images are constant reminders of who we are, where we live, and why we act in particular or peculiar ways. Jane Greenwood relays some advice she gave to her daughter, who is embarking on the same career:

You have to look at everything and evaluate where it belongs in the shape of things. Go and see everything. Never let anything go by that takes your eye that you do not make a mental note of, or put it down in a sketch book. Whatever it is, record it for your memory so that you have all these images to draw on forever. You know, you are always going to be seeing different things, different people, at different times, so that everything that you do, everything that you look at, is valuable. Then you have to start being selective about how you use it.

A strong liberal arts education with the invaluable enrichment of continued life experiences sharpens your abilities to collect and store those images that speak to poetic ideas that transcend material logic. The purpose of gathering information and images, either on a day-to-day basis or with a specific project in mind, is not to copy on stage the vocabulary that defines another time and space, but to understand the synchronicity between the historical period of the play and the contemporary world.

Inspired by Peter Brook, contemporary artists like to bring the play forward, rediscovering it in a more "immediate" context. On "reimaging" the world of the play with an eye and ear toward synchronicity, Douglas Wager says:

[I try] to trace five things (time, space, language, action, and objects) back to the point of origin when the play was written. Also, I try to decide in my own contemporary theatrical vocabulary what I would call the originating impulses that made the play immediate in its own time. I take those impulses and then connect them to the capabilities that I have in terms of my own vocabulary, which has to do with the design and the actors and an ability to interpret the text.

ARTISTIC COLLABORATION

Unlike so many visual artists and musicians, the theatre artist works collaboratively. Actors, directors, and designers influence each other as they prepare a play for production. Often many theatre practitioners find their initial images or creative research is abandoned or reshaped once they begin to work together on a project and exchange ideas. Jenkins offers,

Although I find I have ideas before I actually begin rehearsal those ideas usually do not wind up in the production. I think working on a play is a process, and it is a process that involves everybody. I know a lot of people say "Well, I don't want the prop people here during rehearsal, or I don't want the costume people in rehearsal. I will just tell them what I want." You know, if the theatre is not group effort, what is? These people are paid to help, and I have some of the best help in the world.

For many contemporary theatre practitioners, the director's voice (though still most prominent) has become but one of many voices that contribute to the complex process of preparing a playscript for production. I found this especially true of artists who are interested in exploring the play's poetic images or staging nontraditional productions. Mark Lamos and Richard Jenkins, in particular, remarked how they always attempt to make a conscious effort to remain receptive to the questions, ideas, and concerns of other artists. Too much intellectual preplanning is stultifying. Most artists today tend to agree that the exchanges that happen prior to and during rehearsal (those that occur in a burst of creative energy) are often far more stimulating than those ideas that are the result of solitary thought.

Tori Haring-Smith furthers this point as she recounts how artistic collaboration played an important role in developing the Trinity Repertory Theatre's innovative "reconception" of Williams's play *The Glass Menagerie*. She maintains that although Jenkins's nontraditional production clearly was a collaborative effort, the need to release the play from its traditional interpretation came from the director. Essentially, Jenkins could not accept the narrator (Tom) coming out and convincing a contemporary audience "that he was able to stay in control as he recalled and even revisited his memories—that he could remain outside the story, unaffected by telling it." Sensing that the traditional beginning doesn't address the emotional core of the play, Jenkins felt compelled to see the play anew: "If Williams were writing it today, I feel, he wouldn't choose 'that way' to do it. Knowing his life and knowing what he went through and knowing his feelings about his mother—I don't know how Tennessee Williams feels about his mother—but knowing the play like I do, I know there is a kind of pain in here. I know that kind of pain cannot be put aside easily by the narrator." Preproduction, therefore, included the following questions: "What might Tennessee Williams have done with this play if he were writing it today? What ghosts might he confront now that he didn't confront then?"

Tori Haring-Smith interjected that from the beginning they were interested in how the play dealt with the idea that Tom was "dogged by the memory of Laura." The director, therefore, played with the idea of "letting him see it all." Jenkins explains,

Let him face it; let him face his life. I wanted him to see his life. And how better to do it than stick him in a room alone. Let him watch his sister and the gentleman caller. Let him see his mother cry. Let him get those demons out. He's got to face it sometime in his life. To read it as it was, it didn't mean anything to me. I thought that stage convention was exactly what it was—convention; and maybe it was good twenty, thirty, or forty years ago, but not for me today. It was not a way into the play. And I wanted the play to be alive.

Some of these thoughts and images, therefore, contributed to the discussions that followed, especially those between the director and his designer: "Eugene Lee and I talked about the play taking place in a room somewhere." Eventually Jenkins said, "What about a hotel room?" And Lee responded, "A cheap, cheap hotel." (One can see the "reimaging" process began to produce some fruitful ideas.) The eventual production would find Tom sitting on the bed in his cheap hotel room typing his play. He looked up and noticed the audience, whereupon he read them his opening monologue. Although Williams's lines remained intact, many of the play's icons were replaced by creative adjustments. There was, for example, neither a collection of glass animals nor a fire escape on stage. Haring-Smith recalls how the company worked together to see this play with fresh eyes:

The thing I loved about the hotel room was that he could not be alone in this room— his family was always there. They literally came through the walls at him. We all sat around and we decided that everything that happens in this production had to be in the hotel room. We found ourselves asking: "Why is it in a hotel room? What are the implications of that? Why can't Tom get rid of these images? What is his condition?" I wish I could tell you what Olympia Dukakis [Amanda], Jonathan Freid [Tom], Trish Dunnock [Laura], Dan Welch [Jim], Richard Jenkins, or Eugene Lee, or I brought to the discussions. But I can't, people just threw things in. We just started putting things on the set, and then we would hit a point where someone would say: "I need a tray of dishes, a typing card, a coat, a unicorn, etc." We would find ways to solve the problems. We wanted to be sure that the ending made it very clear that while recalling these memories had been a kind of cathartic experience for Tom, it had not been entirely successful. Later in his life when Tom walks down the street and sees a colored bit of glass, he still sees Laura in that glass.

Theatrical research can be the most satisfying when informed imagination reveals something further about the play's world: its incidents, characters, psychology, objects, rhythms, and so on. Research can also be emotionally rewarding when it validates or expands the artist's early intuitions or when it encourages further "reimaging." Additionally, the process that "informs the artist's intuition" can be artistically gratifying when the actor, director, and designer transfer their poetically enriched and dramaturgically sound imagistic impressions to the stage. The one aspect of research that most artists seem to agree on is the necessary, albeit sophisticated, task of knowing how to use pertinent information in an artistic way on the stage. An imagistic reading that is informed by a dramaturgical analysis can poetically embellish character, time, place, and action in a manner that lifts the play off the page in imaginative, explosive ways.

The artists who work with the playscript's hidden realities create costumes that are more than clothes, lights that tell us more than time of day, props that become more than objects, settings that show us more than locale, and characters whose gestures and movements are psychological manifestations more than examples of everyday behavior. Although it is the task of the actor, director, and designer to tell a good story, the contemporary modernist will tell you that it is also their responsibility to discover ways in which the play's poetic dimensions can transmute the mundane, historical, materialistic world of the play into the transcendent, imagistic world of a theatrical event.

4

Toward Imagistic Cognition

For those who find contemporary interpretive practices troublesome, viewing them as pretentious and largely responsible for egocentric productions, it might be helpful to consider that imagistic interpretations that lead to metaphorical productions are often the product of a dramaturgical textual analysis in which some of the theories of structuralism (especially those that pertain to theatre) play a significant role. Incompetent dramaturgical analysis can result in an egocentric production. Similarly, a production might be labeled "pretentious" if its theatrical images fail to provoke a metaphorical link with the play's poetry.

Perceiving the playscript through the lens of modernism is no longer associated with the avant-garde theatre; it exists in the mainstream of performance theory and practice, particularly in the regional theatres of North America. An imagistic approach to script analysis is most often associated with those artists who denounce the reductive interpretive methods that produce "kitchen-sink" realism. Artists who are intent on exploding some of the naturalism in a playscript by creating a metaphorical mise-en-scène relative to their poetic perceptions concerning the play's inner reality have more than likely been influenced by the theories and practices of modernism. Often stimulated by an immediate imagistic response, these artists inform their imagination by mining each layer of the play's world, ever conscious of how the play's parts work independently and collectively to form its architectonic structure. Careful consideration is given to any dramaturgical research that is nonpedantic and provokes richer, more comprehensive contemporary perceptions about the play's world.

The process that encourages dramaturgical literacy about a given playscript is an evolutionary one; it involves continual coordination between the artist's imagination and cognitive thought. Cognitive perceptual imaging begins when the artist assiduously mines the playscript. Exciting new interpretations often result when artists spend the time needed to decipher its hidden psychology. This process takes into account an intrinsic and extrinsic critical analysis of the playscript; whereas some artists take a good look at the history of the production, others find the historical milieu significant, and a few admit to reading everything they can about the playwright or his/her canon. Most are interested in finding out more about the play's hidden world; therefore, they attend to how the playwright has manipulated the language of the theatre (its signs, poetic images, symbols, metaphors, allusions, myths), as well as to forms, patterns, progressions, and recurring leitmotifs. Artists tend to agree that sound preparation takes months and that there is no set method. All use whatever information and techniques are necessary to attain an intimate connection with the world of the play. Even though most artists find they prefer to have an immediate imagistic response to the text, their initial images are shaped, refined, stretched, and even discarded, once they begin to explore its deep structure and psychology. Generally, artists begin to relax and accept the rigors of a critical analysis when they begin to hear and perceive the script more clearly in their imaginations, as prior imagistic responses by this time have been informed by a thorough dramaturgical analysis. When artists become more secure about their understanding concerning the inner workings of the play, they begin the process of "reimaging" the playscript on the stage—a process that involves the selection and arrangement of metaphorical theatrical images that provoke even further revelations about the play's hidden poetry.

Play interpretation that finds its impetus in the theories and practices of modernism invites criticism from some who argue that when artists set out to discover the playscript's hidden patterns, they imply it is possible to locate meaning or make a statement about the intention of the playwright. Artists who mine the play's images and create metaphorically enriched productions are not interested in closed interpretations; in fact, they recognize that metaphorically enriched productions more than likely encourage reinterpretation. Because interpretation continues to evolve once metaphorical images are presented to the audience, there is little evidence to support the idea that a poetic reading of a play is devoted to fixing, limiting, or reifying meaning. Contrary to closed interpretive methods (genre reproductions or some "concept" productions), a reading of a play that is influenced by modernism finds ambiguity and complexity playing significant roles in a metaphorical theatre that invites reinterpretation. Clarity is at issue only in the way in which artists *order* their subjective perceptions concerning the playscript's hidden poetry.

Like children whose persistent questions indicate their need to discover something more about a world they know little of, theatre artists approach the play with an energy not unlike a child's inquisitive exuberance. When working with the script, interpretive artists find that they are continually asking themselves, "Why?" Why, for example, does it feel as if nothing happens in a Chekhov play? Why does Chekhov insist that Treplev's makeshift stage remain for the duration of *The Seagull*, even though no one uses it for two years? Why does Sorin have a difficult time finishing his sentences? Why do we hear "coughing and hammering" at the beginning of Act One, followed by a dog howling and people singing? When artists question the playwright's choices, they are not attempting to discover "the" answer that results in "the" correct production. Instead, artistic questioning is tantamount to mining the play's world. The director Zelda Fichandler calls the process "an anthropological dig." She likens the words in the text to the surface markings an animal makes; the artist's task is to discover "what kind of an animal made those marks, put all the pieces together and make a world out of it."[1] Artists question because they are searching for unifying threads, recurring leitmotifs, or how the "kernel" of each scene reveals something about the play's inner world. Questioning uncovers the possibility of discovering literary allusions, rhythms, progressions, and patterns; it tells the artist something about how the author manipulates the play's time and place to reveal something further about how the text functions as a whole.

Twentieth-century Russian performance theory and practice has clear perceptions about the nature and function of the "sense of the whole"; therefore, it is not surprising that the Russians have a word to describe this concept. The *zamissel* is, as Zelda Fichandler explains, "the pervading sense.... It's the thought that binds together all elements or the idea. The *zamissel* accounts for the whole—explains every action, every breath, every pulse, every second of the life of the play. It's like looking at a tree. The sap is in every leaf and it's also in the roots. I can spend months looking for the exact *zamissel* or idea or super-objective that will set a play in motion, unlock its hidden conflict."[2] Therefore, as important as it is to have an immediate imagistic response to a play, most artists are quick to dispel any misconceptions about the creative intuition being the sole force behind their reading of a playscript.

The artist's subjective response is tested against the more objective dramaturgical analysis; but no matter how carefully the research is conducted or how imaginatively thought is synthesized with creative imaging, ultimately the production's theatrical images are the artist's relativistic perceptions about the play's story, characters, dialogue, ideas, atmospheres, and the like. However, to ensure that the artist's reading is reasonable and provocative, the more seasoned actor, director, and designer possess an understanding of traditional dramatic structure and theory, a wealth of life experience, and an appreciation of psychology and the visual arts, not the least of which is an astute ability to select artfully and creatively manipulate metaphorical images moment-to-moment on the stage. Many contemporary artists recognize that the communal nature of the theatrical event promotes continual rediscovery; therefore, they resist the temptation to suggest in any way that they have finalized their perceptions. The artist who is interested in revealing something new is often attracted to issues of common cultural concern or the rich poetic core of classical plays. Age-old ideas delivered in new ways inspire additional relativistic perceptions, perhaps because we have found a way to connect the transitory image with the long-term collective memory.

A twentieth-century interpretation of a playscript, influenced by modernism, suggests that the artist has gone beyond the objective linear recording of evidence presented by the playwright and accepts the concept that reality is subjective and relativistic. Thus, a contemporary approach to playscript interpretation would not be complete without a reference to Einstein's thoughts on relativity (especially as it relates to our perceptions concerning time and space). Whereas Einstein's *special* theory on relativity dismisses traditional thought about absolute space and time, offering instead that perception is not absolute but relative to the perceiver's state of motion, quantum theory goes one step further and suggests that when we make the leap to unconscious thought we are, in fact, participating in the creation of reality. In his book *How We Think* (1910), John Dewey proposes that when we are engaged in reflective thinking we make an inferential leap of faith that "involves a *jump from the known into the unknown.*"[3] This shift is referred to by quantum physicists such as Niels Bohr as *quantum jumping.*[4] Artists make similar leaps when they engage their imaginations.

Even when artists feed information about the play's world into their imaginations, they rely less on the logic of linear thought and more on associative perceptions. Seeing and hearing the play in their imaginations, therefore, occur on a metacognitive level or in what the physicist Amit Goswami refers to in his article, "Creativity and the Quantum Theory," as "hyperspace." He continues, "Often when the electron jumps levels and dives into the unknown ocean of hyperspace, it brings back something. Because the electron plunges into another world, something new happens to our world—a brilliant photon. It could be the same with us.... As we plunge into the unknown world, take a quantum leap with our minds, we come in touch with the precious jewels we bring back in a creative act."[5]

Goswami goes on to suggest that "hyperspace" is not unlike what Jung called our collective unconscious. The implications of quantum theory, especially as they relate to Jung's theory of the collective unconscious, are particularly relevant to those interested in the process of artistic cognition, especially as it relates to an imagistic analysis and a metaphorical theatre.

Receptivity to the illusory nature of the playscript's provocative spatial and auditory images implies that an artist leaps from one set of time-space coordinates to another. When theatre artists engage in something akin to "quantum jumping," they are no longer recreating the playwright's world; they are actively creating new worlds. Their active "reimaging" or leaps of consciousness encourage intersubjective understanding. Exploring the potential realities of a given playscript with a creative energy powerful enough to provoke multiple subjective images (the Bergsonian snapshots) is similar to what some quantum theorists would identify as a succession of "qwiffs, flows, and pops."[6] Significantly, in his provocative article "Quantum Drama: Beyond Time and Space," Alistair Martin-Smith reports, "Many quantum theorists use the metaphor of a hologram for describing consciousness."[7] In other words, when artists imagistically perceive the world of the play, they are involved in multidimensional, nonlinear thought guided somewhat by the framework of the playscript; it is only when they manipulate images metacognitively (make up patterns or destroy them) that imaging becomes conscious activity.

Quantum theorists argue that reality is not fixed and logical but instead disjointed and in a state of continual change. The accepted scientific method of verifying reality through causality and objective observation continues to be practiced by quantum theorists. However, these choices "depend upon our minds or, more specifically, the content of our thoughts. And our thoughts, in turn, depend upon our expectations, our desire for continuity."[8] The New Physics would go on to say that order exists in the universe; however, it is not reduced to the causal reality that they define as classical physical physics, or what we associate with the prior theories of materialism and determinism. Instead, they suggest, order is more than a dispassionate account of the physical world; it involves our thoughts and feelings about the physical world. Such things as revolutionary thoughts on how light and color affect our perceptions and the discovery that motion is not continuous dismantled prior assumptions set forth in the Age of Certainty and substantiated an interest in studying how irrationality, chance, imagination, and intuition affect our subjective perceptions. Bohr's position on discontinuity concludes that there can be only an "approximate description of reality" and that our observations create reality.[9] Quantum physics illustrates this point by showing how the "paradoxical cube" can be viewed in a number of different ways:

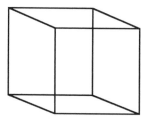

The Paradoxical Cube

When we choose to view the cube in a certain way, our act of observation resolves the paradox. In *Taking the Quantum Leap*, Fred Wolf suggests, "It is only a paradoxical cube when we, observers conditioned to think that everything we see must be solid, insist that 'it' is a solid cube."[10] It can be suggested that reality can appear to be contradictory, paradoxical, and dualistic because more than one person observes a single phenomenon, our perceptions are constantly changing, and objects are in a state of perpetual movement and change. It is very possible, then, that we see what we want to see, what we can see (that which, most likely, evolves from the secure footing of our collective memories).

Quantum theory makes it possible to perceive reality as paradoxical and logical at the same time: paradoxical because there is no such thing as ultimate reality and logical because there appears to be order and a material causality. Bohr's Principle of Complementarity, for example, signified this change in our thinking; Wolf elaborates: "It taught us that our everyday senses were not to be trusted to give a total view of reality. There was always a hidden, complementary side to everything we experienced."[11]   Quantum physics establishes its position concerning the potential of reality: "All of the world's many events are potentially present, able to be but not actually seen or felt until one of us sees or feels."[12] The connection between material reality (what is measurable and repetitive) and the vast resources of the mind (thoughts, dreams, and images) presents the possibility of what Werner Heisenberg called a *"third* or *intermediate reality."* He continues, "The concept that events are not determined in a peremptory manner, but that the possibility or 'tendency' for an event to take place has a kind of reality—a certain intermediate layer of reality, halfway between the massive reality of matter and the intellectual reality of the idea or the image—this concept plays a decisive role in Aristotle's philosophy."[13] Wolf elaborates on the third reality of quantum physics:

It has attributes of both the "in here" and "out there" realities. I think of this third reality as a bridge between the world of the mind and the world of matter. Having attributes, of both, it is a paradoxical and magical reality. In it, causality is strictly behaved. In other words, the laws of cause and effect manifest. The only problem is that it isn't objects that are following those laws (at least, not the ordinary kinds of objects we usually refer to), but ghosts! And these ghosts are downright paradoxical, able to appear in two or more places, even an infinite number of places, at the same time.[14]

In describing matter, the New Physics refers to these "ghosts" as wave patterns; Wolf calls them "qwiffs." He adds that "qwiffs" depend on space and time and that their nature is transitory, multidimensional, and illusional. Similarly, perceiving a play imagistically means that actors, directors, and designers are not dispassionate observers of objective reality. They are engaged, instead, in a creative thought process, receptive to a continuous, paradoxical flow of what amounts to their perceptions of the "qwiffs" and "ghosts" of the play's reality, the metaphorical image.

Playwrights select words, develop dialogue, and suggest physical environments in order to frame what is the broad outline of the play's world. When the dialogue and settings do more than establish the essential descriptive features of character, event, or place, we are struck by the lyrical potential of the work. On one level, the playwright's manipulation of time and space tells the artist something about how the author perceives the outer material reality of the play. On a deeper, more substantial level, the play's images can provoke revelations about the inner psychology of characters, character relationships, and situations. Interpretations informed by material that is hidden within the text's rhythms, images, scenic diction, and atmospheres inspire new readings of not only contemporary plays but also classical ones; in fact, almost any play that has timeless ideas and characters is fertile ground for reinterpretation. The play's images, symbols, and scenic metaphors encourage the creative imagination to find an equally provocative theatrical language that is as explosive as the playwright's material. New readings of plays are the product of aesthetic perceptions that are based on informed imagination.[1] Developing the skill to decipher and work with the play's images can be compared to learning how to play a piano concerto. Because you are emotionally moved by the beauty of the composer's masterpiece, you spend hours coordinating your eyes and fingers with the keys and score; finally, when you technically master the piece, you see the composition anew—reinspired by your informed imagination.

Artists influenced by theories and practices of modernism search for hidden imagistic patterns or leitmotifs deeply imbedded within the play's poetry. Thus, when interpretive artists work with the play's images, poetic allusions, and hidden patterns, they abandon intellectually analytical approaches that would produce naturalistic reproductions. The play's images, which inspire the first creative impressions of the play, are not unlike the fleeting brush strokes of the impressionist painter. They seduce the artist's imagination, provoking the actor, director, and designer to become active participants in the play's world; hence, artists talk about hearing and seeing the play in their imaginations. Moreover, the act of "reimaging" a playscript is a continual one: first occurring in the shadowy recesses the artist's imagination, later becoming part of collaborative thought, and finally resulting in a production in which the audience reinterprets the theatrical images they see on the stage. When the production's metaphorical images evoke additional perceptions from the audience, the staging and all the design elements have been particularly successful in engaging the audience on an emotional level. At the same time, this interpretive method and style of production can stimulate thoughtful reflection, whereby the audience may also consider the intellectual potential of the script's images.

Theatre artists who have been influenced by the theories and practices of Meyerhold, Artaud, and Brecht are more than likely aware of Susanne K. Langer's work with "non-discursive symbolic forms." In her book *Feeling and Form*, she notes that "non-discursive form" has the ability "to articulate knowledge that cannot be rendered discursively because it concerns experiences that are not *formally* amenable to the discursive projection."[15] The rhythms of life and emotional chaos of a character (their emotions, desires, thoughts)—more specifically, the inaction in Chekhov's plays—often resonate in the play's internal progressions, presentational (nondiscursive) scenic images, allusions, and repetitive patterns. For example, the play's dramatic action, what Stanislavsky calls the character's *objective*, is often rendered indirectly in subtext. A silence or pause on stage is frequently a more powerful way to communicate emotional content than the written word; similarly, the rhythm of repartee evokes meaning on stage that escapes the logic of discursive language. Langer doesn't dismiss discursive forms of communication altogether; she does, however, point to the variable nature of dramatic art over other forms and modes of expression. By its very nature drama is incomplete, until, of course, it is brought to life on the stage before an audience. Even then, one could easily argue that the play's suggestive images provoke continual multiple perceptions; thus, it is highly unlikely that a production of a play will communicate a singular idea. Playwrights are more enraptured with the complexities and ambiguities of human nature than with taking a pedantic stand on a particular issue. Whereas the play's social ideas might be responsible for initiating dramatic action, it is the somewhat less than obvious subliminal, emotional world of the character that drives the play forward. For this reason, it is of utmost importance that an author establish a clear and resounding "commanding form," which, Langer points out, "has to govern the crisscross of many imaginative minds, and hold them all...to one essential conception, an unmistakable 'poetic core.'"[16]

The variable nature of dramatic art (its incomplete realities or events as well as the spontaneity of a live performance) separates this mode of art from, for example, the poetic illusion of narrative literature. "The theatre," Langer reminds the reader, "creates a perpetual present moment; but it is only a present filled with its own future that is really dramatic." Unlike the narrative form, the play's progressions create a "virtual future." What Susanne Langer is referring to is her interpretation of dramatic action:

Drama, though it implies past actions (the "situation"), moves not toward the present, as narrative does, but toward something beyond.... Persons, too, in drama are purely agents...makers of the future. This future, which is made before our eyes, gives importance to the very beginnings of dramatic acts, i.e. to the motives from which the acts arise, and the situations in which they develop; the making of it is the principle that unifies and organizes the continuum of stage action.[17]

When artists emphasize how important it is for a young actor, director, and designer to learn how to read a playscript effectively, they appear to have heard Langer's advice: "The lines of the play are the only guide a good director or actor needs.... [They] are really the highlights of a perpetual, progressive action, and determine what can be done with the piece on stage."[18] Careful attention is paid to what words mean, how they are used, and how sentences are constructed and to progressions, allusions, and metaphorical patterns. Playwrights are well aware that their poetry evokes images. The play's "virtual images" (another Langer term) go a long way toward creating an illusion of life as well as helping the script move toward its objective. Imagistic connections are desirable, primarily because they allow us to make emotional connections with the world of the play. Momentary glimpses of the play's life, events, characters, and setting help the audience remember, catalogue, and form impressions about the play as a whole. Because plays are written to be performed, we can assume playwrights know that their range of communication expands to include not only the imagistic word of language, but also scenic means of expression. Often playwrights will utilize whatever discursive and nondiscursive forms of communication they need in order to suggest the elusive reality of the play's core. Learning how to read the text's poetic scenic diction (scenic images and props), therefore, helps the artist comprehend something more about the internal world of the play.

In an insightful monograph, *The Role of Imagery in Learning*, Harry S. Broudy points out: "The arts deal exclusively in images—visual, tonal, kinesthetic. Some are images of things found in the world around us—houses, flowers, clouds, people. Some images can be perceived as merely denotative, much as a photograph or a diagram might be. But in art the images are expected to be connotative also, images not only of recognizable things but of their human import as well."[19] Unspoken human fears and desires (what Ernst Cassirer terms "mythic consciousness," Freud refers to as "dream patterns," and Jung defines as the archetypal forms of our collective unconscious) often find their voice in the nondiscursive metaphorical image. It is important to acknowledge the difference between an image that has little import other than as a signpost and one that has the potential to convey hidden meaning. When an image is only a factual deliverer of information, it is called a sign. A traffic signal is commonly cited as an example of a sign; through common usage, an observer would immediately recognize that this object's descriptive colors represent something specific: to stop, hesitate, or go. If the play's language, story, material objects, characters, and rhythms or an actor's gestures or movements or the director's compositions and orchestrations or a designer's scenic images or costumes surpass the material logic of representational signals and signs, they have the possibility of attaining symbolic significance. Langer says, "A symbol is used to articulate ideas of something we wish to think about, and until we have a fairly adequate symbolism we cannot think about it."[20] Symbolic motifs or metaphorical images are clear objective concepts that reveal something about the play's internal world. Aesthetic perceptions occur when the artist recognizes how the play's "presentational symbols" create patterns and metaphorically suggest something about the text's poetic core.

Following Langer, words or objects have metaphorical resonance when they

1. are more than descriptive, logical, denotative, and representational and elicit a significant emotional response
2. help us explain ideas that we cannot define or that we do not understand
3. clearly and immediately send a message that is a recognizable idea

According to Langer, "We are driven to the symbolization and articulation of feeling when we *must* understand it to keep ourselves oriented in society and nature."[21] She soon cautions, however, that if the "artist chooses for his motif an image or event that is exciting only to him, i.e. as a private symbol, such a use of it would set up no tension *in the work*, but only in his mind, and the intended device would fail."[22] The theatrical image becomes symbolic when its expressive form reaches beyond the logic of discursive thought and helps the audience perceive the complexities and ambiguities of emotional chaos symptomatic of the human condition.

Artists achieve "aesthetic literacy" when they learn how to perceive, as

Broudy points out, "the sensory, formal, and expressive properties of aesthetic images—that is, those that convey human import."[23] Close readings keep the artist from overlooking what could amount to a tantalizing image. Consider, for example, the playwright's initial imagistic sketch—a play's landscape or setting. The opening stage directions of *The Seagull* appear, at first glance, to be nothing more than a physical description for Act One:

> SETTING: *The grounds of Sorin's estate. A broad tree-lined path leading away from the audience to a lake is cut off by a makeshift stage for an amateur performance. The lake is hidden from view. Bushes to the left and right of the stage. Several chairs, a small table. The sun has just set.*

> AT RISE: *On the stage behind a lowered curtain Yakov and other Workmen are heard coughing and hammering. Enter Masha and Medvedenko, left, on their way back from a walk.*[24]

The Seagull's Act One scenic description contains hidden poetic imagery that is especially enticing to an artist who has developed an eye, ear, and mind that is receptive to poetic images. Chekhov uses words to convey a specific naturalistic environment; his detail suggests an interest in depicting a picture of a Russian country home, a dacha, in a clear, straightforward manner. If when analyzing a script for production, the artists assume that scenic descriptions are no more than a way the playwright locates and describes the action, then they run the risk of missing important imagistic connections to the play's hidden poetry. Playwrights are fond of packaging an image so that it conveys subtle messages and assumes multiple levels of meaning; and as symbolic signposts, poetic images help the audience connect with the play's subliminal reality. Timo Tiusanen's *O'Neill's Scenic Images* is a helpful literary study that illustrates how "scenic images" can be used to uncover O'Neill's poetry. Tiusanen defines a "scenic image" as "a scene (or, more often, part of a scene) in which several scenic means of expression are used to achieve an effect charged with thematic significance."[25] The play's material images, therefore, can tell the artist something about the character's internal state or the psychology of the moment. Thus, as Susanne Langer points out, "'Environment' is an invisible constant, but 'setting' is something immediate, something sensuously or poetically present."[26]

These ideas need elaboration to show how scenic images convey meaning on several levels. Consider, for instance, a traditional definition of late-nineteenth-century realism, a dramatic form that requires a certain degree of verisimilitude: a causally developed story, contemporaneous ideas, recognizable characters, believable dialogue, and historically appropriate scenery. Perhaps, the playwright would provide a detailed description of the interior of a Victorian house, including specific objects that locate the action and further identify historical period. The play's story, characters, and spectacle rely on material objects, representational people, and logical syntax to construct a tangible or recognizable reality that conveys a truthful representation of life. A traditional reading of one of Ibsen's realistic plays, for example, would make a case that its physical props and setting help substantiate the material world of realism. The modernist would argue, however, that some of Ibsen's representational objects/signs convey more than a materialistic description of dramatic time or place. An early scenic description in *A Doll House* calls for a Christmas tree, a choice that is interpreted by many to be Ibsen's way of establishing time by materially depicting one of the traditional signs of this Christian holiday. A closer look at the play, however, indicates how the playwright imagistically manipulates the object/sign to say something about Nora's inner psychology. In the beginning of the play, the Christmas tree arrives, and straight away the audience becomes aware of a household happily preparing for what is perceived by many to be a joyous, warm, loving season. Later in Act One, when Krogstad threatens the Helmer household, Nora tries to regain her composure by decorating the tree:

> *Nora:*   (*absorbed in trimming the tree*). Candles here—and flowers here. That terrible creature! Talk, talk, talk! There's nothing to it at all. The tree's going to be lovely. I'll do anything to please you, Torvald. I'll sing for you, dance for you—[27]

Nora's world, signified by the "scenic image" of a Christmas tree, which has been placed center stage, suggests security and warmth—a safe haven for Nora. In fact, her often-quoted childlike impetuosity is motivated by how quickly she denies reality and responds to the Victorian splendor of her Christmas tree—certainly, its magic will chase away the harsh reality of Krogstad's visit.

At the beginning of Act Two, Ibsen asks that the tree be moved to a less prominent position; it is a sign that Christmas is over. However, if the artists recognize the metaphorical significance of the tree as an object/image, they can perceive something about the development of Nora's character. The "scenic image" can now metaphorically suggest that the delicate balance of the Helmer household is in jeopardy. By Act Three, Ibsen tells us that the tree is dying, its candles are burned down, and its ornaments are faded. A compelling argument could be constructed that the Christmas tree has become a poetic metaphor of significant proportion illustrating not only Nora's character, but also her marriage to Torvald: like the candles she placed on the tree, her relationship with her husband has been purely ornamental, soon to flicker and cease to be.

Imagistic messages are conveyed through the play's action, dialogue, and "scenic images." For Anton Chekhov, however, the pause, as well as what appears to be the lack of dramatic action, are equal if not more powerful modes of communication than verbal language or overt physical action. This playwright charges the play's atmosphere by orchestrating his characters, language, props, and scenic images (sounds, scenery, and music) into a lyrical arrangement of significant recurring themes. For example, by developing *The Seagull* through a series of short scenes in which the characters are constantly missing each other; and by selecting syntax replete with ellipses, pauses, and incomplete sentences, the author suggests the frustrating circular or indecisive dramatic rhythms of individuals who are lost and out of control. Chekhov is fond of communicating the human condition in indirect or poetic ways; like Ibsen, he positions his scenic images in ways that signify the inner state of a character. Chekhov's impressionistic, subtle, lyrical, poetic images replace nineteenth-century causal reality with temporal relativism, thus further dismantling the position that authority, materialism, and determinism held as purveyors of truth. In Act Four, when the dead, stuffed seagull is brought on stage and presented to the writer, Trigorin, he does not remember that Treplev killed it because he had nothing better to do or that he used Treplev's earlier words and action as an idea for a short story. The audience or reader, of course, recognizes by this time that the seagull symbolically represents the character Nina. We are also presented with the information that Trigorin (who is interested in finding out how young people behave so he can write about them more accurately in his stories) has had an affair with Nina, has fathered her child, and subsequently has left her. When the preserved dead seagull arrives on stage and Trigorin dismisses any involvement with what is now an object with a richly developed imagistic history, Chekhov not only succinctly underlines the vacuous nature of Trigorin but also poetically suggests one of the play's central issues: how indecisiveness and an unwillingness to recognize and take responsibility for self, others, and art produces continual psychological pain and physical destruction.

When stage directions metaphorically embellish what is to come in the dialogue, they form what Timo Tiusanen defines as a "scenic unit," or "a special kind of scenic means of expression, characteristic of the playwright in question and used by him as an element in constructing scenic images."[28] By isolating a section of the playscript (scenic description, a scene, a motivational unit, a beat) and concentrating on how the dramatist manipulates the play's language, the artist may perceive a microcosm of the whole play. Thus the "scenic unit" helps the artist organize how the play's scenic images metaphorically connect with the play's inner reality.

In Act One of *The Seagull*, Chekhov talks about the woods, a "makeshift stage," and a "lake" that is painted (perhaps) by the rays of a setting sun. The stage directions are an imagistic prelude, a metaphorical teaser, poetically suggesting the role atmosphere will be playing throughout. The opening atmospheric stage directions are punctuated by "coughing and hammering"— odd, harsh additions to what, on the surface, might be interpreted as an overture for a romantic evening in the woods:

Medvedenko: Why is it you always wear black?

Masha: I'm in mourning for my life. I'm unhappy.

Medvedenko: But why? (*Thinking hard.*) I can't understand it...You're healthy.

Your father may not be rich, but he has a comfortable life. My life's much harder than yours—I make only twenty-three rubles a month, minus pension-fund deductions—and I don't wear mourning. (*They sit down.*)

Masha: Money doesn't matter. Even a pauper can be happy.

Medvedenko: In theory perhaps, but not in practice. I've got myself, my mother, my two sisters, and my little brother to support—and all on twenty-three rubles. We need to eat and drink, don't we? We need tea and sugar. We need tobacco. Just try and make ends meet.

Masha: (*looking at the stage*). The play's starting soon.

Medvedenko: Yes. Nina Zarechnaya in a play by Konstantin Gavrilovich. They're in love, and today their souls will merge in the desire to create a unified artistic image. But my soul and yours have no points of contact. I love you. I miss you so much I can't keep away. Every day I walk four miles here and four miles home, and what do I get? Utter indifference. And no wonder. I have no private means and a big family to support... Who wants to marry a man with nothing to eat?

Masha: Ridiculous. (*She takes snuff.*) I'm touched by your love. I can't return it, that's all. (*She holds out the snuffbox to him.*) Snuff?

Medvedenko: No, I don't want any. (*Pause.*)

Masha: What a muggy day. We're in for a storm tonight. All you do is philosophize or talk about money. You think there's nothing worse than poverty. Well, I think it's a thousand times easier to go begging in rags than to...But you wouldn't understand...(5-6)

Mining Chekhov's poetic "scenic images" is one way the interpretive artist can uncover a rich labyrinth of interwoven patterns or leitmotifs that indicate something more about the play's inner action or the psychology of the characters. They become even more provocative when theatre artists discover how theatrical images can create the rich ambiguous texture of Chekhov's world. For example, it is in *The Seagull*'s initial atmospheric "scenic unit" that Chekhov establishes his poetic, multileveled reality: an obvious physical setting for a romantic evening (the woods, a lake at dusk, a strolling couple) and several seemingly inconspicuous sounds ("coughing and hammering"). Chekhov's random, seemingly arbitrary images, however, are far more provocative if they are viewed as part of the larger metaphorical picture. Consider, for example, how a director could enhance the atmosphere of a production of *The Seagull* if the coughing and hammering were orchestrated to foreshadow metaphorically the forthcoming tension between just about everyone in Act One. The opening dialogue between the schoolmaster, Medvedenko, and the love of his life, Masha, are early yet clear examples of what later becomes the predominant psychological makeup of most of Chekhov's players. Although the previous dialogue contains words that signify connection ("unity," "contact," "love"), these characters hardly listen to each other, let alone connect. Generally, Chekhov's plays are known for characters who can neither communicate nor take charge of their lives. Such is the case with *The Seagull*.

As the play progresses, it becomes clear that little, if anything, is accomplished between any of the characters: arguments are left unsettled, problems are dismissed, and characters are evasive or vacillate. Medvedenko wants Masha, but Masha desires Treplev, and Treplev is in love with Nina, and so on; with everyone desiring someone else, and no one getting what they want, the dramatic action appears to be at a virtual standstill. Moreover, the oppressive stillness of the approaching storm is contrasted with occasional thunder, producing a tension-filled atmosphere that echoes the inner psychology of Chekhov's characters.

The earlier images of "coughing and hammering," replaced by intermittent "thunder," have become distant, vague memories. Yet, these "scenic images" metaphorically suggest the annoying early stages of what will become a pounding migraine headache. They reflect the atmosphere produced by the dramatic action in Act One: a series of situations in which Chekhov's characters vie for attention, but the right person doesn't seem to notice, or where there are continual arguments, but no solutions are reached. The play's inner reality is poetically punctuated by "scenic images" (approaching storm, muggy evening, sun setting, hammering, coughing) resulting in an atmospheric leitmotif that is developed further through the application of short scenes, indecisive ellipses, and the terminal Chekhovian pause. As provocative as "scenic units" might sound at this stage, Tiusanen cautions that "not all scenic means used by a playwright are scenic units, but only those repeated with some regularity." He continues, "When trying to approach a playwright's world it is significant to notice certain consistent elements that seem to be symptoms of relatively lasting characteristics. Scenic units are signs of artistic continuity, scenic images of variety and fresh creation."[29]

How do artists who are influenced by modernism keep their subjective perceptions from digressing into expressions of self-indulgent pretentiousness? Contemporary artists, who see the play's world through the prism of modernism, have been influenced by Stanislavsky's ideas concerning objective and through line of action as well as Francis Fergusson's interpretation of Aristotle, especially those ideas that address dramatic action. Even at the end of the twentieth century, theatre in North America continues to subscribe to many of the theories that produced psychological realism. Artists turn to Stanislavsky's idea of objective (the character's needs, wants, and desires) when scoring the character's development; they find it especially helpful in understanding the progression of the play's story. It was the literary critic Fergusson who, in his *Idea of a Theater* (1949), made the connection between

Aristotle's dramatic action and Stanislavsky's objective and super-objective. Whereas Aristotle provides us with no clear definition of action, Fergusson devotes a great deal of his book to studying how dramatic action relates to the play as a whole. He views dramatic action, not unlike how Stanislavsky interprets objective, as "the object which the dramatist is trying to show us, and we must in some sense grasp that if we are to understand his complex art: plotting, characterization, versification, thought, and their coherence." He makes reference to the Moscow Art Theatre's use of the "infinitive phrase" as a way in which we can comprehend dramatic action, citing that in the play *Oedipus* the central action would be "to find the culprit."[30]

Many artists I interviewed stressed that after their initial reading and emotional reaction they concentrated on what is going on or happening in the play. The "key question in theatre," especially for the costume designer Robert Morgan, "is not really what are people saying, but what are they doing?"[31] Zelda Fichandler perceives the playscript to be held together by "a knot of will and need" located somewhere in "the pith of the play."[32] After the artists find and follow the development of the character's needs, desires, or wants moment-by-moment, or beat-by-beat, they know a great deal more about how the play is constructed and what drives it forward. Although Jay Halio writes about the problems of interpreting Shakespeare, in *Understanding Shakespeare's Plays in Performance*, he too addresses the problems of subjectivity and clarity as well as historical validity and contemporary significance; therefore, his thoughts about classical interpretation bear mentioning here. Halio finds, "The through line of action provides the consistency of point of view, the thread on which the various scenes are strung, but it need not rigidify the acting or the interpretation of the whole so that new insights and representations are prohibited."[33]

Theatre artists might not mention their indebtedness to Aristotle's *Poetics* (ca. 325 B.C.) directly when they talk about approaching a play for production. Admittedly, scholars have found fault with the sketchy nature of some of Aristotle's theories in the *Poetics*; some question its legitimacy, arguing that, at best, this seminal work is incomplete; others suggest it might be a collection of lecture notes intended to be passed on to those students who were knowledgeable about Aristotle's teachings. Recently there has been inquiry into the possibility that *Poetics* was not written by Aristotle but by those who were commenting on his ideas. Although the definition of some of his key concepts (*mimesis, katharsis,* and *hamartia*) provoke continual controversy, Aristotle's definition of the six elements of tragedy (plot, character, thought, diction, song, and spectacle) nevertheless provides modern artists with one strategy by which they can study the foundational structure of the play's world.

Artists who infuse new life into a play by giving a playscript an alternative reading would find Aristotle's extended ideas concerning the function of *mimesis* (imitation) provocative, especially if one considers Gerald Else's contention that as Aristotle moved away from copying life to suggesting something more, he was making the transition from copying in the Platonic sense to creating.[34] The last three Books of the *Poetics* are even more titillating for a metaphorical director and designer; in Book XXIV, for example, Aristotle suggests "the poet should prefer probable impossibilities to improbable possibilities" (xxiv.10).[35] Reality, for Aristotle, is the process of becoming; his view, which Marvin Carlson summarizes in *Theories of the Theatre*, is one that perceives "the material world [as] composed of partially realized forms, moving—through natural processes—toward their ideal realizations. The artist who gives form to raw material thus works in a manner parallel to that of nature itself and, by observing the partially realized forms in nature, may anticipate their completion." Artists don't copy reality; they show the things of life as they "ought to be." Thus, Carlson adds, artists free themselves "from accidental or individual elements."[36] Hence, Aristotle offers in Book IX his position of what distinguishes poetry from history: "Poetry, therefore, is a more philosophical and a higher thing than history: for poetry tends to express the universal, history the particular" (ix.3).

Contemporary artists who are interested in what Aristotle called universal look for issues in the play that are timeless. The costume designer Jane Greenwood addresses what in the past is present today.[37] Similarly, Zelda Fichandler finds herself asking how the material is connected to the gestalt of the moment politically, socially, and emotionally. She adds: "I try to give the audience the sense of discovery that I had by sharing my astonishment of finding something so human and revelatory about why we are alive."[38] Determining cross-cultural connections is a significant issue in contemporary performance theory; what is important for the young artist to realize, however, is the extent to which modern theories and practices have been influenced directly or indirectly by Aristotelian theory—especially by his ideas concerning *mimesis* (imitation), universality, and *katharsis* (purgation).

It was during the Renaissance that Aristotle's ideas concerning dramatic theory were recognized and unequivocally accepted as a means of measuring a play's dramatic merit. Since then many scholars, as well as artists/theorists, have joined the neoclassicists and reinterpreted Aristotle, generally challenging his views on tragedy, action, *katharsis*, and unity. Although much has been written concerning whether Aristotle's theories are applicable to drama written in the twentieth century, his elements still serve to help many Western artists understand how the play's parts work to reveal something about it as a whole. Many artists first experience a play on a metacognitive level; however, they understand that their relative perceptions, which find their voice in the ambiguous nature of a metaphorical theatrical image on stage, are helpful only insofar as they have been inspired by dramaturgical literacy. As stated earlier, Aristotle's ideas about plot, character, thought, diction, spectacle, and song are the critical tools most artists refer to when they reconcile how the parts of the play interrelate and tell us something about the play as a whole.

A brief review of Aristotle's elements is appropriate at this point to illustrate why artists engaged in scoring a playscript might view this over-2000-year-old theory as beneficial in the organization and testing of their initial imagistic perceptions.

Contemporary artists tend to interpret Aristotle's

- *mythos* or "Plot" ("the arrangement of the incidents" [vi.6]) as fable, story, or action
- *ethos* or "Character" as the individuals who tell the story
- *dianoia* or "Thought" (sometimes translated as politics) as the character's beliefs and feelings or those ideas, themes, or meanings inherent in the context of the play as a whole
- *lexis* or "Diction" as the play's language
- *melos* or "Melody or Song" as incidental music or internal dramatic rhythms (progressions, tempo, etc.)
- *opsis* or "Spectacle" as scenery, costumes, props, lights, etc.

Aristotle begins by pointing out that Tragedy is "an imitation of an action" that is "serious, complete, and of a certain magnitude...having a beginning, middle, and an end" (vi and vii). The play's plot consists of the events that detail and develop the play's action. Action is difficult to understand because today's students of theatre immediately tend to associate action with physical action (such as a car chase) or stage business (the physical movement of a character on stage, for example, Nora's Tarantella in Ibsen's *Doll House*). Aristotle views tragedy as

an imitation, not of men, but of an action and of life, and life consists in action, and its end is a mode of action, not a quality. Now character determines men's qualities, but it is by their actions that they are happy or the reverse. Dramatic action, therefore, is not with a view to the representation of character: character comes in as subsidiary to the actions. Hence the incidents and the plot are the end of a tragedy; and the end is the chief thing of all. (vi.9-11)

Physical business should not be construed as a part of action unless that business contributes, then, to the overall understanding of the play. If a physical action contributes to the plot, it can be part of an external overt action. If the action is not physical but psychological in nature and it contributes to understanding the play's events, then this type of action is internal.

Internal action is best understood when detailing the characters' needs, wants, and desires. An example would be Treplev's need to win his mother's love in Chekhov's *Seagull*. Throughout the play's dramatic narrative or plot, Treplev's primary need is evidenced in the structuring of the play's events; its significant actions develop logically (through cause and effect); have a beginning, middle, and end; and sustain our interest. Here the action is both internal and external. An example of the internal action is Treplev's desire for his mother's love, and an example of an external action is his suicide at the end of the play. Aristotle states that change happens when the character moves either from good fortune to bad or from bad to good. It is the play's action, coupled with the sequencing of the play's events, that propels the play forward in time and initiates response and change from its characters. When artists can retell the playwright's story, understanding how its action contributes to the development of all of Aristotle's elements, they begin to sense they have discovered something about how the play has been framed by the playwright—the rhythm of its heartbeat. Whereas Aristotle referred to plot as "the soul of a tragedy" (vi.14), many of today's practitioners refer to this aspect of analysis, especially when they sense an interrelationship between dramatic action and plotting, as finding the play's "pulse." Robert Morgan, for example, spends a significant amount of time determining what drives the scenes. He feels that "unless you get at the root of what moves each scene forward, what makes the next scene possible, you don't understand what the dynamic thrust of the play is. If you don't understand that, you run the risk, as a designer, of telling the wrong story."[39]

The next act of imitation occurs with the characters—in particular, how their needs, wants, and desires help in realizing the dramatic action by moving the plot forward. Aristotle cautions that a character's actions, like the plot, should be necessary, probable not irrational (xv.6 and 7), true to life, and consistent (xv.3 and 4). Additionally, characters go through reversals or recognitions; Aristotle separates the latter into five types: signs, revelations, memory, reasoning, and natural means (xvi). Through recognition the character undergoes "a change from ignorance to knowledge" (xi.2). Much of Aristotle's concept of character is drawn from what constitutes a hero in a Greek tragedy, that is, an individual of noble birth who falls into misfortune by "some error or frailty" (xiii.4). *Hamartia* is another controversial term that is viewed traditionally as part of man's mortality and more recently interpreted as an error in judgment. Many of Aristotle's ideas (his concept of what makes a tragedy, the construction of recognition scenes, and development of rational characters), if strictly observed, have little in common with the ideas put forth by modern or contemporary dramatic theory, let alone performance theory.

Dramatic art, from the fourth century B.C. onward, has remained interested, however, in Aristotle's ideas on universality. Plays are rarely successful unless their characters' needs, desires and wants are immediately accessible and clearly presented to the audience. No one understands this better than the artist who presents the play on stage. Consider, therefore, how important it is for the actor, director, and designer to identify and trace the character's action throughout the play, noting how it becomes the pulse of the plot.

What Aristotle classifies as *dianoia* is dismissed in short order in the *Poetics;* he refers the reader to the discussion in the *Rhetoric.* Most theatre practitioners interpret this element to mean the thoughts or meanings that evolve when one experiences the play as a whole. Generally, thought, like character, has broad appeal because both address issues that relate to humanity at large. There are plays that exhibit fairly obvious meanings. Thorton Wilder's *Our Town*, for example, is about those moral issues (love, marriage, family, and death) that say something about the beliefs and value systems in "Small Town, U.S.A." A play like *Death of a Salesman*, however, has caused critical controversy because its central meanings cannot be limited to any one major theme. Some critics focus on what happens when the protagonist, Willy Loman, loses his grip on reality because he has no moral values or ideals, whereas the playwright, Arthur Miller, counters with the premise that he is full of ideals, he just does not know how to attain them. Because plays aren't vessels that are limited to a singular meaning, it is not important that the interpretive artist becomes intent on discovering the one issue that is universally perceived as the theme. What is essential, however, is that the actor, director, and designer take the time to discover what particular thoughts are evident in the playwright's work and how they are integral to the play as a whole. The artistic director of the Actors Theatre of Louisville, Jon Jory, notes the importance of defining the play's "theme." He calls the approach "old-fashioned"; however, notice how he scrutinizes his subjective perceptions against a thorough working of the play's parts:

My first order of business when I approach a playscript is to define the theme. However, the process I am trying to describe is like an image on water—it changes, of course, as you work on the play before and during rehearsal. I'm not so naive as to believe that simply because I define it, that's what is in the play. Obviously there is a difference between the play itself and those who receive it. I find once I find the pervasive theme it is always a theme that I'm wrestling with in my own life. So there is a mirror there. It's not an objective process. But I want to find something thematically that allows me to judge each scene, in light of the scene, and relate the scene to the theme. What I do is, I will experimentally write down my two- or three-sentence themes, then I will thumb through the play. And when I find out that Act Two, scene two simply seems to have nothing to do with what I'm talking about, I go back and work on the theme some more.[40]

In Books XIX through XXIII, Aristotle considers diction, or the language of the play. In fourth century B.C., plays were written in verse and heavily relied on poetic imagery, rhyme, metaphor, apostrophe, jest, and epigram; yet Aristotle does not analyze "the language of lyric poetry in any of his extant writings."[41] He states that the diction must be clear and jargonless, with the goal being metaphor. Today, the language of plays remains highly selective and crafted, relying on image, symbol, and metaphor to communicate in a poetically clear manner. However, Chekhov introduced to the Moscow Art Theatre the potential of silence (the Chekhovian pause) as a different but equally powerful form of communication, whereupon Stanislavsky found it necessary to develop the concept of subtext. Consequently, the actor has been for a century exploring the possibilities of communicating thought without the aid of the written word. Modern dramatic theory and practice have found that nonverbal gestures, movements, illogical sound and silence, and physical objects have been powerful subliminal forms of communication capable, in many instances, of surpassing the limitations of discursive language. The theories and sometimes the practices of Meyerhold, Artaud, and Brecht, as well as the work of other playwrights (Ibsen, Chekhov, Strindberg, Maeterlinck, Yeats, Pinter, O'Neill, Williams, Shepard), then, seem to have adjusted Aristotle's notion of diction to include the possibility of nondiscursive communication. Good analysis work, therefore, depends on how carefully you read and understand how the play's "total language" (verbal and scenic images, metaphors, allusions, and myths) has been manipulated to evoke the hidden world of the play.

When Aristotle talked about song or melody, he was referring to how Greek plays were chanted or sung, not simply spoken. The dithyramb has been replaced, in most cases, by the written word, and today song or melody is used incidentally or indirectly to enhance mood. Characters might sing, play records, or play a musical instrument; a director might ask for music before and after the play, between acts or scenes, or underneath dialogue to help create the right atmosphere. Although it is no longer common in Western theatre for characters to sing or chant dialogue, the internal poetry of the play often gives the impression that the playwright has orchestrated its hidden patterns much like a musical composition. Rhythms are created in dialogue or in monologue through repartee, sounds, and silences. The playwright can further control rhythm by calling attention to physical sounds: the explosion in Shepard's *Curse of the Starving Class* or the breaking of the harp string in Chekhov's *Cherry Orchard*, or the city noises in O'Neill's *Hughie*. Indirectly, Aristotle's melody or song is interpreted today to mean the way the playwright has suggested and the theatre practitioner has orchestrated progressions, leitmotifs, rhythms, and sounds (verbal and nonverbal) in order to enhance the psychology of the play's plot, characters, thought, diction, and spectacle.

Aristotle speaks of spectacle as something one adds to the text, the play's visual elements: its scenery, costumes, lighting, makeup, and props. Its value is not unlike that of the other dramatic elements: Spectacle is another way of seeing, understanding, and enhancing the play's plot, characters, thought, diction, and song. Effective use of spectacle can tell a story, create ideas, help to delineate character, facilitate rhythm or movement on stage, and accentuate language (verbal and nonverbal). Some playwrights offer elaborate suggestions concerning the play's mise-en-scène (such as Tennessee Williams's opening description in *The Glass Menagerie*), whereas others might not paint an elaborate scenic picture but will instead delineate the need for specific scenic elements (such as the Christmas tree in Ibsen's *Doll House*). The author's use of spectacle can be a way of speaking metaphorically about the play and should not be ignored or dismissed. Generally, it is correct to assume that everything playwrights ask for or speak about is there for a reason; it is part of their way of communicating; it is part of the poetic language of the dramatist.

Although Aristotle doesn't speak directly to the issue of artistic synthesis, he does offer some thoughts on unity: "a whole, the structural union of the parts being such that, if any one of them is displaced or removed, the whole will be disjointed and disturbed" (viii.4). Unfortunately, Aristotle doesn't talk about performance; however, his thoughts on unity are not unlike Adolphe Appia's concept of balance and synthesis. Effective communication is the goal of most artists. In *Hughie*, for example, O'Neill orchestrates the hollow sounds and silences of New York City in the dead of night in a way that echoes the existential loneliness of two characters in a deserted hotel lobby. Aristotle might not speak directly to the issue of synthesis; however, many playwrights have discovered that the interrelationship of Aristotle's elements is a powerful way to address directly both the intellect *and* the emotions of the audience. Artistic communication is equally desirable to the audience; therefore, they mine the play's parts until they have an intimate knowledge of how the script works as a whole.

Richard Hornby's *Script into Performance: A Structuralist Approach* (1977) is a helpful study for those interested in how the theories of Structuralism (as Hornby interprets them) address issues of reinterpretation, the nature of the playscript, and its relationship to performance. (Hornby capitalizes Structuralism to indicate that he is not talking about the traditional concepts of dramatic structure.) Although Hornby's book appears to be aimed more toward students of dramatic literature who might direct than toward designers and actors, it is clear he has thought deeply about the relationship between dramatic theory and production. Hornby's reading of Structuralism focuses on how the content (the parts) of a playscript form "patterns," "structures," and "webs of relationships," which upon being revealed in performance produce new thoughts about the play. Hornby views Structuralism as part of the New Criticism movement (T. S. Eliot, I. A. Richards, William Empson, L. C. Knights, G. Wilson Knight, F. R. Leavis, to name a few). Hornby sees the Structuralists' position as one that perceives "a work of art—a play, a poem, a painting, a film—as an interrelated process rather than a thing or a collection of disconnected things.... Structuralism finds the essence of a work in the relation between parts rather than in the parts themselves; these relations form patterns or 'structures' that define what the work truly *is*."[42] Significant to this study is Hornby's argument that effective play interpretation necessitates that the artist carry out a thorough organic or "intrinsic"[43] examination of the playtext and develop the ability to make "imaginative leaps."[44] For Hornby, "Structuralism is far more *style* than fixed method. It is never a single thing, but rather a way of making connections, or 'functions,' between different things."[45] Eschewing interpretive processes that offer a fixed set of rules, Hornby (like so many creative artists) prefers whatever eclectic approach might provide access to the inner workings of the play's world; Structuralism is thus one way an artist can begin to understand a playscript. According to Hornby, Structuralism, in relationship to playscript analysis, "1. Reveals something hidden, 2. Is intrinsic, 3. Incorporates complexity and ambiguity, 4. Suspends judgment, [and] 5. Is wholistic."[46] Like the Structuralists, theatre artists Adolphe Appia, Richard Wagner, and Constantin Stanislavsky were interested in discovering the connection between the play's parts and a "sense of the whole." Though Appia was not a playwright, Hornby makes the argument that his early twentieth-century designs are not unlike the approach of a Structuralist, who finds value in an organic relationship between the play's parts and the "sense of the whole." Hornby adds that Stanislavsky's work with objective is an example of an artist who appears to be using a Structuralist approach and methods in creating a character. When actors use a character's objective to give direction to the dramatic action, they utilize something that is *"hidden"* to reveal an understanding of the script and character. It is *"intrinsic"* because it draws on material from the script and not external facts. Hornby continues, "It can *incorporate complexity and ambiguity*, since unlike other acting systems it deals easily with situations where the character says something different from what he means; it *suspends judgment*, since it requires no 'typing' of a character or ethical comments on his behavior but instead tries objectively to ascertain his particular desires; and it is *wholistic*, since it views all aspects of performance as interconnected"[47] (italics added).

When theatre artists make something from an existing blueprint, they should come to the material fresh, willing to participate in a process that seeks to identify how the threads of a fabric are woven together. Because Structuralism is a method of critical associative thinking that considers how the play's parts organically combine to form its whole, it is in contrast to other more traditional forms of play analysis that create isolated categories to describe dramatic structure: rising and falling action, acts, scenes, beats, climax, French scenes, reversal, cognition, and denouement. (Hornby classifies the traditional categories as examples of "surface structure" that are not very illuminating to the performer.)[48] Hornby argues that what is far more significant is a critical analysis that focuses on the exploration of the play's "deep" or "hidden" structure (its progressions, patterns, and relationships). The Structuralist, Hornby adds, sees the text as a "complicated mosaic" open to multiple interpretations. "The standard, obvious views will always be limited or prejudiced; he attempts to get at something more profound. If he is successful, this more profound view is of course *no longer hidden*; it may even, with time, become blatantly obvious, requiring other critics to try new approaches."[49] An artist who works with the play's poetic images is not unlike the Structuralist critic: both are concerned with revealing something about the play's subliminal world. Whereas an imagistic encounter with the text's "hidden" poetry might sound mystical, both the Structuralist and the imagistic interpretive methods use materials already available in the text. However, the less apparent structures make themselves available only when the artists know the play well enough that they can identify significant structures (leitmotifs, patterns, "scenic units").

Some artists find it valuable to use French scenes, noting (among other dramaturgical classifications) the beats and climatic moments throughout the play. While Hornby expresses concern about the limitations of analyzing a play's "surface structure," he also notes that the use of such scoring is helpful if it reveals a "hidden" pattern or structure. My interviews indicated that many artists feel strongly about scoring the playscript; several artists (designers in particular) cited Lester Polakov as the artist/teacher who introduced them to a rigorous approach to play analysis. Years of experience would later allow them to adapt the process to fit their needs. Taking the time to sit down and score the play (the visual orchestration of the play's parts) might appear to some to be too academic an approach, one that prohibits or diminishes spontaneous commingling with the script on an emotional level. Polakov, I feel certain, would correct that hasty assumption by offering that he finds his way into the world of the play through both his imagination and a methodical scoring of the play's action. Polakov's approach begins with finding some way to indicate a "non-objective representation of the feeling of the play." He continues,

It can be shapes or forms, some do sculptures; it's really an abstraction of the feeling of the play. The graphic image is a way of getting to your unconscious memories. I tell people it is like having a reservoir of ideas in your mind, which are mostly unconscious. It is like dropping a fish-hook and fish-line and pulling up something, and that is what the play is like. I did a summer stock production of *On a Clear Day You Can See Forever,* and my graphic image was "a mirror with a memory." This is a play about a psychoanalyst who goes back into a girl's previous life. And I thought somehow that sounds good, I can use that as a graphic image.

Polakov's "non-objective" or initial "graphic image" is followed by a written statement in which he describes what he thinks the playwright is writing about. When Polakov scores the play, he is looking for how the play's internal structure relates to his initial "graphic image" and statement.

I break the script down into steps or beats [actor's beats], and that is the story in the script. That's the action. I number each beat in this column. Then I group the beats into episodes or French scenes and they are numbered in this column. In another column I write the subtext of each beat. In the last column I list the physical needs. Those are the physical objects you don't want to forget—like a large kitchen table. Sometimes I put the initials of the author after it to remind myself that he said those are necessary. Later, I may have a better way of doing it.

Polakov also identifies the point at which the play begins, which he calls the "the attack" or "where the chief dramatic question is asked." He adds that when the protagonist is asked this question it is simultaneously presented to the audience. It can be suggested, therefore, that by locating "the attack" in the script and highlighting that significant moment on the stage the artist can suggest to the audience a path that will guide them into the world of the play. He later locates in the playscript where the protagonist finds the answer to the question; he calls this point "the crisis." That answer is followed by a more difficult question: What is the protagonist going to do? Identifying the resolution in the playscript becomes the next task. This designer makes it quite clear that he designs the play around "the attack, the crisis, and the resolution."[50]

Artists who score the playscript find the activity to be more propitious than mundane; they recommend it as a way to test their immediate imagistic responses with the play's mechanics. In short, interpretive artists who prefer not to work against the playscript or to tell a peripheral story actively score the play so they can understand how the play's parts work as a mechanism. Although Robert Morgan was not one of Lester Polakov's students, he considers his costume score as part of his homework: "I go through the play scene-by-scene, and I try to understand each scene in relation to the larger structure of the play: how long it is, what happens in it, who is in the scene, and what you understand at the beginning of the scene and what you understand at the end of the scene. Every scene has to move the play forward somehow."[51] Some artists spoke about how they titled each French scene. When they go back and read their titles, they find themselves asking, "Does each scene's title have something to do with their impression of the play's theme?" The title becomes a shorthand way to test their understanding of how each scene works with the play as a whole. Thomas Skelton, who was a student of Lester Polakov, uses the title of each scene as a quick form of identification. He finds this method particularly useful when he is in the process of physically lighting the production and he can't take the time to stop and study the script; he glances at the title of the French scene and immediately he recalls the essence of the scene through a rich progression of images.[52]

Scoring encourages the artist to work closely with each scene, identifying significant moments, lines of dialogue, and object/images that fuel the play's dramatic action. Contemporary artists are interested in the genetic makeup of a scene; their search for the essence of a scene is similar to what Sullerzhitsky, at the beginning of this century, calls the "kernel." The "kernel" of one individual scene might be repeated in another; sometimes they reappear throughout the play, forming patterns and telling the artist something more about the play's hidden rhythms, atmospheres, and ideas. Zelda Fichandler finds the "kernel" of the scene significant in informing movement on stage. She elaborates, "You'd be surprised how bodies fall into beautiful patterns if they know just what they are doing and who they want to be near or not near.... Geography pulls people, needs pull them, hunger pulls them, antipathy or friendliness pulls them. The polarities in life make shapes and forms."[53]

Generally, when artists score the playscript they are applying some of the traditional categories of dramatic structure to organize or frame a moment. Scoring produces a microversion of the playscript; it affords the artist the opportunity to take a closer look at the poetic structure of a particular moment (beat). When the artist produces a score that consists of a series of moments, poetic images function in a different way, some forming leitmotifs illustrating the flow of the play's inner poetry. Stepping back and reviewing a completed composition provides a more comprehensive picture of how the playscript works externally, and a subsequent bird's-eye view of the score as a whole can elicit an immediate impression about how the play is structured both externally and internally (Aristotelian critical framework and "surface structure" as well as "hidden" patterns and leitmotifs). Similar to the director or designer who titles French scenes or works with a written statement that says something about the playscript as a whole, artists might find it helpful, Hornby suggests, to sketch their version of the playscript's "unifying principle"—"a *statement* (possibly in the form of a diagram, formula, or phrase)" as one way to immediately "*grasp the significance of a playscript as a whole.*"[54]

The wholistic approach to interpretation set forth by the "New Critics" is one that looks at the "intrinsic" nature of the work itself, whereas the traditional "extrinsic" criticism of the late nineteenth century, as Hornby reports, tends to look at everything outside the work: "its historical background, including the life of the author; genre, leading to excessive generalizing at the expense of the particular; philosophy, especially ethics, reflecting that nineteenth-century tendency to make moral lessons out of everything; character, taken out of the context of the work and analyzed like that of a real person." The New Critic focuses on a detailed examination of the "intrinsic" nature of a work of art "in isolation and in considerable detail."[55] Hornby, aware that the position of the New Critic has been cited by many as being too limited, is reluctant to soften his position, especially when he speaks of the stage director who, he emphasizes, "should limit himself to analyzing the particular playtext...suspend value judgments, historical considerations, discussions of genre, philosophical speculations, and the like."[56] Hornby argues that an intrinsic analysis is generally superior because "a Structuralist critic of literature" is forced to take a closer look at how the play works—especially its ambiguities and complexities. He continues, "[They] will not try and isolate and define an element." Instead, they will note how the play comes together: the interconnected relationship of "a theme to a character, or a character to another character, or a setting to an action."[57] In a structural analysis every detail is important, especially minor ones. Hornby points out that unlike the play's major details, which are required for telling the story, it is "the minor details [in which] the playwright is most free to express himself."[58]

An interpretation of a play's text originates with a close reading, and a metaphorical director or designer is interested in an analysis that might offer something that has never before been revealed; however, many might take issue with Hornby's position that "extrinsic" criticism is irrelevant in discovering something new about the play's world. Artists are generally well read and conversant with dramatic form, aesthetics, music, and art as well as with those psychological, philosophical, sociological, and historical issues that expand their understanding of the human condition. Therefore, it would be foolish to suggest that information outside the play would not take, at the very least, a subconscious role in play interpretation. Equally significant is the position of the playwright who prefers not to write in a vacuum and who therefore is consciously or subconsciously aware of the traditions of literary genre. A case also could be made that playwrights write, generally, because they are in some way affected by and have something to say about the cultural milieu that informs their plays. Moreover, many North American regional theatres, aided by their dramaturgical staffs, spend a considerable amount of time preparing for production. The previous chapter addressed some of the ways artists work on a playscript when they prepare for production: Some review everything (documents, music, the visual arts, film, etc.) that will give them a better understanding of the play's cultural history; some admit to reading critical scholarship about the play; others talk about reading material about the author and/or other plays in the author's canon; and most spend a great deal of time with pictorial references that relate to the play historically. Actually I heard a great deal about how research, *if used in a creative way*, played a significant role in how artists prepared a playscript for production.

Developing a sensitivity to the playscript's cultural and historical context can be an asset to those interested in how the play's cultural milieu has played a role in developing the psychology of the play's world. Frequent trips to museums and a knowledge of music can stimulate a curiosity about the past, as well as suggest how the past relates to the present and, perhaps, to the future. Developing a literacy in the visual arts stimulates imaginative thought about how persons in another society carried themselves (the ways in which they sit, stand, and gesture tell the viewer something about movements, patterns, and interpersonal dynamics). Additionally, a study of the manners, customs and dress of a given period may help in relating such discoveries to the playscript and understanding more about the characters' psychology. Musical literacy aids the artist in finding dramaturgical rhythms; moreover, the ability to recognize that the play's rhythms have something in common with the music of the period enhances the artist's sensitivity concerning the play's historical time. For example, exploring late-nineteenth-century Russian music, art, architecture, and fashion can enlighten the artist's critical awareness of a Chekhovian landscape.

In particular, Chekhov's friendship with the Russian impressionistic artist Issac Levitan exposed him to the world of impressionistic thought. A worldview that perceived reality in a state of continual change, or as fleeting moments, must have been intriguing to a playwright who was interested not in what was being said but in what was left unsaid, not what was done but what was left undone, and not in the play's external actions but in what was occurring below the surface. The play's external realism (people eating, drinking, and playing cards on stage, as well as the environmental sounds), which was so attractive to Stanislavsky's early thoughts on this subject, we now know was subsequently seen as an elementary or pedestrian way to reveal the psychology of those characters. Like the impressionist artist intent on suggesting a temporal world over a physical world, Chekhov's play only appears to be simple and quiet. In truth, the world consists of layers of complex, ambiguous images and symbols that, upon closer study, reveal a transitory sinister environment capable of silently destroying its characters.

An imagistic interpretation that is informed by dramaturgical literacy goes beyond the production of the broad outlines of a given time period; an artistic sensitivity to the cultural mood of the period is a crucial factor in an analysis that results in the synthesis of imagination and information. Immersing oneself in the world of the play places the artist in a position to discover how subtle poetic images and overt physical objects work together to form dramatic structure. Whereas contemporary modernists might label a production pedestrian if it simply duplicates the materialistic outlines of the play's world, they recognize that extrinsic information, if viewed in creative ways, can help in revealing aspects of the play's hidden reality. Some might find fault with Hornby's insistence, then, that elaborate character biographies and improvisations of events outside the playscript are irrelevant because they are a form of "extrinsic" analysis. (Consider, for example, Ming Cho Lee's portrait gallery.) However, eventually Hornby amends his position on the value of "extrinsic" information, generally accepting it if it is part of the creative act of interpretation, "made means to its end, which is a construction of a vision of the work-in-itself."[59]

Ostensibly, Hornby is concerned that if artists don't work with the play's organic structure (accepting that its ambiguities and complexities are, in part, responsible for multiple and contradictory meaning), they might fall into the trap of producing a "concept" production. Like many performing artists, Hornby finds "concept" productions to be "crude and reductive." He continues, "Such productions find a modern equivalent for a single aspect of the playscript—Lear's power struggle or Phaedra's marital jealousy—and ignore all the rest, the multiple levels of meaning, the contradictions, the quirks, the resonances that occur when particular characters operate in a unique world. It is not necessarily bad to turn something old into something new, but it is disgusting to turn something subtle and complex into something simple-minded and dull."[60]

Many artists (especially those I interviewed) preferred not to talk about "concept" productions, suggesting their aversion to a play reading that can produce overly glib, too pat, ill-prepared, or pedestrian forms of theatre. A careful reading of a playscript involving a thorough working of a play, especially the synthesis of imaginative thought (images) with information (ideas), was their preferred approach—one that tends not to produce closed interpretations, warmed-over reproductions, or oversimplified productions.

"Concept" productions can be the unhappy result of a hasty analysis, whereupon the artist (usually the director or designer) panics and tries to "fix" the parts of the play that appear to be unclear, unnecessary, or difficult to understand. Or sometimes the production team will go in another direction; fearing the play might bore the audience, they attempt to make the playscript more accessible by updating the material—adjusting the play's time and space until it is more recognizable to a contemporary audience. While a modern-dress, Americanized version of *The Seagull* might diminish an undergraduate's criticism of Anton Chekhov's play as being historically irrelevant and too far removed from the consciousness of a contemporary American audience to be of any value, one wonders how placing this play in the twentieth century on an estate in the Berkshires (for example) would elicit significant new insights about character relationships, let alone sensitively capture the play's poetic world. In fact, such a radical departure from late-nineteenth-century Russia would trivialize most of Chekhov's conflicts between old forms and new. It is difficult to identify an example of an American dacha that would convey the isolation of Sorin's estate, much less evoke the magical reality of Russian provinciality, or to imagine how a contemporary reading of this playscript would help an audience understand the isolation Treplev feels as he lives out his life far from the mainstream of society.

Although successful "concept" productions can offer new perspectives, they are a dangerous proposition, as Hornby cautions, if they suggest reification or closure or so emphasize one point that the playscript's subtlety, complexity, and artistic ambiguity are lost to heavy-handedness. Effective play analysis "reimages" the play as a whole, and resulting metaphorical productions evoke multiple, not singular, perceptions. Updated plays, called "simile productions" by Robert Brustein, can be worthwhile projects. (Consider the 1920s version of Congreve's *Way of the World* in 1992 at the Huntington Theatre Company in Boston, or JoAnne Akalaitis's controversial subway-setting production in 1984 of Beckett's *Endgame* at the American Repertory Theatre in Cambridge.) Brustein finds, however, that "simile productions" tend to be more successful if they focus on topical issues in classical plays or are "thematic," not "ornamental." And while Brustein acknowledges that "updating" a production might be a part of metaphorical theatre, he adds, "it is rarely the basic device."[61]

Finally, Hornby argues that unity is not at issue for the Structuralist. Whereas the neoclassicist sets out to fix Shakespeare's disunity by adjusting the play's time, place, and action, the Structuralist perceives the play's structure as a web of interconnected parts, at once unified, "but not in the older sense of uniformity."[62] Hornby's Structuralist vision is more like Gestalt psychology: both support the sensual perceptions of imagery; both propose that we experience the world wholistically; both find that novel insights are the result of our ability to recognize the structural characteristics of a given event. While there is no satisfactory translation of the German word *Gestalt*, Gaetano Kanizsa suggests a translation could be an "'organized structure,' as distinguished from 'aggregate,' 'heap,' or simple 'summation.'" Kanizsa continues: "When it is appropriately translated, the accent is on the concept of 'organization' and of a 'whole' that is *orderly, rule-governed, nonrandom*. This concept is opposed to that of a merely *arbitrary*, *random*, and *unstructured* grouping. But in addition to its being used to describe the product of a process of organization, the term 'gestalt' also indicates the structural properties of the process itself."[63]

It is not surprising, therefore, that Hornby would not overlook Structuralism's connection to Gestalt psychology: "The Rorschach text, for example, shows that the human mind is capable of perceiving unity even in random blobs of ink."[64] The purpose of this book is not to study the relationship between current work in Gestalt theory and an imagistically informed critical analysis of a playscript. I do intend to suggest, however, that the artist who perceives a playscript in a creatively informed yet subjective manner has more than a little in common with the cognitive perceptional context of Gestalt psychology. For example, the Gestalt position champions that learning (insight) occurs when we observe relationships, clusters, or patterns. The Gestalt psychologist Wolfgang Köhler's investigation with chimpanzees during World War I leads to his concept of insight: a creative moment resulting after one stops and reflects on a situation, event, or problem, when at once there is a sudden flash of insight. Thought, synthesis, and evaluation lead to what the Würzburg school describes as the "A-ha experience."[65]

The artist who works associatively with the text's images, exploring their interrelationships, weaving informative thought with imaginative perceptions, seeing new possibilities instead of frozen views, is receptive, then, to a Gestalt vision of the play ("a sudden flash of insight"). Even when artists respond to the playscript as a unified whole, they maintain that there is still no way this experience should suggest a recovery of artistic intention or indicate that they have found *the* (one-and-only) way a playscript should be interpreted. Briefly, the modernist would insist that an imagistic reading of the play's world is preferable over an interpretation that conceives space as absolute, simply because in no way do images limit or define. Images are subjective, and often unconsciously informed, sensations that emerge when the artist reacts to the play as a whole. It can be suggested, then, that an artistic perception of the play's world, which is informed by modernism, is a Gestalt configuration of its content.

Noel McInnis, in his article "Gestalt Ecology: How Do We Create Our Space?" reminds the reader that because the Newtonian world order sees "external spectacle" or reality as separate from the "internal spectator," it then can be measured objectively, measured in a reductive way "in which wholes are separated into their respective parts. Reality is then structured, for purposes of communication, into linear, sequential, cause-and-effect arrangements of the data gained from this piece-by-piece examination of the external world. Properly standardized by such a structural process, reality is thus thought to be communicable to all people with rational minds, whose interpretations of reality will then be in complete agreement."[66] The reductionist position offers the whole as the sum of the parts: a specious assumption in today's complex world—no human being can keep track of the multitudinous array of parts that make up a whole. "Symbiotic interaction is a *process* which inevitably assumes that the whole is different from the sum of its parts. Such interaction," McInnis continues, "can be comprehended only by perceiving the parts of a process in relation to one another as well as separate from one another."[67] Similar to Gestalt psychology, an imagistic interpretation responds to the dynamic energy of an event; such is the case when the artist experiences the playscript's integrity. Moreover, this interpretive process may lead to perceiving the play's organic unity as both a theoretical base and a significant force initiating intermittent imagistic responses, in part responsible for the "A-ha experience." Finally, metaphorical theatrical images (psychological gesture, profound scenic images, revelatory tableaux vivants, etc.), those that invite reinterpretations, are the physical manifestations of a Gestalt experience.

Imagistic theatre, especially as informed by contemporary modernism, is not devoted solely to the process of perceptual associative "reimaging"; it is also a theatre that seeks to ponder thought-provoking issues about the complexities of the human condition. An imagistic production that supports the vision of the metaphorical director and designer champions a theatre that in revealing the play's poetry has not diminished the possibility for social action. For example, in *Reimagining American Theatre*, Robert Brustein argues that the metaphor's expansive realities "represent a poetic avenue to the truth."[68] The suggestive, reverberant nature of a metaphoric interpretation can increase our ability to understand, if not to solve our problems. Brustein supports this point by citing earlier the ancient argument between Plato and Aristotle, which he interprets as "whether the theatre has importance as an instrument of moral and political action, or whether it is an imaginative experience with no apparent usefulness beyond the purgation and exaltation (*katharsis*) of its audiences." He continues by adding that whereas the Aristotelian theatre is "complete and self-contained, designed to spend and discharge the passions of the audience," the Platonic theatre invites a more active political participation, to the extent to which "the audience, excited to passion by the spectacle before it, emerges into the world to resolve these tensions through some form of active intervention."[69] The controversial issue between art and politics is, for Brustein, resolvable if one considers the metaphor as "a bridge where politics and theatre meet." In his essay "Politics and Theatre" he offers these thoughts: "Art encompasses politics but refuses to affirm it. The artist lives in compromised reality, but he lives in another world as well, the world of the imagination, and there his vision is pure and absolute.... Politics demands resolution; dramatic art is content to leave us in ambiguity. The consequences are unreconciled opposites, tension, inaction—but also the metaphysical joy which comes from a pure truth, beautifully expressed."[70]

It is true that dramatists are not in the business of solving problems. Through the rich metaphorical texture of their plays, they present issues and are careful not to take sides. Brustein cites numerous examples in which Ibsen and Chekhov refute any assumptions that they stand for a particular social cause or a philosophical view; instead, they present social problems (such as the development of an individual) rather than political solutions. Both playwrights claim they are artists, not philosophers, and although they might have opinions, they mask their personal judgments through presenting contrary points of view and in artistic ambiguity. Plays such as *Ghosts, A Doll House, An Enemy of the People, The Cherry Orchard, The Three Sisters,* and *The Seagull* indicate that their authors had a sense of moral responsibility and that in some instances they even dared to present current social and political issues. However, as Brustein points out, "these opinions are never the personal property of the playwright; they belong to the people who express them, and exist, in Aristotelian fashion, to reveal character."[71] Chekhov made it clear in his letters that he was an objective observer of life. He believed the audience, not the playwright, should be the judge; therefore, he seems hardly a candidate for a theatre informed by Plato. Yet Brustein suggests that Chekhov's dramas, as well as those of other modern playwrights (Ibsen, Shaw, Brecht, Beckett, van Itallie, Kopit, and Genet), are metaphorical; therefore, their theatre can function in poetic and politically responsible ways. The suggestive yet reverberant nature of the metaphor has just the right ambivalent quality to present a problem without solving it. Brustein's contention is that, within the imaginative metaphor, Platonic ideas can mingle with Aristotelian form to the extent that the theatrical metaphor provokes interest long after the audience has left the theatre.

A contemporary reading of a play, then, especially one that results in a metaphorical production, is not unlike the modern metaphorical playwright: neither particularly uses metaphors to solve problems; instead, they imaginatively suggest what the problems are. Thus, theatrical metaphors have become one way in which the artist can project the world of the play into a larger context. We tend to identify a modern design as one that creates a poetic interpretation of reality through a collection of images that function in metaphorical or presentational ways. The tableaux vivants and artful gestures, in addition to scenic images, present the artist's subjective imaginative interpretations in ways that suggest symbiotic relationships between past and present-day societies. When metaphorical directing and design provokes "active intervention" with the world of the play, it does so in a way that neither reproduces reality nor presents pedantic ideology. To that extent, and perhaps that alone, the artist who gives a playscript an imagistically informed reading is discouraging mindless entertainment by encouraging the audience to become actively involved in understanding more about the play, its world, and the human condition.

5

Reimaging *The Seagull*

Artists influenced by modernism find that their initial response to the world of
the play is an imagistic one. When images form and commingle, they stimulate
the artist's creative thought, and the actor, director, and designer begin to sense
something about the play's internal reality. Imaging seduces the artist's creative
spirit, encouraging participation in the interpretive act of "reimaging" the play's
world. A way of becoming more intimately involved with the play's heartbeat
is to contemplate how the playwright's use of allusions and scenic images
poetically embellishes ideas about the story, characters, language, rhythm, and
scenic descriptions.

The goal of an artist's journey into the playscript is to emerge with an artistic
vision that makes a poetically resonant statement. The artist who is interested in
metaphorically revealing something about the playscript's inner reality and
suggesting its poetic equivalent on stage therefore develops the ability to weave
words, characters, ideas, situations, rhythms, gestures, and atmospheres into
theatrical images.

A rapid reading of *The Seagull*, for example, might lead one to think that
Chekhov's world is uninteresting, morbid, or terribly vapid. A closer reading
reveals that this playwright's poetic vision contains subliminal dramatic action,
enigmatic characters, elusive morality, delicate rhythms, and sublime "scenic
images." Only when artists become actively involved with the inner workings
of *The Seagull* can they appreciate how this playwright could write
passionately about a society, yet maintain a distanced subjectivity.

Some of the material in this chapter has appeared in two of the author's articles, "Imaging *The
Seagull*'s Faustian Leitmotif" and "Seeing *The Seagull* Again," *New England Theatre Journal* 4
(Spring 1993): 39-48, 128-31.

This chapter offers a dramaturgical analysis of *The Seagull*. The intention is to suggest some of the ways artists might use creative research to inform their initial response to the playscript. The process that is offered is not meant to imply a singular, rigid methodology. Instead, the rigors of a deep interpretive analysis suggest how the artist who is sensitive to the nuances of images and the complexities and ambiguities of hidden structures envisions what we perceive as metaphorical theatre. The quotations that appear throughout the text, the periodic questions that occur at the end of some sections, and the remaining body of dramaturgical material illustrate some of the ways artists might work with the play and corresponding dramaturgical information. This material is intended to provoke images, not to dictate process. For example, the questions found at the end of a section are meant to be only suggestions that may provoke further questions. They relate to those issues, objects, and ideas that might help the artist understand something more about the play's world. Questions are part of the overall process; they don't occur in any particular order.

Furthermore, when artists work with the script's internal patterns (its structures, leitmotifs, progressions, allusions, images), they often explore cultural and literary images that illuminate their perceptions. Most artists, especially those influenced by modernism, agree that their understanding of the play's inner world can be furthered by creatively mining the images found in the play's external cultural history. This bilevel approach, therefore, is useful for artists who are interested in becoming more aware of a play's poetic energy.

The Seagull has been selected as a case study because it is one of the most poetic, expansive, and challenging works within the naturalist/realist tradition. It is not surprising that Chekhov's comedy continues to find an audience almost a century after its first production. Near the turn of the twenty-first century, the ideas and images that are part of Chekhov's hundred-year-old play have a contemporaneous ring: New forms continue to challenge traditional thought, imagistic theatre provokes continual controversy, and the yearnings, struggles, and betrayals attributed to Chekhovian characters remain elusive and alluring. Further, *The Seagull*'s rich poetic structure surfaces as an invitation to ponder how an imagistic approach impacts on traditional textual methods of playscript analysis and performance practices.

Oftentimes, first impressions and perceptions about a proposed production of *The Seagull* have led many to connect this play to late-nineteenth-century thoughts about naturalism and realism. After all, Chekhov's work was embraced by Nemirovich-Danchenko and Stanislavsky and produced at a time when the Moscow Art Theatre was focusing on a truthful depiction of reality on stage. Some have made the case that this playwright depicts plot, character, situation, and idea by carefully motivating each event and selecting and arranging the material objects to convey the logic of materialism. Other interpretive artists would argue that Chekhov's world is filled with fragile, lyrical images that can only *suggest* the depth of his character's frustration. These artists have discovered that this play is neither linear nor causal, but filled with ambiguous leitmotifs, a rich imagistic world, and complex hidden patterns.

*The important truths in Chekhov's plays are those which are left unsaid,
or allowed to emerge obliquely, in indirect hints, from deeps of silence
or understatement.*[1]

—Ronald Bryden

Many artists find their way into the play's world imagistically; they find that
the play's images provoke an endless stream of spontaneous snapshots that
encourage the development of a metaphorically enriched production. A mise-en-
scène that is the result of an informed imagistic reading not only stimulates
additional discoveries about the poetic nature of Chekhov's world but also
provokes the imagination of an audience and encourages further "reimaging."
Numerous artists have recounted how important it is to be immediately
stimulated by something in the playscript. It could be an image—how the
playwright manipulates time and space, the emotional landscape of a particular
character, the play's ideas, or the like. Often an artist's first impulse will be an
emotional one. Olympia Dukakis, for example, is intrigued by how Chekhov
deals with time and what it does to people: "I'm interested in how time changes
the characters, how they lose their dreams, and how they keep improvising their
lives. There is such yearning in every character in Chekhov. And they all feel
such betrayal. They have to regroup. Nina, for example, has to accept something
about the reality of her life so she can go on. You know, it's not what we
thought in our youth. It's not fame and fortune. It's about work, carrying those
crosses, having faith and endurance."[2]

Many artists find that their way into the play begins with a spontaneous
reaction that produces a series of images. Not only do they find that their
initial response is a personal one, but many also insist that their immediate
connections will more than likely relate to some issue they are working on
themselves or one that is timely. Consider, for example, what Richard Jenkins (a
director who enjoys breaking performance traditions) found tantalizing about
Chekhov's *Seagull*. Jenkins offers, "There is no right or wrong in this play.
There's no judgment. You don't really know who Chekhov agrees with. So I
think it gives you the freedom to really let these characters come alive."[3] Tori
Haring-Smith (Jenkins's dramaturg and translator) describes Jenkins as an
individual who is interested in contemporaneous connections and collaborative
spontaneous "reimaging." In particular, she recalls that Jenkins not only wanted
to break away from a more traditional rendering of Chekhov but also expressed
an interest in exploring the play's comedy, which has eluded and mystified
many who have attempted to produce *The Seagull*.[4]

On a different note, director Douglas Wager found his curiosity heightened
when he noticed the absence of traditional form in Chekhov's play. Because he
produced *The Seagull* in an arena space, he saw an opportunity "to blow the play
apart visually and get rid of some of the obligations or conventions that have
been attributed to this playwright through the use of a proscenium stage." Wager
decided, "Chekhov was breaking form almost for the sake of breaking form, and
not understanding (while he was writing) why he was writing the way he was

writing. But he knew what he didn't want—anything that smelled of melodramatic convention."[5]

> *The comedy has three female roles, six male roles, four acts, a landscape*
> *(a view of a lake), much conversation about literature, little action and*
> *five tons of love.*[6]
>
> —Anton Chekhov

Artists speak of taking their first impressions and testing them against the manner in which the playwright tells the story, creates characters, uses language, develops ideas, and manipulates time, space, objects, and images. Aristotle tells us that plot is responsible for ordering dramatic events in a way that unifies dramatic action. Writing out the plot might seem tedious; however, it can be an informative way to discover something more about how the playwright constructs the story.

PLOT

Act I

The Seagull is about a group of individuals who lead unfulfilled, monotonous, frustrating lives. As the play opens we find they all have gathered at Sorin's estate beside a beautiful lake. Here each character strives for a better life; however, no one knows how to attain it. Sorin's nephew (Treplev) writes a play in hopes of gaining his mother's (Arkadina) respect and winning the admiration of an aspiring actress (Nina). The play is performed as the moon rises by the lake in the midst of a forest that surrounds the estate. Treplev's play is filled with images and symbols; its new form alienates most of the audience— at least enough of them for Treplev to feel he has been a failure in front of not only Arkadina and Nina but also the famous writer (Trigorin) who is his mother's lover. A disappointed, distraught Treplev runs off into the forest, pursued by a young women (Masha), the only one who loves him unconditionally. The performance abruptly ends, leaving its audience to make their way back to the house—but not before Trigorin has a fateful meeting with Nina; Arkadina obsesses about her age; Sorin expresses a need to make something more out of his life; Dr. Dorn, the family friend, remarks that he has enjoyed Treplev's play; and Medvedenko, the schoolmaster, calls for plays to be written about teachers.

Act II

Several days later we find Trigorin indulging in his favorite activity, fishing, while Sorin sleeps, and a bored Arkadina reads de Maupassant out loud (to those who will listen) in the hot noonday sun. Still overwrought by the events of his play's premiere and Nina's rejection, Treplev challenges Trigorin to a duel. Later, he shoots a seagull and throws it at Nina's feet. Arkadina, fueled with jealousy, paranoia, and guilt, uses the excuse that no horses are available for a trip to town to incite her fury and cause her to decide to leave the estate immediately. By chance, Trigorin meets Nina and tells the impressionable young actress about his life as an artist; she responds by telling him she would do anything, live anywhere, if only she could experience such a life. Trigorin is charmed; however, he does nothing but write down some more tidbits he has observed that might be useful in future short stories. Arkadina ends the act by announcing that she has decided to stay, a decision that delights both Trigorin and Nina.

Act III

Between Acts Two and Three, Treplev unsuccessfully tries to shoot himself, and Masha decides to marry Mevedenko and forget Treplev. When Act Three begins, Sorin begs his sister Arkadina to help Treplev by giving the boy some money; in turn, Treplev asks his mother to help Sorin by giving *him* some money. Arkadina rejects both of their pleas. Treplev longs for his mother's love and attention and begs her to forget Trigorin; she rejects his requests. Crazed with jealousy, Arkadina begs Trigorin to return to her and leave the thought of Nina behind. Trigorin agrees; they decide to leave the estate for Moscow. However, shortly thereafter Trigorin again meets Nina (who has decided to become an actress) and arranges to meet her in Moscow.

Act IV

Two years pass, but little has changed on the estate: Masha has married Mevedenko and borne a child; Polina (Masha's mother) remains in love with Dr. Dorn even though she has been married to Shamraev for a number of years; Dr. Dorn has gone abroad on an extended holiday; Treplev is a published author; and Sorin remains an old, sick man whose procrastination has been instrumental in allowing his life to slip through his fingers. We discover that Treplev is still in love with Nina. However, not only has she had a disastrous career on the stage, but she has also had an affair with Trigorin, which produced a child who died shortly after birth. The characters reveal how their dreams have dimmed or in some ceases been abandoned when faced by life's harsh realities. Arkadina returns to the dacha to see her ailing brother, Sorin. While Trigorin and Arkadina are having dinner, Nina enters. Although life has proven disappointing and harsh, she implies she has benefited from her experiences. Not realizing Treplev still loves her, she tells him about her love for Trigorin. Although she cannot accept his love, she attempts to comfort Treplev by showing she still remembers lines from his first play. But Treplev is lost in his own loneliness and fear. Unlike

Nina, he does not know how to give his life meaning. He exits, and shoots himself.

Assessing the Plot

Chekhov develops his story primarily through a series of short scenes, snapshots of moments that tell the story and shape the characters' lives. Two years pass, in which little seems to happen. Chekhov uses the plot and its characters to call attention to a play devoid of physical action. For example, the characters tell the story through their actions; although those actions are complete (they have a beginning, middle, and end), they give the impression of being incomplete because little happens. In true Aristotelian form, Chekhov uses his characters to drive the plot. However, because this plot and its characters seem bogged down in indecision, Chekhov inverts traditional action by showing the *consequences* of the characters' actions rather than the actions themselves. In that sense he writes a play of nonaction or, as David Magarshack calls it, "indirect action."

Questions

- What is the attraction of Moscow?
- Why do these characters want to leave the country?
- What is the significance of valerian drops?

CHARACTERS

> *The demand is made that the hero and heroine should be dramatically effective. But in life people do not shoot themselves, or hang themselves, or fall in love, or deliver themselves of clever sayings every minute. They spend most of their time eating, drinking, running after women or men, talking nonsense. It is therefore necessary that this should be shown on the stage. A play ought to be written in which the people should come and go, dine, talk of the weather, or play cards, not because the author wants it but because that is what happens in real life. Life on the stage should be as it really is, and the people too, should be as they are and not on stilts.*[7]
>
> —Anton Chekhov

The plot focuses on a group of individuals who sit about and talk of their problems, needs, and desires; however, they are at a loss as to how they can change their dreary lives. Chekhov's action appears misleading: on the surface nothing much happens, but if you look at the composition of the plot (how the scenes are constructed and work together to create the structure of an act) then it becomes clearer how Chekhov's lack of external action is only a diversion that permits the action of his internal world to go unnoticed. The action of the plot is driven by characters who cannot move forward, who continue to make the same mistakes. Their action is repetitive and frustrating, yet it reinforces the play's general action.

Aristotle mentions that characters' needs are responsible for telling the story and are part of dramatic action because they drive the play forward in time and space. Chekhov states that his characters are filled with "five tons of love"; their appetites, however, are rarely satisfied. Even though they yearn for emotional, physical, or artistic fulfillment, their existential fears keep them from doing anything substantial about facing their wants, needs, and desires. Yet they continue talking about a better life and/or pining over a lost love. The play moves forward in time despite how much they avoid their real problems or mismanage their energies. It only appears that there is no dramatic action because their misguided choices keep anything significant or healthy from happening to their lives, yet below the surface of things the reasons for their "inaction" indicate that a great deal is going on in the psyche and souls of these characters. What initially seems uninteresting, then, is actually a cunning manipulation of the play's dramatic ideas and a means by which Chekhov creates dramatic tension. It is true that often his characters never get to Moscow, become famous, or marry the people with whom they are in love. Because they never take personal responsibility, their lives give the appearance of being colorless, directionless, and empty.

> [Chekhov] might have hoped for productions whose actors buried themselves in the individual emotions of his people, yet showed that such absorption in private feelings made them ridiculous, as a man who thinks the earth is flat because he walks on it flatfooted is ridiculous. As Chekhov said, it was all there on the page. His characters condemned themselves in their own actions, their own egocentricity.[8]
> —Ronald Bryden

The characters' motivations and rhythms might not be obvious immediately; nevertheless, they are responsible for initiating the play's dramatic color, interest, movement, and passion. Because Chekhov's dramatic action is not an obvious or overt part of the construction of the play's plot, characters, theme, language, song or spectacle, it only seems as if this playwright eliminated the dramatic conventions that traditionally are responsible for driving the play forward and giving it a direction or a specific meaning. For example, Chekhov's characters continue to express their needs; however, their talk becomes stale as their wants become too familiar. We might not see any physical action in Chekhov's plays, but we do feel and see the psychological effects of the characters' "inaction": Masha marries a man she does not love because she cannot face the inevitable fact that Treplev does not love her; Treplev commits suicide because he has never experienced any love from his mother and now has lost Nina's love; Trigorin comes back to Arkadina because he is essentially a spineless man who cannot face that he has ruined a young girl's life. These examples from *The Seagull* go on and on and point to how the psychological nature of Chekhov's dramatic action might be subtle, but nevertheless packs enough power to shape these characters' destinies.

Chekhov claims to have no political, religious, or philosophical views, yet his characters often speak with authority. For example, Dr. Dorn does talk to Treplev about the importance of a play having a clear-cut idea. Later, Chekhov undercuts Dr. Dorn's authority, questioning his medical competency. This is a device Chekhov uses throughout his plays. For Chekhov, truth is an elusive issue that permeates the play's fragile, complicated, and mercurial nature.

A study of the characters who inhabit Chekhov's rich environment reveals patterns created by the playwright to illustrate the play's action. For example, in *The Seagull* there are nine major love triangles:

- Masha—Medvedenko—Treplev
- Treplev—Nina—Masha
- Treplev—Nina—Arkadina
- Nina—Trigorin—Arkadina
- Nina—Trigorin—Treplev
- Dr. Dorn—Polina—Nina
- Shamraev—Polina—Dr. Dorn
- Sorin—Nina—Trigorin
- Sorin—Nina—Treplev

None of these relationships is ever resolved, yet they remain in place throughout the entire play. These nine simultaneous love triangles create debilitating lives that contribute both to the level of the characters' frustration as well as to the static action of the play.

Determining each of the characters' actions illustrates how the playwright tells the story and reinforces the play's general action. For example, Arkadina's need to be the center of attention, her fear of growing older, her love/hate relationship with her son, and the unstable relationship she has with Trigorin are all documented early in Chekhov's dialogue and his notes. Identifying the motivations that drive this character to say and do what she does helps in understanding who this person is. Asking why she says what she says and pinpointing when she says it and to whom tell a great deal about what fuels her passions. But character analysis can also be a helpful way to identify the play's dramatic form.

Character analysis begins with reading the play and noting what the character says and does and what others say about that character. Looking deep into the needs, desires, and wants of each personality in *The Seagull* reveals the reasons behind their complex relationships, why there are no resolutions, and what precipitates their fights. Their behavior patterns are replete with jealousy, paranoia, and anxiety. Many artists find their way into the play's world by exploring how the character's psychology stimulates physical responses and evokes visual or aural images.

Sketching the Character

In nature descriptions you must go after tiny details, grouping them in such a way that once you've read them you can close your eyes and see a picture.... In the domain of psychology, more details. But heaven keep you from clichés. It's best to avoid describing the characters' psychic states, which should be clear from their actions.[9]

—Anton Chekhov

Irina Nikolaevna Arkadina (Trepleva by marriage) is an actress, Treplev's mother, and Sorin's sister; she is in love with Trigorin (a famous writer) and is visiting Sorin's estate in all four acts. Act One takes place at dusk into early evening just as the moon is rising in the forest that surrounds the dacha. Arkadina, as well as the rest of the cast, is attending the premiere performance of her son's play. The play has a single performer, Nina, a young, nymphlike girl who aspires to be an actress.

We hear about Arkadina before she arrives. Sorin tells us she is in a bad mood. Treplev offers the reason why she is "bored" and "jealous:"

> *Treplev:* ...She's dead set against me, my play, and the performance, because her novelist might find Nina attractive. She doesn't know the first thing about the play, but she hates it.
>
> *Sorin:* (*laughing*). You're imagining things. Really...
>
> *Treplev:* It annoys her to think that Nina will get the applause. Even on that tiny stage. (*Glancing at his watch.*) She's a psychological oddity, my mother: unquestionably talented and intelligent, capable of weeping over a novel, reeling off all Nekrasov by heart, nursing the sick like an angel—but try praising Duse in her presence. No! She's the only one you can praise; she's the only one you can write about, shout about, rave about in *Camille* or *The Fumes of Life*. But here in the country there aren't any opiates like that, so she's bored and edgy and thinks we're all her enemies, we're the ones to blame. She's superstitious too: afraid of three candles, of the number thirteen. She's a miser: she's got seventy thousand in a bank in Odessa, I know it for a fact. But try and get a loan out of her—she'll burst into tears.
>
> *Sorin:* You're so convinced she's against the play you can't think straight and all. Calm down. Your mother worships you.
>
> *Treplev:* (*pulling the petals off a flower*). She loves me, she loves me not; she loves me, she loves me not; she loves me, she loves me not. (*He laughs.*) See? My mother doesn't love me. Why should she?

What she wants is to live, love, wear bright clothes. And here I am, twenty-five—a constant reminder she's not so young as she used to be. When I'm not around, she's thirty-two; when I am, she's forty-three. That's why she hates me. Besides, she knows I don't accept her theatre. She loves the theatre. She thinks she's serving mankind, a sacred art, but as far as I'm concerned the theatre today is all rote and delusion. When the curtain goes up on an artificially lit room with three walls, and those great talents, those priests of sacred art, show how people eat, drink, love, walk, and wear their jackets; when they take stock lines and stock situations and try to squeeze a moral out of them, a smug, homespun, over-simplified sort of moral; when they serve up the same thing in a thousand variations, over and over and over again—then all I can do is run, flee, the way Maupassant fled the Eiffel Tower, afraid its vulgarity would rot his brain.[10]

It is clear in reviewing Arkadina's actions in Act One that she wants and desires to be the center of attention; she does not abandon this need throughout the play. Initially she achieves her goals by playing an impromptu scene from *Hamlet* with Treplev:

Arkadina:	...O Hamlet, speak no more: Thou turn'st mine eyes into my very soul: And there I see such black and grained spots As will not leave their tinct.
Treplev:	...Nay, but to live in vice, To seek out love in sin's pernicious depths. (14)

Shortly thereafter she dismisses the importance of Treplev's play by incessant interruptions. Because she cannot stand not being on the stage herself, she eventually brings the performance to a halt with her silly questions, supercilious attitude, and contemptuous laughter.

Arkadina:	I smell sulphur. Is that part of it?
Treplev:	Yes.
Arkadina:	(*laughing*). I see. Quite an effect.
Treplev:	Mother!
Nina:	He longs for human company...
Polina:	(*to Dorn*). You've taken off your hat. Put it back on or you'll catch cold.
Arkadina:	The doctor's taken off his hat to Satan, father of eternal matter.

Treplev: (*flaring up, loudly*). That's it! The play is over! Curtain!

Arkadina: What are you so upset about?

Treplev: That's it. Curtain. Bring down the curtain! (*Stamping his foot.*) Curtain! (*The curtain comes down.*) I'm sorry. I overlooked the fact that only a select few may write for the stage and act. I've encroached on a monopoly. I...I've...(*He tries to say something, but gives up and exits left.*) (16-17)

The evening begins harmlessly enough with the premiere of her son's play. She should be proud, but in truth, as both an adult and a mother she behaves badly. She is more concerned with her personal life. She is filled with the anxiety that she could lose everything (career and Trigorin) if she grows old and is no longer attractive and charming enough to be the center of attention. Note how as the scene continues her fears intensify her anger.

Arkadina: What's the matter with him?

Sorin: You've wounded the boy's pride, Irina dear.

Arkadina: What in the world did I say?

Sorin: You hurt his feelings.

Arkadina: He said himself the play was a lark. Well, I treated it like a lark.

Sorin: Even so...

Arkadina: And suddenly he's written a masterpiece. Really now! So it wasn't a lark. He put together this extravaganza and choked us with sulphur to make a point...He wanted to teach us how to write and how to act. What a bore! The thrusts at my expense, the gibes — really, they'd try the patience of a saint. He's just a moody, headstrong little boy.

Sorin: He only wanted to please you.

Arkadina: Is that so? Then why didn't he pick an ordinary play? Why did he make us sit through that decadent delirium? I'm perfectly willing to put up with delirium for the sake of a joke, but why all those claims for new forms and a new era in art? I don't see new forms; I see bad temper.

Trigorin: A writer writes as he feels, as he can.

Arkadina: Well, let him. Let him write as he feels, so long as he leaves me out of it.

Dorn: Thou art angry, Jupiter...

Arkadina: I'm not Jupiter; I'm a woman. (*She lights cigarette.*) And I'm not angry. I'm just sorry to see a young man wasting his time like that. I didn't mean to hurt him.

Medvedenko: There are no grounds for separating spirit from matter. What we call spirit may well be the sum total of material atoms. (*To Trigorin, animatedly.*) You know what someone ought to do? Write a play about the life we schoolteachers live. Put *that* on the stage. It's a hard life, a hard life. (17-18)

In the forthcoming dialogue, Arkadina changes the subject, talks about the past, and other people—anything that will keep her from dealing with the nagging awareness that she is Treplev's mother and that she has behaved badly. She knows she should do something, but reacting in a responsible and loving way would imply motherly love, maturity, and growth. Arkadina does nothing. Leaving to search for her son would take her out of the limelight and make it impossible for her to keep a watchful eye on Trigorin.

Arkadina: True enough, but let's stop talking about plays and atoms. What a divine evening it is! Listen, everybody. Is that singing? (*She listens attentively.*) Lovely!

Polina: It's from the other side of the lake. (Pause)

Arkadina: (*to Trigorin*). Come and sit here next to me. Ten or fifteen years ago we had music and singing on the lake all the time, every night almost. There are six estates bordering the lake. I still remember the laughter, the noise, the gunfire...And the romances, the romances...By the way, the *jeune premier*, the idol of all six houses was none other than (*Nodding towards Dorn.*)—that's right, Dr. Dorn. Oh, he's still fascinating, but back then he was irresistible...Dear me, now my conscience is bothering me. Why did I hurt my poor boy's feelings? I'm so upset. (*Loudly.*) Kostya! Kostya, darling!

Masha: I'll go and look for him.

Arkadina: Would you, dear?

Masha: (*exiting to the left*). Konstantin Gavrilovich! Yoo-hoo! Konstantin Gavrilovich!

(*Nina comes out from behind the stage.*)

Nina: We're obviously not going on with it, so I may as well come out. Hello, everybody.

Sorin:	Bravo! Bravo!
Arkadina:	Bravo! Bravo! We all loved you. With those looks and that beautiful voice it's a crime for you stay buried in the country. I'm certain you've got talent. Certain, do you hear? It's your duty to go on the stage.
Nina:	Oh, it's the dream of my life! (*Sighing.*) But it will never come true.
Arkadina:	Who can tell? Here now, let me introduce you to my friend, Boris Alexeevich Trigorin.
Nina:	Oh, so pleased to meet you...(*Flustered.*) I read everything you write...
Arkadina:	(*giving her a seat next to them*). No need to be flustered, dear. He may be famous, but he's a simple soul. See? Now he's flustered too.
Dorn:	We can open the curtain now, can't we. It's eerie closed like that.
Shamraev:	(*loudly*). Yakov! Open the curtain, will you? (*The curtain opens.*)
Nina:	(*to Trigorin*). Strange play, isn't it?
Trigorin:	I didn't understand a word. But I did enjoy watching it. Your acting was so sincere. And the scenery was beautiful. (Pause.) There must be a lot of fish in that lake.
Nina:	Yes.
Trigorin:	I love to fish. There's nothing I like more than sitting on a riverbank in the late afternoon, watching my float bob up and down.
Nina:	But I thought that once an artist had experienced the joys of creation he'd be immune to all others.
Arkadina:	(*laughing*). Don't talk to him like that. Whenever people say nice things about him, he gets terribly flustered.
Shamraev:	Once when I was in Moscow at the Opera, I heard the great Silva go down to a low C. And it so happened there was a bass from our church choir up in the second balcony, and suddenly—imagine our amazement—suddenly we hear "Bravo, Silva!" a whole octave lower...like this (*In a deep bass.*) Bravo, Silva!...You could have heard a pin drop. (Pause.)

Dorn: The angel of silence must be overhead.

Nina: Well, I'd better be going. Good-bye.

Arkadina: Going? Where? It's so early. We won't let you.

Nina: Father is expecting me.

Arkadina: No, really. He's impossible. (*They kiss.*) Well, that's that, I suppose. We're so sorry to see you go.

Nina: You can't imagine how hard it is for me to leave!

Arkadina: Somebody ought to see you home, dear.

Nina: (*frightened*). Oh, no! No!

Sorin: (*to Nina, beseechingly*). Please stay!

Nina: I can't, Pyotr Nikolaevich.

Sorin: Just an hour and all that. Really now!

Nina: (*hesitating, nearly in tears*). No, I can't. (*She shakes hands with him and exits quickly.*)

Arkadina: The poor girl. Apparently her mother left all her enormous fortune to her husband—every last kopeck—and now he's gone and signed it over to his second wife. The girl hasn't a thing to her name. It's disgraceful. (18-21)

By the end of Act One, Chekhov has presented the reader with substantial information, and artists can begin to sketch Arkadina in their imaginations. We know, for example, Arkadina has retained the spotlight by relying on her youthful charm and her career on the stage. Recently, however, she has been reminded of her age by both her son's presence and the spirited neophyte who is the sole performer in her son's play. As she knows she is avoiding being a responsible adult, she feels guilty. A combination of fear and guilt only exacerbates her paranoia and anxiety. In many ways Arkadina'a behavior exemplifies what happens when our deepest desires cannot be fulfilled. She chooses neither to be a good mother nor to face her mortality; her existential indecision, in part, contributes to the "inaction" and tension in Act One and her relationship with Trigorin.

All the major characters in *The Seagull* suffer from the anxiety and pain of not getting what they want. Because Chekhov weaves their wants into a web of ever-present overlapping love triangles, every moment of the play contains the stress of a group unable to acknowledge the fears that keep them from facing the harsh reality that they are not getting what they want. Ultimately the characters (with the exception of Nina) lose their freedom to move on and grow because they do not take responsibility for the actions and choices they have made in life.

Because they are trapped in their own insecurities they are evasive and vacillate (most never take stands or synthesize ideas). Arkadina's ever-present need to be in control and the center of attention forces her to focus on maintaining her youthful looks, being witty and charming, and keeping her money intact. Her lack of personal insight fuels her insecurities, keeps her from making mature decisions, and ensures that she will continue to make the same mistakes. Being aware of the existential crisis inherent in Arkadina (and the other characters) makes it easier for the actor, director, and designer both to understand why these individuals do and say what they do and to determine why they cannot seem to say or do anything in particular that will lead them out of their agony. The conflict between their yearnings and their indecisive actions creates most of the play's internal tension and contributes to some of its external comic rhythms.

Questions

- Why are the characters filled with anxiety?
- How does the concept of "inaction" impact on character development (gestures and movement)?
- How does their individual pain affect their relationships with other characters?
- What are this period's customs and rituals (the duel, festivals, holidays, and games)?
- What are the educational backgrounds of these characters?
- What are the relationships between parents and children?
- What are their religious beliefs?
- Are there issues of class structure?
- What are the economic realities?
- What are the traditional roles and responsibilities of men and women?

THOUGHT

> *Anyone who says the artist's field is all answers and no questions has never done any writing or had any dealings with imagery....*
>
> *You are right to demand that an author take conscious stock of what he is doing, but you are confusing two concepts:* answering the questions *and* formulating them correctly. *Only the latter is required of an author.... It is the duty of the court to formulate the questions correctly, but it is up to each member of the jury to answer them according to his own preference.*[11]
>
> —Anton Chekhov

Chekhov writes about Russians at the end of the nineteenth century. In *The Seagull*, he focuses on the characters' tedious, repetitive, anxiety-ridden lives.

However a sensitive reading of this play tells us that it also emphasizes two important elements, namely, art and love. Here are some of the issues:

Art
- new forms *versus* old forms
- the competition between the neophyte and established artist
- hollow art, philosophical art, art-for-art's-sake
- artisan and artistic art, commercial art

Love
- love of art
- love of self
- unrequited love (the nine love triangles)
- parent-child love
- love of work
- love of fame

In the pursuit of art and love, these characters' lives become a tangled mess of misguided and ill-conceived accumulations of wants, desires, and needs that can never be fulfilled. *The Seagull*, like all of Chekhov's plays, is difficult to analyze because he does not take sides and point a finger at a singular cause or an evil or good individual. No character becomes a hero or villain; all have flaws and strengths. Because Chekhov does not illustrate a point of view, it is difficult to determine who is to blame. The Chekhovian world is neither simple nor rational. Instead, Chekhov's vision parallels the impressionist thought and form in that it is as elusive and as varied as human perception can allow.

Questions

- At the end of the nineteenth century, what was happening in Russia (artistically, historically and philosophically)?
- What was the artistic climate like?
- What is the production history of *The Seagull*?

DICTION

In the numerous short scenes that make up *The Seagull*, arguments are left unsettled, problems are not faced, characters do not listen to each other, nor do they speak in complete sentences (much less have a conversation that reaches closure). This tiresome chaos is punctuated often with a "Chekhovian pause" or silence—virtually a stop in action. Chekhov's language (his syntax, grammatical style, and use of the pause) keeps the play from moving forward. But it is not only Chekhov's dialogue, with its pauses, silences, and inept communication skills, that is devoid of action, it is also the way in which

Chekhov phrases the utterances that stops the play's momentum. For example, Sorin's inability to complete sentences, is punctuated by the use of ellipses: "Um...and all that...um...if you know what I mean..." (58). His linguistic style indicates an interruption in thought and illustrates how Chekhov continually reinforces the general action of the play by creating a language and suggesting a style of delivery that is indecisive and hesitant. Sorin's shorthand-like speech and the dramatic device of the pause or silence are effective linguistic techniques that enhance the play's ideas, expand the nature of these characters, and tell the story. (More on language follows in the section on spectacle.)

Chekhov uses dialogue and the obvious absence of dialogue to communicate ideas directly and indirectly. For example, his use of pauses and silences frames the moment, forcing the audience to attend to the actor's subtext and physicalization. Chekhov's intention was to create a play whose subtle nuances would give the impression of life "not as it is, but as it appears in our dreams." His transitory, ambiguous, momentary theatrical images give the impression that nothing is going on, but in actuality, a great deal is happening and being communicated.

Questions

* Why do these characters speak in such simple sentences?
* Why does Arkadina use such melodramatic language in her scene with Trigorin in Act Three?
* Why are patronymics and nicknames used?

MELODY OR SONG (RHYTHM)

The Seagull has specific musical references: We hear singing across the lake; Treplev plays the piano; Shamraev tries his hand at mimicking a famous singer he once heard; Dr. Dorn sings lines from Gounod's opera *Faust* (1859).[12] Additionally the orchestration of dialogue within an act (length of scenes, the internal pace of a scene, a well-timed pause or silence, and the movement from one scene to the next) can be an effective form of dramatic rhythm. In this play the movement between the scenes is challenging—to the extent that its ephemeral world might be lost in a heavy-handed scene change.

Even this play's "inaction" is filled with information about dramatic rhythm and is a rich resource for discovering how the playwright created tension in a play in which there appears to be a lack of activity. These characters give the impression that their lives are static because they only talk about what they want, do not make decisions, get sidetracked, or use inappropriate ways to achieve their goals. A case could be made that, overall, this repetition creates a rhythm. These characters do not take stands or make plans that might initiate change; they also never relinquish what they want (no matter how ridiculous), which gives the impression that they are spinning their wheels. The psychology that causes this redundant entrenched behavior of traveling in circles and never getting off center creates a particular rhythm. Repetitive misguided and ill-founded desires create circular, downward-spiraling rhythms somewhat similar to the motion of a spinning top.

Questions

* Why does Dorn sing from Gounod's *Faust*?
* What is the traditional music of late-nineteenth-century Russia? Does any of this music have a contemporaneous quality?

SPECTACLE

> *Chekhov appreciated the surface glitter of experience but infused it with a vision of a more universal understanding of the world. His parallel among the Impressionists finally rests not with the intricate brushstrokes of Monet but the more complicated vision of Cezanne. Where Chekhov never allows his characters to speak for* one point of view, *Cezanne aspires to paint canvases which comprehend the rhythms of nature, the architecture of the object world while acknowledging the vagaries of human perception.*[13]
>
> —John Lahr

Chekhov's plays have physical environments that are as static as his character's lives. His language, scenic metaphors, and images create atmospheres that reveal more information about the drama's structure, passion, and poetry. His images are both tangible (visual and aural) and intangible (feelings and ideas). They function together and separately to further the play's general action, as well as to suggest that Chekhov's dramatic structure is lyrical, somewhat impressionistic, delicate, and ambiguous. When the artist scores *The Seagull*, it becomes obvious that Chekhov is speaking through a collection of quiet yet powerful images. For example, not only is there rich imagery within the language of the playscript, but also Chekhov orchestrates the dialogue in concert with the play's objects, scenic descriptions, sound effects, and music to form a larger lyrical arrangement of *über*-images that emotionally charge the theme and atmosphere. It is no wonder that Chekhov's plays have been called works about atmosphere and mood. Because he lyrically weaves images with atmospheres and moods, they become powerful visual, aural, intellectual, and emotional communicators. Additionally, Chekhov's images, moods, and atmospheres are devices that support the "inaction" in his plays.

Assessing the Scenic Image

When Chekhov uses a scenic image or symbol to suggest the character's inner feelings, he is talking to his audience indirectly or poetically. The combination of various scenic images throughout this play, especially those of an environmental nature (e.g., the moon, lake, or forest that surrounds the dacha, as well as the heat of the sun, the raging storm and so on), intensifies Chekhov's intent by stating metaphorically the internal action of the play. For example, Chekhov places the action in Act Four within the confines of the house, two years later, and while a storm is raging and howling outside. We know there are giant waves on the lake, that it is pitch-black outside, and that there is a significant amount of wind. However, we do not know what time of year it is; there is, ironically, no mention of snow or rain. Drawing from the existing images and an analysis of the play, several specific interpretations are possible. First, relatively nothing has changed, except for minor alterations. Masha and Medvedenko are married and have a child, and the drawing room has been adapted to facilitate Treplev's writing. Everything else has stayed the same, and the characters still desire a life they are not living. The environment has brought the characters inside, both emotionally and physically. Forced introspection confirms that they are emotionally bankrupt. Treplev tells Nina he has lost faith: "You've found your way, you know where you're headed. I'm still rushing about in a maze of dreams and images with no idea of who or what any of it is for. I have no faith. I don't know what my calling is" (71). To intensify the turmoil, existential emptiness, pain, and death, Chekhov brings the action, or lack of it, inside one room and permits the storm to rage around them. The storm—a scenic image—intensifies their personal reality by depicting the rage, loneliness, or confusion that each character embodies. More powerful perhaps is what is poetically more subtle and established through contrast. The storm with all its power surrounds the dacha; it forces the characters inside. As it restricts their action, the storm becomes a "scenic image" that reinforces not only the idea that Chekhov's characters are incapable of controlling their lives but also the idea that their environment is stronger than they are and has the potential of controlling their destiny.

In Act Four when the dead, stuffed seagull is brought on stage and presented to Trigorin, he does not remember that Treplev killed it because he had nothing better to do, nor does he remember that he used Treplev's action and words as an idea for a short story. The audience or reader, of course, recognizes that the seagull poetically represents the character Nina. We also know that Trigorin (who is interested in finding out how young people act so he can write about them more truthfully in his plays) has had an affair with Nina, fathered her child, and abandoned her. When Trigorin does not remember that Treplev has shot the seagull and that this action and his words triggered an idea for a short story,

Chekhov not only succinctly underlines the vacuous nature of Trigorin but also indirectly points to one of the play's central issues: the unwillingness of this society to take responsibility for self, others, and art and how that indecisiveness has led to existential pain and destruction.

Questions

- What is a dacha? What does it look like? Who goes to a dacha?
- What does the countryside of Russia look like? What are the pastimes, hardships, and so on of its people?
- The play takes place inside and outside. Why?
- Where is intermission?
- What is the current fashion (country and city)? Are there any current fads? Do they relate to today?
- What do the furnishings look like?
- What are the methods of transportation and communication?

ALLUSIONS TO IMAGES

Chekhov uses allusions in *The Seagull* to provoke communal connections to our primordial instincts. He uses them sparingly, and often they are hard to analyze because of their ambiguous tone. However literary allusions are part of this script's fabric and play a significant role in furthering the rich pattern of imagery, mood, atmosphere, character, and plot development. In his article "Chekhov's *Seagull* and Shakespeare's *Hamlet*: A Study of a Dramatic Device," Thomas G. Winner explores Chekhov's use of literary allusion to create a "tragedy about mediocrity, a mediocrity which is sharpened in our minds by the constant allusions to *Hamlet*."[14] His article details Chekhov's specific references to *Hamlet* and demonstrates how Chekhov sometimes inverts Shakespeare's original intent to create dramatic situation and character that contain irony, satire, and emotional depth, as well as timeless appeal. Chekhov paraphrases, alludes to, suggests, and uses specific lines from *Hamlet* in *The Seagull*. Although Winner carefully details Chekhov's obvious and not-so-obvious connections to this Shakespearean play, he does not explore any connections to *Faust*.

Specific references to *Faust* are not frequent in Chekhov's writing. However, the spirit of the Faustian legend appears in his short stories, especially "The Black Monk." It is the central character, Kovrin, in "The Black Monk" who sees himself like "the great men of history and thinks of himself as striving for all-knowledge, like Faust." Although the character who appears as the Black Monk has been identified by Thomas Winner in *Chekhov and His Prose* as Mephistopheles, and this analogy certainly supports Chekhov's interest in drawing upon literary allusions from *Faust*, Winner later adds that, "unlike Faust, Kovrin is a mediocre man who only masquerades as an intellectual giant. He repeats that he cannot live without his work, but he is never able to proceed beyond outlines of his writings."[15] How then do the Faustian images in *The Seagull* create an atmosphere that not only supports Chekhov's aesthetic but also elicits a commentary on society's responsibility to self?

The Metaphorical Image

In *The Seagull*, Chekhov creates several *über*-images that are significant enough to charge the play's atmosphere emotionally. (It is no wonder that his canon has been referred to as plays about atmosphere and mood.) Masterfully weaving scenic images with atmosphere and mood, Chekhov orchestrates commanding visual, aural, intellectual, and emotional communicators within the "inaction" of his play. In preparing *The Seagull* for production, an artist influenced by the practices of modernism might become stimulated by the allusion to *Hamlet* and *Faust* as well as by periodic Faustian images. Chekhov uses Faustian allusions sparingly and even inverts their connections; however, his fleeting and enigmatic interest in the power of allusions allows his drama to go beyond the limitations of a traditional realistic production. *The Seagull's* resiliency depends upon a series of images and allusions that are intended not to puzzle but to provoke both understanding and a more poetic portrayal of humanity and society.

The Seagull's Faustian Leitmotif

The Seagull's connection to *Faust* is not unlike the play's impressionistic and poetic "inter" workings: both operate in terms of suggestion rather than direct parallels and, in turn, both are responsible for creating the play's mood and atmosphere. It appears that Chekhov's interest in *Faust* is similar to his attraction to *Hamlet*. Both allusions serve to embellish the play by creating images and a foreboding atmosphere that furthers the theme. The first specific reference, Dr. Dorn's singing of "Tell her, tell her for me, O flowers, do..." (24 and 28) from Gounod's *Faust*, is found twice in Act Two but is not sung in Acts One, Three, or Four. Although some might dismiss the doctor's song as a peculiar trait and therefore inconsequential to the play's meaning, its appearance suggests a leitmotif that is significant in uncovering both the play's poetry and hidden meanings. In addition, two other allusions to *Faust* are evident: the seduction of a young girl and the plucking of petals from a flower accompanied by the recitation, "She loves me, she loves me not."[16] Other connections are more subtle and only reminiscent of Faustian themes, such as malevolent self-serving characters and significant demonic images.

As Trigorin's connection to Faust is merely suggested, any attempt to trace specific direct parallels would be fruitless. There is, however, a general similarity in their weakness of character, their desires to be great men, and the obsessiveness that surrounds their work. Trigorin is unlike Faust in that he is said to be a simple man who would love to be a great literary force but whose pedestrian talents are not equal to the genius of Faust. Here, Chekhov inverts a possible connection to Faust and, like his similar inversion with *Hamlet*, the result is filled with elements of satire.

Not only is Trigorin a mediocre artist who poses as a substantial writer, he is, in general, a fool: His actions are far from comic, and his vacuous personality is horrifying. He is remiss in accepting responsibility for self and his art. In Act Three, he tells Arkadina, "I have no will of my own..." (50). His spinelessness, lack of control, confusion, and possible possession connect him to Faust. Ironically, Trigorin's passionate description of his life in art endears him to Nina. In part, he says:

Success? I've never liked myself as a person. I don't like myself as a writer. And the worst of it is I live in a kind of daze and often don't even understand what I write... What I do love is this water, the trees, the sky. I have a feeling for nature. It arouses a passion in me, an irresistible urge to write. But I'm not just a landscape artist; I'm a member of society as well. I love my country and my people. As an author, I feel duty bound to speak out about the people, about their sufferings, their future, about science and the rights of man, and so on and so forth. I try to cover them all, I do my best, but there's always someone after me, angry with me, and I rush back and forth like a fox at bay. I watch science and society forge ahead while I drop further and further behind, like a peasant running after a train. And then I start feeling I'm no good at anything but landscapes and when I do anything else I'm an impostor, an impostor to the marrow of my bones. (36-37)

Trigorin's aforementioned love for nature is a subtle but significant reference that connects Chekhov's aesthetic to symbolism, as well as accentuates Trigorin's artistic blindness toward nature and its relationship to art.[17] Chekhov knew that life, like nature, is constantly changing and evolving. Any effort to stop time, as so many of the characters attempt to do in *The Seagull*, makes action mechanical and comic. For Bergson, a human being attempting to stop time was comic; however, "for the symbolists...as for Goethe in *Faust*, it becomes horrifying. Driven by a desire to capture the moment, to stop time in its course, man grows incapable of joining the eternal flow. Haunted by the limited scope of his lifetime, bounded at either end by the involuntary acts of birth and death, he is obsessed with the concerns of the moment."[18] Although the ridiculous qualities of stopping time may shed some light on why Chekhov called *The Seagull* a comedy, Trigorin's attempt to stop time and his obsession with the moment have some tragic consequences. At this point, Chekhov's position as a symbolist is clear, and his allusions to *Faust* are striking, especially with the seduction of Nina.

There are no direct parallels in plot, scene, or language construction that connect Faust's seduction of Marguerite (or any other Faustian heroine) to Trigorin's seduction of Nina. However, the Trigorin-Nina seduction scene at the end of Act Two has a sinister atmosphere that is the result of an accumulation of previous internal images. Eager to rediscover his youth and to collect new literary material, Trigorin seduces Nina. In her passion to become an actress, at any cost, Nina falls prey to Trigorin's advances. Her abandonment is evident when she presents to Trigorin a medallion inscribed with a passage from his book, *Days and Nights*. The line reads, "If ever you should need my life, come and take it" (47). On Nina's behalf, some excuse can be made on the grounds of her age; however, Trigorin's impropriety, lack of control, and irresponsibility for self, others, and his art display a hollow morality that is both inexcusable and foreboding.

Trigorin is similar to Faust in that his curiosity becomes a justifiable reason to exploit others to gain personal satisfaction and power. Trigorin gathers material for future short stories by writing down what he sees and hears. In particular, he records the actions of Nina and Treplev, but that alone does not satisfy his curiosity. He also must seduce Nina to discover young love and how girls of Nina's age think and feel. It appears there are no limits to scientific inquiry when ego and power are the ends to justify the means. At the play's conclusion, when Trigorin does not recall his request to have the seagull stuffed, it becomes metaphorically clear that he prefers not to take responsibility for his actions. At the core of this play's theme is the issue of irresponsibility, and Trigorin is not the only offender. He is, however, the character who bears the strongest resemblance to Faust.

If further connections can be made, they are in terms of character weaknesses and in atmosphere. Chekhov stresses human responsibility for self, and in *The Seagull* that responsibility includes the artist's role in the evolution of art. This position is promoted at the end of Act One when Dr. Dorn instructs Treplev, "A work of art must have a clear-cut, well-defined purpose. You must always know why you are writing. If all you do is paint pictures, if you have no definite goal in mind, you'll go astray. Your talent will be the end of you" (22). While Dorn, early on, stresses clarity to Treplev, Nina later concludes that art is not about fame and glory but consists of hard work, perseverance, and faith. Both Treplev and Trigorin have unclear, self-centered artistic goals.

Chekhov preferred to see men and women in Russian society as responsible for, and involved in, their fate and certainly not as the victims of their environment. For Chekhov, "Man's tragedy...lies primarily not in any absolute helplessness before his fate, but in the fact that he is continually affirming fate's autonomy through abdication of his own responsibility."[19] Humanity's tragic vision is reinforced by *The Seagull*'s characters, language, and plot construction. Human inability to take responsibility for self weakens Chekhov's characters to the point that they cannot communicate effectively and are not in control of their own lives; consequently, they leave themselves open to fate, chance, and their own evil natures.

Like Faust, typical Chekhovian characters are ineffective and vulnerable because they are irresponsible, lack initiative, and have a desire to stop time and live in the past or for the moment. Examples of indecisiveness, lack of communication, and an inability to face reality have been mentioned earlier by citing peculiarities in character development, plot, and language construction. At this point it is important to mention that the accumulation of all these dramatic devices produces a resounding atmosphere that is a further reflection of a decaying middle-class Russian society.

The effect of Chekhov's atmosphere is difficult to appreciate fully unless one is viewing a production. Victor Emeljanow, in *Chekhov: The Critical Heritage*, concurs, stating that

it is impossible to guess how effective [the plays] are on the stage, the delicate succession of subtle shades and half-tones, of hints, of which they are composed, the evocation of certain moods and feelings which it is impossible to define, — all this one would think would disappear in the glare of the footlights, but it is exactly the reverse which is true. Chekhov's plays are a thousand times more interesting to see on the stage than they are to read.[20]

It is clear in production that *The Seagull*'s sluggish, chaotic, despondent, and troubled atmosphere is synonymous with the characters' inner turmoil and that of the play itself. What is revealed further in production is how Chekhov allows atmosphere to become more than a reflection of dramatic action by granting it a poetic quality of its own. Throughout the four acts of *The Seagull* the atmosphere gains momentum and poetic potential. For example, the storm becomes not only a reflection but a controlling force in poetically detailing dramatic action. Chekhov develops atmosphere through imagery—some of which can be attributed to *Faust*.

Lev Shestov finds an association between Chekhov's characters in *The Seagull* and its atmosphere. He adds that Chekhov's mature characters, especially Trigorin, tend not to like their work, "but, as if they were hypnotized, they cannot escape the influence of an alien power. The monotonous, regular, and mournful rhythm of life has lulled to sleep their consciousness and their will."[21] The sun and Dr. Dorn's singing of *Faust* promote a leitmotif that suggests poetically how these characters, because of their weaknesses, are running the risk of being susceptible to forces outside of themselves. The sun's heat drains them of energy and initiative and inhibits their mobility; therefore, the sun, as a scenic image, helps to create the play's theme. The sun is also a component of their environment that is, in part, responsible for the play's atmosphere. Because the characters in *The Seagull* lack the incentive to move inside and remain outside immobilized by the heat of the sun, the sun assumes a powerful position. As Chekhov tips the scales to favor the sun's hypnotic power, the characters not only become weaker but also relinquish further control of self, to what can be interpreted as a force of determinism. Dorn's references to *Faust* are then significant, as they can be understood as a poetic commentary on both the atmosphere and the characters' relationship to their environment.

Chekhov's characters are filled with relentless desires; they are struggling continually to reach experiences that are better than what they have; however, they lack the direction, stamina, and honesty that will allow them to attain their goals. Faust had knowledge, but that wasn't enough for him; he continued to search for fulfillment at all costs, whereas Chekhov's characters are not sure what they want. Their misguided desires, however, create an atmosphere that evokes a similarity to *Faust*. Like the character Faust, Chekhov's characters show more ambition than strength, and they try to stop time and become obsessed with the moment. Not only do these characters create an air of helplessness that is embellished poetically by the image of the sun, but the *Faust* allusions permeate the atmosphere and poetically suggest how these characters are vulnerable to outside forces that are capable of both possessing their will and directing their actions.

Throughout Act One of *The Seagull*, further Faustian connections are suggested in terms of imagery. Satan is referred to in Treplev's play. There are lines in *The Seagull* that mention Satan's blood-red eyes, as well as these specific references: "Satan, the father of eternal matter...in my fierce, unyielding battle with Satan, the epitome of material force...Behold! My mighty enemy draws near: Satan. I spy his fearsome crimson eyes..." (16). Dr. Dorn's reference to the magic lake (23), the howling of a dog (21), and the approaching storm all help to establish that "something" is in the air. Chekhov himself suggested that "the smell of sulphur and the imagery of cold and satanic spirits [should] linger over the rest of Act I."[22] What Chekhov accomplishes in terms of "interaction" in Act One is to plant the seeds of an atmosphere of malevolence that are then cultivated in Act Two and finally bloom in Act Four.

In sum, Chekhov's *Seagull* has certain subtle allusions and scenic images that are common to *Faust* (emphasis on the seduction of a young girl, existential despair, music, line references), as well as imagery (the magic lake, dogs howling, approaching storm) that creates an internal and external malevolent atmosphere and mood. Although it has been said that Chekhov doesn't localize evil, Trigorin bears some association with Faustian characteristics.

Chekhov does carefully construct suggestive allusions. These allusions, together with dark scenic images, create a substantial atmosphere; because atmosphere plays an important part in realizing *The Seagull*, its dramatic purpose and function demand attention. There is no Mephistopheles character, like the Black Monk, in this play, but nevertheless a sinister quality seems to linger in the air. It can be offered that, through the "interaction" of scenic imagery, Chekhov creates a malevolent atmosphere that furthers the theme. Moreover Chekhov's atmosphere is double-edged: It is reflective of a society lost in its own indecision and misguided desires, and it is an independent force that can be interpreted as determinism. Chekhov's dramatic structure helps to portray a society that has abdicated responsibility and placed power outside of human will. His characters become potential victims of environment, fate, and their own evil nature.

Chekhov uses atmosphere to intensify the human struggle. It is more than a scenic image that reinforces the play's theme or inspires Faustian allusions; in effect, *The Seagull*'s atmosphere is a scenic image, charged with Faustian allusions, that can be interpreted as a force powerful enough to control human destiny.

Perhaps the suggestion of Faustian themes and images throughout *The Seagull* is meant to haunt the play's atmosphere so that it both aids in manipulating the action of each of the characters and reminds successive generations of potential weaknesses. Also, it can be suggested that Chekhov's use of imagery, allusion, and atmosphere creates an environment charged with the poetry of impressionism. By weaving Faustian allusions and scenic illusions into the play's fabric, Chekhov expands the play's reality to suggest further possibilities concerning *The Seagull*'s provocative "indirect action."

Existential Images

An existential reading offers some direction to those who are attempting to produce this play. It corresponds with Chekhov's love for humanity and his relentless search for a more inclusive understanding of the world. Chekhov's interest was, in part, in illustrating how we must take responsibility for our lives, in particular, our individual wants, desires, and needs. If not, we can become filled with some of the same anxiety, paranoia, and fear that ultimately paralyzed his characters in *The Seagull*. When they neither faced who they were (their age, abilities, significance, and mortality) nor comprehended the facts of their existence (what situations affected their being), they lost their individual freedom to make good choices about their future and lives.

Douglas Wager's 1991 production of *The Seagull* at the Arena Stage in Washington, D.C., was not influenced by a reading of Gounod's *Faust*; however, his production revealed (as did a subsequent discussion with the director) that he was aware of the importance of Chekhov's images in creating a theatrical world that poetically suggested the characters' inner turmoil. Ming Cho Lee's set, Arden Fingerhut's lights, Susan R. White's sound, and several of Marjorie Slaiman's costumes delicately painted a Chekhovian landscape where fragile images created a dreamlike impressionistic state. The following includes remarks made by Douglas Wager to his cast prior to rehearsal:

Man is the animal who creates. He creates out of a need to evince the meaning of life, to bring form and simplicity to the confused world of experience; to embody his history, his destiny in metaphorical terms; to discover pure intention in the senseless chaos of living; to discover the human value of an inhuman universe, to measure the real world in terms of his own inner reality.

Man creates with his imagination. All wanting erupts from the most intimate corners of our heart and our wanting is transformed, brought to life by the imagination.

Chekhov said, "He who wants nothing, hopes for nothing and fears nothing cannot be an artist." *The Seagull* is a play about art. Art is at the center of the play. Four of the characters are actors or writers. Everyone talks about art, and yet these characters fail to see the very life they are failing to capture which is all around them, amply supplied by Chekhov.

The Seagull, in the words of biographer V. S. Pritchett, is "an alluring mixture of the poetic and the dire, an extravagant and disturbing dream." It is an ironic, mysterious, existential, and astonishing meditation on the question of the artist's metier. It is seemingly plotless, a morally neutral tale, ambiguous in tone, and non-judgmental of its characters. There appear to be no clear villains, no true heroes; no one is valued for us; events are not fully explained.

Yet, *The Seagull* is at once a work of genius. Breaking with dramatic forms familiar to his day, Chekhov created the first truly modern existential drama; a play not dependent upon plot; an emotional and psychological landscape peopled with a cast of dear, deeply self-deluded souls caught up in the throes of what Dr. Irvin Yalom, author of the recent book, *Love's Executioner*, calls "Destiny pain. Existence pain; pain that is always there whirring continuously just beneath the membrane of life. Pain that is all too easily accessible... "

Yalom goes on to say "Our deepest *wants* can never be fulfilled, our wants for youth, for a halt to aging, for the return of vanished ones, for eternal love, protection, significance, for immortality itself."

"Basic anxiety," he says, "emerges from a person's endeavors, conscious and unconscious, to cope with the harsh facts of life, the 'givens' of existence." (There are four that concern us here):

1. The inevitability of death for each of us and for those we love
2. The freedom to make our lives at will
3. Our ultimate aloneness
4. The absence of any obvious meaning or sense to life.

We tend to cope with these "life truths" through denial. There is potential humor in the behavior of denial and inevitable pain in the consequences of it.

I believe Chekhov (a physician himself) understood this objectively and intuitively, creating in *The Seagull* a painfully ironic symphony of denial, of wanting, played by a rich ensemble of characters each caught up in their own personal perceptions of reality, which, in the end, they are hopelessly unable to share with one another.

Thornton Wilder said of Chekhov's plays, "Nobody hears what anybody else says. Everybody walks in a self-centered dream." Indeed it can be said that these characters dream their passions, they speak them, but they do not live them; their dreams simply collide.

The play is peopled by characters hopelessly in love with characters hopelessly in love with still other characters, yet the ugliness of being unloved lurks at the center of everyone's being. In Chekhov love is something that either once was or will be: it never just *is*. He asserts that (as in his own life) love alone does not provide a firm foundation for the creative life. Creativity becomes the only salvation for the individual, yet art can warp and destroy the very life it draws upon. In *The Seagull* the word talent is the touchstone by which the characters evaluate themselves and one another. Yet, to be talented is not necessarily to be a superior person, according to Chekhov.

The play is a testimony to the absurdities of the human condition. All grandiose plays are doomed to failure and it takes a superhuman effort to throw a footbridge across the abyss separating dream from reality. This is the struggle of the artist

Chekhov so brilliantly articulates in *The Seagull.*[23]

IMAGING *THE SEAGULL'S* HUMAN HISTORY

In that period when artists are engaged in working with the script prior to beginning rehearsal (which is well before the director makes introductory comments to a cast), many find it productive to go back into human history and discover when the act of imagination took place. Artists use research to uncover more about their initial impulses or to pursue synchronicity in time, space, objects, language, and action. Whereas some find the cultural "dig" unnecessary, other artists view "external" research beneficial in discovering, as Douglas Wager points out, "if there are any points of contact common to my emotional response to the material." He continues, "I think [one of] the director's functions is to discover the emotional narrative within the story that has the most explosive points of contact with a contemporary audience as opposed to serving as a curator or as an act of historic curiosity."[24]

As mentioned earlier, Wager's dramaturgical work included a trip to London to attend the Hayward Gallery's exhibition "Twilight of the Czars." Wager also listened to Rachmaninoff's *Isle of the Dead*, reviewed symbolist poetry and paintings, and viewed three Russian films: *Slave of Love, Unfinished Pieces for Player Piano*, and *Dark Eyes*. He continues,

The films are very *cinema verité*. They are not useful in terms of well, let's do the scene like this. It's a deceptively unconstructed visual approach. And I thought it was very liberating in that regard, because I felt that temperamentally everything I was reading, researching, and watching was mitigating against a kind of dark, sepia-toned sentimentality, which is maybe the pedestrian way you think of Chekhov; it is what you worry that you are going to see.

Wager had the help of the Arena Stage's dramaturgical staff (Laurence Maslon and his assistants), who compiled a series of critical articles that they loosely titled "Gull-arama." Wager recalled that the most effective articles on Chekhov and *The Seagull* were the ones that corresponded to what he was interested in, those by Laurence Senelick. He also looked at the Nemirovich-Danchenko/ Stanislavsky casebook study on *The Seagull*, which was published in 1952. However, the most significant contemporary influence for Wager was Irvin Yalom's, *Love's Executioner: And Other Tales of Psychotherapy*. He continues,

The hypothesis that this author sets out to prove is the frame for understanding the characters in Chekhov's play. Because my intuition was telling me that since psychology itself was in its infancy when Chekhov wrote *The Seagull*, as well as the fact that he really was a physician and was able to keep (I thought) a healthy, kind of objective point of view about his characters who are not completely tragic nor completely comic, not overly moralized, pre-judged, or sentimentalized in any way. They are, however, acutely and painfully observed.

The life and death struggle is whether or not people can integrate their dreams with reality. Once I hit on that and looked back at the historical perspective of the movements in art, literature, science, and philosophy in this sort of pre-Revolutionary environment that Chekhov was living in, it connected with Senelick's hypotheses about Chekhov's borrowing from his own life and actually satirizing aspects of his own culture. It also connected Yalom's hypothesis about denial. I then had a very strong world of ideas to measure each event in the play against.

Wager adds that, after reading symbolist poetry and listening to Rachmaninoff's *Isle of the Dead,* he began to see more clearly the turmoil inside Treplev. "I think Chekhov views Treplev's turmoil on two levels: externally it is ridiculous, and internally it is the most explosive and dangerous emotional well in the play." Wager recounts that he found his way into the play through visually creating the turmoil Treplev was experiencing.

Research, then, can be much more than the collection of informational data. If used in imaginative ways it has the ability to help the artist become more intimately involved with the play's sources of inspiration. What is significant about this type of research, however, is not that a line, character, or situation connects directly to history or the playwright's life. Instead, artists seek provocative biographical images so that they might meet the author in their imagination. Dropping into the playwright's world affords the artist the opportunity to sense the artistic temperament that shaped the play. For example, Chekhov's friendship with the Russian impressionistic artist, Isaak Levitan (1861-1900), exposed him to a world of impressionistic thought. This aesthetic must have been stimulating to a playwright who was concerned not about what was said or physically accomplished, but what was left unsaid or undone—specifically, not the play's external action but what was occurring below the surface.

> *My holy of holies is the human body and brain, talent, inspiration, love and personal freedom—freedom from force and lies—whatever form the last two may take. Had I been a great artist that is the line I should like to have followed. I am not a liberal, or a conservative or an evolutionist or a monk. I should like to be a free artist, that's all. I hate violence and lies of any kind. Phariseeism, stupidity and licence are to be found not only in middle class homes and police stations. I see them in science, in literature and among young people.*
> *...An artist must judge only of what he understands.*[25]
> —Anton Chekhov

Biographical Images

Anton Chekhov was born in Taganrog in 1860. He was one of six children who were terrorized by an authoritarian father whose quick temper and puritanical churchgoing influenced, in particular, his son's views about love, authority, and religion. Chekhov's grandfather was a serf, but he managed to buy freedom for himself and his family; later, Chekhov's father would work hard to try to establish himself as a shopkeeper. In a century's time, Chekhov's extended family rose from serfdom to members of mainstream Russian society by becoming part of the medical, teaching, artistic, and literary professions. Chekhov, himself, was educated to be a medical doctor, and he did practice. However, his major contribution was as a prolific writer and philanthropist as well as a sensitive interpreter of his beloved Russian society. Chekhov's hometown was about 750 miles from the culture of Moscow, but despite its provinciality, it did have several schools, a cathedral, a library, and a theatre that housed touring companies. There is little to indicate in Chekhov's early life that he was destined to become an artist. Having a playful imagination, however, he could be found enjoying a good practical joke, being the class clown, attending the productions of those theatre companies that ventured to Taganrog, and being part of original plays that were staged at home. It is probably safe to assume that young Anton did whatever he could to escape the harsh realities of a domineering father and the boredom of a provincial town.

> *Perhaps it should be remembered he was writing at a time when the society around him was decaying, restless and frustrated. After the exhilaration of the reforms which had taken place in Russia in the 1860's, Russia was in the doldrums before the storm of the Revolution and Chekhov caught this mood of his times. Many of his stories and characters reflect it, since he was one of the most truthful of writers, but time and again he points beyond to a hopeful future, and his natural optimism shines through.*[26]
>
> —Pauline Bentley

By 1879, he was in Moscow studying medicine. Obviously Chekhov did not devote all his time at his desk to absorbing medical details, because a year later he managed to publish his first short story. Then after completing his third-year exams, he vacationed in Voskresensk, where it is reported that he spent much time in post offices, gentry homes, peasants' taverns, or even at the justice of the peace. There he watched people and collected biographical material, anecdotes, and images that gave some hints about their lives and relationships; he was on the lookout for anything that might give him some inspiration for a new story. Throughout his life Chekhov had an insatiable desire to study people. In 1890, for example, he traveled to Sakhalin (an island off the coast of Siberia) to observe the penal colony there; additionally there are many reported incidents of his asking friends to tell him anecdotes that might give him an idea for a short story. In 1884 Chekhov graduated from medical school, but not before he finished his first full-length play, *Platonov*. A collection of short stories (under the pseudonym of A. Chekhonte) soon would be published; in the same year, its young author would embark on a medical career and would be free, at last, from his obscure and humble beginnings.

Censorship has long been an issue for Russian writers, and Chekhov was no exception. However, perhaps both because his medical training required that he remain distant and because he believed art and politics should be separate, his perceptions or comments about society were always ambiguous, impartial, or harmless enough to escape the censors' eyes. He painted life with an objective but loving brush; his strokes were light—just enough to capture life but never strong enough to point an accusing finger. He never took sides; his work is about the rich and the poor, the enlightened and the ignorant, the talented and the not-so-gifted, the young and the old. These people exist side by side, influencing, contributing to, and sometimes destroying each other's lives. In his acclaimed biography, *Chekhov*, Henri Troyat describes Chekhov's unbiased collection of characters as

Society's loose change. To one and all he gave the pitiful misadventures befitting their pitiful characters, yet with a series of seemingly insignificant remarks he was able to hint at the mystery behind their gray exteriors. He made the absurdity of everyday life unmistakably plain without ever putting it in so many words. No speech for the prosecution, no speech for the defense. The raw truth. Photographic. Moreover, his bag of tricks seemed inexhaustible: there is no repetition whatever in the entire massive portrait gallery.[27]

> *All I wanted was to say honestly to people: "Have a look at yourselves and see how bad and dreary your lives are!" The important thing is that people should realize that, for when they do, they will most certainly create another and better life for themselves.*[28]
>
> —Anton Chekhov

In 1895, when Chekhov embarked on *The Seagull*, his letters and biographical material provide substantial information to indicate that he initially was relying on his friends' as well as his own life experiences to inform his work. He never tired of people; his kindness and an insatiable interest kept him involved: he watched them, talked to them, listened to them endlessly when he was sick or well. Their presence or actions might tire him, depress him, or frighten him; however, he passionately wanted to experience life, so he put up with long hours and, sometimes, inconvenient conversations. Biographical material reveals Chekhov's desire to seek the truth behind actions, feelings, and relationships as well as to find ways in which he could create that truth in literature and on the stage. However, Chekhov felt that if he merely copied life, he failed as an artist; therefore, he used life's experiences as a springboard into his imagination, from which he developed his unique aesthetic.

Research reveals that there are many connections between Chekhov's life and the reality of his play *The Seagull*. Chekhov has a way of using life images to help tell the story and reveal the characters' psychology. For example, we read that Chekhov visited his friend Levitan when he learned that he had attempted suicide and was depressed. After becoming involved with a wealthy older woman, Levitan found himself caught between the affections of the woman and those of her daughter. Violent arguments between the two women over his favors caused his abortive suicide attempt. Afterward, Chekhov found his friend looking "deathly pale" with a bandage around his head, fortunate that he had suffered only a slight, superficial gunshot wound. Another interesting anecdote about Levitan is that apparently he once senselessly wounded a woodcock, which Chekhov then had to kill—after which they went home and had dinner. Both instances became part of Chekhov's "literary larder" and reappear in *The Seagull*.

When creating his characters Nina and Trigorin, Chekhov was influenced by information he had about an affair between his own friends Lika and Potapenko. At the play's first reading, the actors who were aware of the unfortunate affair between Lika and Potapenko not only noted this apparent correlation but found further connections when they brought up how much Arkadina resembled Potapenko's wife. Clearly, Chekhov's imagination was imprinted with an event that was rich with psychological implication and emotion—one that would later surface in *The Seagull*.

Additionally, an admirer of Chekhov's, Lydia Avilova, once sent him a "watch fob in the form of a book" on which she engraved on one side "*Stories and Tales* by A. Chekhov" and on the other side "page 267, lines 6 & 7"—a reference to a sentence ("If ever you have need of my life, come and take it") in Chekhov's "The Neighbors."[29] Obviously, this moment is captured in Act Three of *The Seagull* when Nina presents Trigorin a medallion with the same inscription. These are some of the blatant connections that can be found in Chekhov's biographies and letters to illustrate how instances from his life found their way into his plays. Also peppered throughout this research material are references to actual lines or ideas found in the play that Chekhov gives to characters of either sex. Time after time, *The Seagull* provides examples of Chekhov's obsession with the problems of creativity, boredom, and the loss of the soul.

> *We have neither immediate nor remote goals, and there is an emptiness in our souls. We have no politics, we don't believe in revolution, there is no God, we're not afraid of ghosts, and I personally am not even afraid of death or blindness. No one who wants nothing, hopes for nothing and fears nothing can be an artist.*[30]
>
> —Anton Chekhov

Unfortunately, the premiere production in St. Petersburg of *The Seagull* (1896) was unsuccessful; the actors had neither the time nor the technique to understand and convey the play's delicate tone. In that first, ill-fated production, Chekhov watched the actors who had failed to memorize their lines mutilate all the subtle nuances in his play by indulging in a grandiose, bombastic, theatrical style of acting.

The actors playing these characters were confused. They were concerned that the audience would lose interest because nothing seems to happen in Chekhov's play. How painful it must have been for Chekhov to listen to actors moan about his characters and know that the director did not understand his artistic form. Additionally, the 1896 audience was confused; they came to watch one of

Russia's leading comic actresses do a benefit production of a comedy that was to follow the premiere of *The Seagull*. It is not hard to understand why the audience jeered, the critics scoffed, and Chekhov ran from the theatre, vowing he would never write another play.

> The Seagull *is a work whose conception, freshness of ideas and thoughtful observations of life situations raise it out of the ordinary. It is life itself on stage with all its tragic alliances, eloquent thoughtlessness, and silent sufferings—the sort of everyday life that is accessible to everyone and understood in its cruel internal irony by almost no one, the sort of life that is so accessible and close to us that at times you forget you're in a theater and you feel capable of participating in the conversation taking place in front of you.*[31]
> —Letter to Chekhov from A. Koni after the premiere performance

Despite Chekhov's rather inauspicious beginning as a playwright, he eventually did write other plays, win literary awards, and live to see a successful production of *The Seagull* at the Moscow Art Theatre. Chekhov might have thought that he had left the theatre, but those in theatre did not leave Chekhov. In particular, Nemirovich-Danchenko pursued him and, after much talk, persuaded Chekhov to let his fledgling theatre produce *The Seagull*. It seemed like the perfect play for a theatre that was interested in bringing a sense of truth and reality to the stage and reforming the dismal state of Russian theatre. This time there would be twenty-six rehearsals, a talented cast, a serious director, and a theatre that was in danger of closing if it failed to create a successful production.

Chekhov agreed. The actors were noticeably nervous and concerned when the sickly playwright visited rehearsal. Chekhov, however, enjoyed their work and must have thought that, at last, the actors understood him. He even felt comfortable enough to make some suggestions. To Stanislavsky (who was concentrating on achieving a new theatrical form, psychological realism) he offered that there should be a little less realism and more attention paid to suggestion. However, Stanislavsky was interested in developing internal and external realism. He wanted to revolutionize staging in the Russian theatre, and he did so by embellishing any stage device (e.g., the sounds of crickets chirping) that would create a sense of naturalistic truth, or reality, on stage. Yet, Chekhov's dramatic form defied the limitations of nineteenth-century realism. His impressionistic collection of images and provocative symbols suggested the complex nature of inner reality. Nevertheless the play and production were a success; at last Chekhov had his play, and the Russian theatre had a new playwright.

BREAKING THE MOLD

Mining *The Seagull*'s images, as we have seen, can stimulate the artist's imagination, contributing to the development of a metaphorically enriched production. A reading that has been influenced by the interpretive practices of contemporary modernism not only evokes the play's poetry and stimulates additional discoveries about the psychological nature of Chekhov's world but also provokes the imagination of an audience and encourages further reimaging. Consider, for example, the recent imagistic explorations of two metaphorical directors, Douglas Wager and Richard Jenkins.

Wager's production gave Chekhov's play an existential focus. His point of view seemed reasonable insofar as Chekhov's vision suggests we should take responsibility for our lives, in particular, those fears and desires that sometimes, if neglected, can paralyze our actions. Because most of these characters (with the exception of Nina) do not realistically confront their problems, they end up repeating the same mistakes. When we opt not to face our existence, we lose our freedom to make good choices and end up living in a dreamlike world, susceptible to repetition, chaos, and forces outside of ourselves that can shape our destiny.

The previous points were clear in Wager's staging. Actors moved in repetitive and cyclical patterns that physicalized Chekhov's ideas about those who search relentlessly and at all costs for identity, love, fame, or power. There was the traditional blocking, in which Chekhov's characters constantly missed each other. What was more interesting, however, was the director's innovative metaphorical staging. For example, at the close of Act Two, the actress playing Nina sat on a swing, laughing and twirling in circles as she said, "I must be dreaming" (38).

Wager felt that his "way into the play was through Treplev and the turmoil he was experiencing." The scene changes were orchestrated as "emotional narrative." To create Treplev's turmoil and disconnection, the panic of being unloved and trapped, Wager decided to place the intermission at the end of Act Three. Moreover, he choreographed the changes between Acts One and Two and between Two and Three, to focus on Treplev's emotional crisis. Between Acts One and Two, for example, Treplev was caught in a pool of light after he shot the seagull; later, between Acts Two and Three he was left briefly sitting alone among a random (yet-to-be-arranged) collection of dining room chairs; finally during Act Four, after Nina leaves, he walked slowly offstage, up a raked platform, and into a pool of white light, ostensibly to commit suicide. Whether it was the simple action of Nina turning in circles on a swing or the more complex act-change études that orchestrated Treplev's aloneness, Wager's staging attempted to create images that heightened the existential chaos, anxiety, and aloneness found in Chekhov's play.

Wager understands Chekhov's ambiguous tale that has neither a hero nor a clear-cut villain, and whose action is a delicate weaving of unexplained or absent events. Because he perceived Chekhov's characters as involved in existential despair, it is clear why he chose scenic images to score an atmosphere filled with emotional chaos. Wager spoke of being inspired by the impressionistic, existential, mystical images in Treplev's play: "Satan, the father of eternal matter" and "My fierce, unyielding battle with Satan, the epitome of material force" as well as "a dog howling," the "approaching storm," "a smoke filled stage," "the smell of sulphur," and "the devil's eyes." Wager not only embraced these images but embellished them by having Treplev create, for example, the devil's eyes when he enters shod in what appear to be *Cothornoi* footwear, wearing a hooded cape, and waving lanterns for the devil's eyes. Meanwhile an ominous sound track underscored Nina's rendition of Treplev's play. She appeared in a diaphanous white dress that no doubt taunted Trigorin by revealing subtly her nude body underneath. Also it is worth mentioning that the characters entered through a large gate that, viewed by itself, might signify the entrance to the garden area of the estate. However, because Act One is so filled with powerful imagistic subtext, and this production chose to score that litany of images, the presence of the gate may have signaled the entrance to some place of more telling importance.

The atmosphere of Act One was initiated by those obvious, youthful, and heavy-handed dramaturgical images found in Treplev's play; however, because this production was enriched by a director's point of view, Wager saw how Chekhov's images could be orchestrated to suggest visually and audibly the various layers that formed the characters' existential crises. The final effect was a production whose images suggested the presence of a dark force that lingers just below the surface of these characters' lives. Because this playwright does not take sides or give his audience any clear-cut answers to life's problems, the ambiguous tone of his play is matched by the suggestive nature of his images. Wager's existential reading is not unlike an interpretation that uncovers Faustian allusions; both are means by which one can uncover more about this play's rich resources in an attempt to mine further its complex reality.

Richard Jenkins's 1992 production of *The Seagull* at the Trinity Repertory Theatre in Providence, Rhode Island, was unlike Wager's existential reading. Jenkins's directorial images and Eugene Lee's metaphorical design were bold and often humorous. Their imagistic work not only liberated Chekhov's play from the dullness of naturalism but continued to play with the transitory nature of this author's poetic vision.

At times, the characters seemed as if they were painted with broad brush strokes—like a Kirchner painting. In the next instant, I felt they weren't characters, but simply people—like the audience members I could see on either side of the thrust stage. The characters seemed crisper, and some relationships were more sharply defined than what one might expect from a more poetic version of this play. For example, Chekhov's famous love triangles were apparent, but in this production they seemed to be more shocking, desperate, funny, and pathetic.

Jenkins's view of *The Seagull* was a collection of sharply defined moments: a brief glimpse of the moon captured the illusion of night, or the sound of Nina's footsteps as she circled behind the audience heightened the anticipation of her first entrance. For a brief instant, I would be touched emotionally by some heart-rending moment (the naïveté of young love or the exuberance of two neophytes preparing to shock and impress the world with *their* vision of theatre). Then shortly thereafter I would find myself laughing at them as they tried to create the symbolism in Treplev's "new" play with the heavy-handedness of naturalism mixed with melodrama. As an audience member, I found myself reconnecting with the play's emotional reality. Dr. Dorn spoke directly to the audience, telling us he liked the play and asking us to help him encourage Treplev by applauding his next entrance. As I moved in and out of the play's world, as both a willing participant and an observer, I found myself asking, "Am I watching this play, or am I part of its action?" Obviously, this production caught the spirit of Chekhov's statement, "People will only become better when you make them see what they are like."

This production provoked new perceptions about the predatory nature of humanity, especially when we are frightened, unloved, lonely, and lost. Jenkins chose to highlight Treplev's existential crisis by making it a result of his mother's emotional abuse. Arkadina has rejected her son for years. The audience witnesses firsthand her dismissal of Treplev's fledging work. However, in this production, she adds insult to injury when in Act Three she demands he stifle his tears after she brands him a "nonentity." When Jenkins freezes that moment, we understand something about how this mother diminishes her son's self-worth by denying his pain. Arkadina's vacuity doesn't end here; when she should be comforting her son, she asks him to comfort her. For example, her next line ("My dear child, forgive me") is followed by Treplev running to her side. This director found the emotional core of their debilitating relationship, and the effect was not only painfully on target but timely. No wonder there is no love in his life; no wonder that he struggles as a writer unable to connect with his characters or write with authority. Her ineptness at mothering continues to be outrageously shocking when in Act Two, scene two, Arkadina confesses (within earshot of Treplev) that she has not read her son's latest published writing. Treplev numbly walks away and turns to his writing. Does he feel that his love for his art somehow will fill the void in his heart? Although he finds no comfort in that diversion, Treplev does discover something about writing: "Yes, I'm gradually coming to the conviction that it doesn't matter whether the forms are new or old. A man has to write without thinking about form at all—he has to write from his soul."

This production was refreshing because it was as unpredictable, chaotic, unfinished, and irrational as Chekhov's world. There was no magic lake or illusionistic storm in this production, yet the director and designer created images that were magical and poetic: Rugs became walls, and Treplev's study was as cluttered as his mind.

Because this production never lost sight of Chekhov's humor or his more serious ideas about love and art, the characters seemed more pathetic than tragic. Chekhov had something to say to his audience; he wanted them to wake up and see how dull, boring, and misdirected their lives had become. Jenkins caught the playwright's spirit and brought his play forward in time. Therefore, it is not surprising that he has Nina tell the audience, after the comic antics of the beginning of Act One, scene two, that these famous people aren't so special; they behave as does everyone else in life. What was surprising, however, is the gunshot that followed her speech; it stunned the audience. In particular, it broke the comic rhythm and focused our attention on Treplev's bloody shirt hiding the dead seagull (which he had shot because he had nothing better to do), and the upcoming scene with Nina and Trigorin.

One of the most magical moments and powerful images comes at the end of Act One, scene two. Nina is so enraptured by Trigorin, the famous writer, she neglects to hear how unhappy he is. Jenkins paced Trigorin's Act One, scene two, speech so extraordinarily fast that the audience had to listen very carefully to hear how this artist, although seemingly successful, is trapped by his art. (Jenkins places this scene inside a circular bench.) Nina, like the other characters in this play, can't hear the truth. She is mesmerized by his fame and glory. Nina's downfall begins when Trigorin (the fisherman) senses a catch: Perhaps this young girl might be interested in a potential relationship with an older, successful playwright. Nina knows she has sparked his interest; left alone on stage, she can barely contain her excitement, ending this act with the line, "It's a dream." When a trapdoor opens and she disappears abruptly through the floor, Jenkins demonstrates metaphorically what can happen when we aren't thinking clearly about life, love, and our careers.

My only objection to this production was the reappearance of Nina and Treplev at the end of the play. Because Jenkins has Nina dancing with Treplev after he has shot himself, you are left wondering whether she has prevailed or even endured. Yet, the ambiguity of this last image was compelling. I had always thought that Nina's reentrance and speech at the end of Act Two, scene two, suggested that this young actress was not doomed like the rest of these characters. Then I remembered that this Nina had curiously punctuated the word *"all"* in her line, "all living things have come to a mournful end." Was she encouraging Treplev to end his life? Was she telling him that she would end hers? Jenkins's last image forced me to rethink what I thought about Nina's potential to grow and change. Does hard work and perseverance mean an artist will become successful, especially today? Or does this image suggest that caring about each other (love) is what will keep us from destroying each other? Jenkins left the conclusions up to the jury, the audience.

6

The Question of "Auteuring"

I don't think there is a style that is frozen in the play and you hack it out. It is just like reality—it changes depending upon when and who is looking at it. There is no absolute reality. Even naturalism is a style. A style is "the time" you're looking at, "the person" looking at it, "it" itself, "the time" it was read. So it is all these interactive things. Style is the basic language of the theatre. To find the one for this production, at this theatre, at this time, in this month, in this year, with this company, by this playwright, of this particular play, and written in this particular year is a layered process.[1]

—Zelda Fichandler

In no way do I intend to bring closure to the complex issue of play interpretation with this chapter. My overall intent when I began this study was to explore some of the ways professional artists work with a playscript in preparation for production. My inquiry stopped short of the theories and practices of radical "deconstructivism" in order to offer some perspective on the interpretive methods of artists who perceive the playscript though the prism of the dramaturgical theories and the theatrical practices of nineteenth- and twentieth-century modernism. Yet, in many ways it is difficult to determine what separates the modernist from the postmodernist, especially the modernist of the late twentieth century. For example, the metaphorical artist whose imagistic analysis often results in "reconceiving" the playscript is not that far removed from the interpretive practices attributed to the postmodernists who "deconstruct" the play. Whether artists "reconceive" or "deconstruct," they often raise the ire of those who believe the artist's role is to reproduce the playwright's intent and *not* to auteur the script. Therefore, one of the main concerns today is whether the production's conceptual weight overshadows the playscript. At this point, the issue of who authors the script has become an explosive and complicated matter; certainly, it is worthy of a far more detailed treatment than what can be offered in this study. The following, I hope, will stimulate further thought, inquiry, and scholarship, especially as it relates to the theories and practices of contemporary play production.

Provocative theatrical images that suggest something new about the play's poetic infrastructure attract the eye of the modernist. This artist, especially the contemporary metaphorical director or designer who has been part of, but not wed to, the cultural environment of postmodernism, champions an interpretation of playscripts that is devoted less to *mimesis* and reflection and more to the roles that temporality, subjectivity, collaboration, and informed imagination play in creative thought and practice. Currently, theatre artists who prefer to explore the poetic images within the playtext, rather than to create traditional works, are under attack by traditionalists because metaphorical productions give the impression, to some, that these artists have rewritten the play. Critics feel that their "radical" interpretive process borders on "authoring" the production, yet contemporary modernists claim that their metaphorical approach is meant to release or rediscover the playscript's impulses. Naturally the process is controversial; it raises issues of artistic arrogance, distortion, and self-indulgence. For these artists, theatrical interpretation is subject to multiple perceptions; therefore, it is not uncommon that they question the logic of an interpretive process that would attempt to determine either the playwright's intent or create an accurate historical representation of the play's world. A reading of a classic play, for example, that attempts to reveal something new or to rediscover more about its original impulses or cultural energy will more than likely be controversial, scorned by critics as an example of a production whose artists did not trust the author's work. Such an example is a production I discussed earlier in this book, Trinity Repertory Theatre's *Glass Menagerie*. Jenkins's "reconception," although it was innovative, was not without controversy. The reviews were mixed, and he met a certain degree of resistance. He mentions, "I heard one guy in the lobby exclaim: 'It says right in the script that it's their apartment in St. Louis! My God, I almost got up and walked out when I saw the set.'" Jenkins responds:

Of course I knew Williams's stage directions. But the next question you ask is "Oh, okay, they're not doing it that way. Why are they doing it this way? Let's see what they're doing." But you know you get a lot of resistance. It's like you're doing it only just to do it. Or you're doing it to be a pain in the ass. Or you're doing it for no good reason. I hope I am not doing it for no good reason. I think the worst kind of theatre in the world is the type that is done for no good reason.[2]

Nearly a century ago Chekhov remarked to Stanislavsky that theatre is art; it is not meant to be an actual depiction of life. In other words, what the audience sees on stage should not attempt to be a comfortable representation of reality whose predictability lulls us to sleep. Art invites reactions. By the end of the twentieth century, the interpretive artist finds that reproducing or mirroring the playwright's world on stage has little to offer a creative artist whose vision has been shaped by modernism. Furthermore, theatre in North America will be facing an audience in the twenty-first century who, unlike the gentleman in Jenkins's audience, will decipher images at an alarming rate. More than likely, this viewer will not immediately reject a production that disregards traditional interpretive practices such as finite meaning, representative dialogue, and a logical interaction of time, space, and action.

Anne Bogart's one-and-only season (1989-1990) as Trinity Repertory Theatre's artistic director was controversial and commercially unsuccessful. Her season alienated most of the theatre's long-standing audience. However, Bogart noticed that younger audience members were having little trouble deciphering her "deconstructed" version of Maxim Gorky's play *Summerfolk*:

There is a [party] scene...where you could hear one person starting a sentence and on the other side of the stage somebody is talking to somebody else, and then somebody starts [talking] over there, and everybody is sort of moving all at the same time. It's choreographed fairly complexly. It was unbelievable to watch. The older subscriber audiences couldn't follow it. They just couldn't begin to know what was going on, and they kind of gave up. Whereas, the younger audiences and high school kids had no problem. They reacted to and could follow every single part of it. They got all the jokes.[3]

Bogart presented the Providence, Rhode Island, audience with a season of "deconstructed" or nontraditional theatre featuring the director and designer as auteurs. The stage productions (adaptations and "deconstructed" versions of novels, classics, and modern plays) followed much of the innovative thought and practice that is associated with postmodernism.

In *Reimagining American Theatre*, Robert Brustein tells us that "the most controversial issue in the theatre today continues to be the reinterpretation or 'deconstruction' of celebrated classical plays by conceptual directors." He continues:

There is no theatrical activity that more inflames purist sensibilities in criticism and the academy—nothing that stimulates as many caustic generalizations about the debasements of modern culture. Perhaps because "deconstruction," as an assonant noun if not as a method, is so perilously close to "destruction" and "desecration," the standard purist posture is that of Switzers before the gates of the Vatican, defending sacred texts against the profanations of barbarians. The irony, in this contemporary war between the ancients and the moderns, is that both sides are really devoted to the same aesthetic purpose, which is the deeper penetration of significant dramatic literature. The difference is in the attitude.[4]

The "playwright-god" has been challenged by those theorists and artists who perceive the process of play interpretation as derivative and never ending. Essentially, the position of "playwright-god" diminished when the avant-garde theatre artists in the late 1960s and 1970s began to ask certain questions: 1. Is it possible to determine accurately the playwright's intention? 2. Does the playwright imitate (mirror) or reinterpret an action? 3. What role does subjectivity play in script analysis, especially in a world where the word has lost its representational value?[5] Because the hierarchy is no longer sacrosanct, the traditional interpretive process is suspect. For the postmodern "deconstructivist," the text holds no hidden singular meaning that, through analysis, is discovered and later revealed to the audience. Uncovering the play's theme implies order, closure, and fixed meaning, and these artists reject the possibility that any playscript has a singular truth or permanent phenomenon hidden within the text waiting to be discovered.

Although the playwright retains copyright, postmodern "deconstructivists," in particular, dispute the author's claim that the playtext is original. In his article, "Is Theatre under Deconstruction? A Retroactive Manifesto in a Language I Do Not Own," Stratos Constantinidis offers the following: "'Writing' is an endless process during which the 'author' becomes a 'reader' and the 'reader' becomes an 'author.' The exchange of roles between 'authors' and 'readers' subverts any original or final authority.... Each 'text' repeats 'texts' prior to it, and it does not express the intention of an individual author who poses as the origin of all meanings. Shakespeare's playtexts, for instance, re-write other 'texts.' In sum, all writing involves re-writing."[6]

If one accepts that playwrights present, through their texts, their subjective impressions of life, it follows that imitation is subject to the author's interpretation. Furthermore, as the play moves from playtext to rehearsal-text to performance-text, the script is constantly being rewritten by those who are affected by its world. Because playscripts are in a continual state of reinterpretation, meaning is, at best, subjective. On the issue of subjectivity, therefore, both the modernist of the late twentieth century and the postmodern "deconstructivist" share an interest in reconsidering the hierarchy associated with traditional interpretive practices. It is in the following areas, however, where the postmodernist clearly challenges the position of the modernist.

Directors, designers, and actors who "articulate sign-systems which re-present the playtext," "master space and time in rehearsal," and attempt to bring meaning, order, and closure to a playscript by making it "an organizing center of reference" are referred to by Constantinidis as *logocentric*:

Like the playwright who allegedly renders the universal *Logos* intelligible in a playtext, the director makes sure that the designers and actors render the playtext's *logos* intelligible in rehearsal and performance. The notion that this principle of structure and order (*logos* or *Logos*) transcends all "texts" ranks meanings to a primary, secondary, or tertiary status. The logocentrists believe that, by working backward and upward through the chain of "texts," they can arrive at the primary (original) meaning of the playwright (*logos*) or, of the divine universe (*Logos*), in an act of revelation. In other words, the logocentric director controls the creativity and expression of the designers and actors in the name of the playwright's *logos* or of the universal *Logos*. Logocentric theatre artists look backward, not forward.[7]

Thus, the "deconstructive" postmodernists would object to, for example, the early modernist theories and practices of Adolphe Appia, whose thoughts on "organic unity" suggest that the interpretive artist should locate the meaning the playwright had placed in the playscript and then find ways to represent that meaning on stage.

As I have mentioned throughout this book, theatre artists who favor the theories and practices of modernism cannot agree on any *one* way they approach or work with a playscript in preparation for production. One would think, then, that because the postmodernists dismiss many of the theories and practices of modernism, they would have nothing in common with the interpretive practices of modernism. There are, however, some similarities that deserve mentioning. The metaphorical position of today's modernist and postmodernist is, most likely, the result of artistic creative interactions and collaboration. Both interpretive camps feel most comfortable when the artist has an immediate connection with the play; both explore the play's images. Besides their imagistic work, both need to bring, in some way, the play forward in time. Historically outlining a particular period or specific space holds little value to interpretive artists whose relativistic perceptions result in theatrical images that either explore, from the contemporary modernists' point of view, the play's poetry or, as is the case in postmodernism, reject the possibility of consistent historical reference. The theatrical images of, for example, Robert Wilson's postmodern productions "quote history out of context to shatter conventional narrative."[8] Thus, an Appiaesque approach (the interdependence between artistic idea and production form) is no longer valid to any artist who views the act of interpretation as one that *presents*, not represents, the world of the play.

Postmodern "deconstructive" performance theories differ insofar as they clearly reject the organic, synthetic, structural organization that is associated with previous interpretive methods. Yet, their nontraditional productions involve artists who are dramaturgically literate. Not only do they know how to explore a playscript and playwright, but they are also capable of adroitly accessing, transmogrifying, and expressing on stage a broad spectrum of visual and aural theatrical images and metaphorical moments. "Deconstructing" a classic does not mean, therefore, that postmodernist artists will abandon the dramaturgical dig. Quite the contrary. Like the contemporary modernists, they are not interested in merely reproducing representational data. These artists mine the play's resources, searching for inspirational impulses that afford them the opportunity to expand the play's world. For example, Anne Bogart's "deconstructivist" productions reject most of what is associated with illusionistic representational theatre, yet she eagerly explores the playwright's world. She states, "As a director, it is my great joy and obligation to enter inside the playwright...to translate what that person saw into theatre metaphor."[9]

Plays that have a production history are especially inviting to the contemporary theatre artist who finds little interesting or creative about reproducing a historical replica of past productions. Briefly, these artists feel that a truthful representation of France in the eighteenth century or America in the post-Depression era is virtually impossible. Even with the best intentions, theatrical research is always processed subjectively; these artists hear and see yesterday in the context of today. Contemporary modernist and postmodernist theatre artists do agree, however, that if they research historical periods they are doing so with the intention of discovering what about the past is present today. They then explore theatrical ways in which to present their subjective perceptions. For example, their metaphorical work often produces commanding images that physicalize their perceptions about the play. Additionally an imagistic mise-en-scène, replete with metaphorical resonance, is one in which the director or designer works to encourage other perceptions about the playscript's cultural energy or poetry through a collection of metaphorical moments.

Therefore, contemporary artists will often dismiss the playwright's scenic descriptions in order to see the play anew. They may also look for ways to dismantle the play's logic or those icons that have for so many years defined and limited its meaning. When a playscript is not seen as a recipe, it challenges the artist to find something in its world that speaks to its audience today. For example, Anne Bogart struggles to discover, "Who needs the play now? For whom should this play be an exorcism?" She prefers to "shake" or "interrupt" the playscript "until something occurs, and something true emerges from the play," whereas the director Martha Clarke talks about "intuiting images."[10]

The process of "reconceiving" or "deconstructing" a playscript is generated by conceptual artists who find artistic pleasure in discovering why a playscript persists in being valuable, relevant, and great. "Texts develop fullness of being," Brustein notes, "only through the continuing intervention of collective minds." He continues, "They are not frozen in time, they are subject to continuing discovery, and each new production generates others in response. It is the proper role of theatre to let us look at plays through a variety of perspectives rather than in a single authorized form. It is also the function of criticism. Both act as prisms through which to view the limitless facets of great works of art."[11]

Like the postmodernists, the contemporary modernists find that their initial response to the world of the play is an imagistic one. When images form and commingle, they stimulate the artists' creative thought; and the actor, director, and designer sense something about the play's poetry. Imaging seduces the artists' creative spirit, encouraging them to participate in the interpretive act of "reimaging" the play's world. Because these artists use their research in creative and collective ways, it can stimulate further "reimaging" or can shape, focus, and clarify their initial momentary perceptions. In that sense, there is some crossover between contemporary modernism and postmodernism. But, unlike the postmodernist Robert Wilson, who often reshapes the play's world beyond recognition, the contemporary modernist, in general, does not rewrite the play. Instead, these artists mine the play's resources not in an attempt to discover how the playwright envisioned the production, but rather to encounter how the play's images reveal something new about the play's world.

Those who remain influenced by contemporary modernism differ from the postmodernists insofar as they continue to follow Stanislavsky's principles, especially his work with the super-objective, objective, and through line of action. Most look for the kernel of each scene and the play's "*zamissel.*"[12] Attention is paid also to recurring patterns (leitmotifs), especially as they relate to the play's images and ideas. Although these contemporary modernists rely on subjective perceptions concerning time and space when approaching a play for production, they test their immediate imagistic response against what they have discovered about the play's world (its internal structure and cultural history) to see if their initial response reveals something about the play's inner poetry.

Such a response or analysis, influenced by the ideas and practices of contemporary modernism, creates on stage a "sense of style" that is identifiable more often than not by a singular image or a collection of unified/metaphorical/presentational images. Because these artists "reimage" existing playscripts, they become more than interpreters in the traditional sense. However because they function as a cocreator, they give the impression, to some, that they are auteuring the playscript. A more correct assessment of the process would be that in "reconceiving" the play's world, these artists select poetic images in the script that suggest the timeless issues inherent in the human condition. For the contemporary modernist, therefore, the interpretive process does not involve a reconstruction of the play's world; instead, it embraces those images that encourage additional exploration, new perceptions, and further "reimaging." Therefore, the artist who is interested in viewing the playscript through the prism of contemporary modernism might take issue with those who think their intent is to order, bring closure to, or attach a specific meaning to the play's world. If a metaphorical interpretation suggests that the artist has in some ways authored the production, chances are they have done so, as Robert Brustein suggests, "to penetrate the mystery of a play in order to devise a poetic stage equivalent."[13] If truth is possible on stage, it becomes so because the interpretive artist has touched, for an instant, the soul of humanity through theatrical images that in some way seduce, suggest, and reverberate.

Notes

CHAPTER 1

1. Tom F. Driver, *Romantic Quest and Modern Query: A History of the Modern Theatre* (New York: Dell Publishing, A Delta Book, 1970), ix.

2. Martin Esslin, "Modernity and Drama," in *Modernism: Challenges and Perspectives*, ed. Monique Chefdor, Ricardo Quinones, and Albert Wachtel (Urbana: University of Illinois Press, 1986), 63.

3. The more common spelling of the word is "holistic." However, Merriam Webster's Collegiate Dictionary, 10th ed., recognizes *wholistic* as acceptable. As this study is interested in how the play's parts work together to create "a sense of the whole," *wholistic* is a better choice.

4. Stanley Trachtenberg, ed., *The Postmodern Moment: A Handbook of Contemporary Innovation in the Arts* (Westport, Conn.: Greenwood Press, 1985), xii.

5. Silvio Gaggi, *Modern/Postmodern: A Study in Twentieth-Century Arts and Ideas* (Philadelphia: University of Pennsylvania Press, 1989), 19.

6. The contemporary modernist approach to play analysis signals another shift in play interpretation. These artists find momentary imagistic perceptions so valuable they encourage continual imagistic exploration. Imagistic interpretations and metaphorical productions encourage the audience to discover, for example, what of the past is present today. Artistic "reconceptions" of classical playscripts should not be confused with deconstructivism. It is easier to accept the contemporary modernist's "reconception" because these interpretations do not carry the assumptions of deconstructivism.

7. Robert Brustein, *Reimagining American Theatre* (New York: Hill and Wang, 1991), 116. Brustein states, "Directors who are fond of similes assume that because a play's action is *like* something from a later period, its environment can be changed accordingly."

8. Ibid., 148.

9. See Richard Hornby, *Script into Performance: A Structuralist Approach* (Austin: University of Texas Press, 1977; paperback edition, New York: Paragon House Publishers, 1987), 21-25 (page citations are to the paperback edition). Hornby's *Script into Performance* is valuable for his argument concerning genre criticism and the creative process.

10. The actor/director/theorist Mikhail Chekhov was one of the first twentieth-century artists to clarify how the "psychology of style" is dependent upon the artistic synthesis of information with imagination. The synthetic process is referred to by Mikhail Chekhov as creating "a sense of the whole."

CHAPTER 2

1. Robert Brustein, interview by author, tape recording, Boston, Mass., 8 November 1990.

2. Henri Bergson, *Creative Evolution*, trans. Arthur Mitchell (New York: Random House, 1944), 344-45.

3. Arnold Aronson, "Postmodern Design," *Theatre Journal* 43, no. 1 (1991): 2.

4. Fredric Jameson, "Postmodernism and Consumer Society," in *Postmodernism and Its Discontents: Theories, Practices*, ed. E. Ann Kaplan (London: Verso, 1988), 17. Jameson claims modernism is a thing of the past, linked to a bygone age in which individualism, associated with competitive capitalism, the nuclear family, and the emerging bourgeoisie, was possible.

5. Although some plays and productions (burlesques like *Cyranose de Bric Brac* and musicals like *Dames at Sea, Little Mary Sunshine*, and *No, No, Nanette*) have done just this and have been commercially successful and stylistically sound, it is important to clarify that these pastiches had within their broad sense of production style an understanding of the period they were imitating and satirizing. Therefore, in that sense, these plays have within them a "sense of style" that is not insubstantial or incorrect.

6. See Michel Saint-Denis, *Theatre: The Rediscovery of Style* (New York: Theatre Arts Books, 1960), 67. Saint-Denis perceives style as part of the psychology of the play's construction. The psychology of the style implies the play's inner meaning, its heartbeat, or its significant reality.

7. William Fleming, *Arts and Ideas* (New York: Holt, Rinehart, Winston, 1963), 674.

8. Samuel Montefiore Waxman, *Antoine and the Théâtre-Libre* (1926; reprint, New York: Benjamin Blom, 1964), 16-17 (page citations are to the reprint edition).

9. Marvin Carlson, *Theories of the Theatre: A Historical and Critical Survey, from the Greeks to the Present* (Ithaca: Cornell University Press, 1984), 275.

10. Ibid., 278.

11. Emile Zola, *La Fortune des Rougon*, vol. 1 of *Les Rougon-Macquart*, ed. Henri Mitterand (Paris: Editions Fasquelle et Gallimard, Bibliothèque de la Pléiade, 1960), 3, quoted in William J. Berg and Laurey K. Martin, *Emile Zola Revisited* (New York: Twayne Publishers, 1992), 10.

12. Waxman, *Théâtre-Libre*, 20.

13. Ibid., 128-29.

14. Quoted ibid., 138.

15. Carlson, *Theories of the Theatre*, 277.

16. Waxman, *Théâtre-Libre*, 175.

17. See Marvin Carlson, *The German Stage in the Nineteenth Century* (Metuchen, N.J.: Scarecrow Press, 1972), 91-161.

18. John Osborne, *The Meiningen Court Theatre, 1866-1890* (Cambridge, England: Cambridge University Press, 1988), 160.

19. Ibid., 89.

20. Carlson, *German Stage*, 169.

21. Osborne, *Meiningen Court Theatre*, 161.

22. Ibid., 155.

23. Ibid., 165.

24. Ludwig Barnay, *Erinnerungen*, vol. 1 (Berlin: n.p., 1903), 276, quoted ibid., 163.

25. Osborne, *Meiningen Court Theatre*, 146.

26. Ibid., 146-48.

27. Oliver M. Sayler, *The Russian Theatre* (New York: Brentano's, 1922), 249.

28. Constantin Stanislavsky, *My Life in Art*, trans. J. J. Robbins (n.p.: Little, Brown and Company, 1924), 171.

29. Constantin Stanislavsky, *An Actor Prepares*, trans. Elizabeth Reynolds Hapgood (New York: Theatre Arts Books, 1948), 66.

30. Vladimir Nemirovich-Danchenko, *My Life in the Russian Theatre*, trans. John Cournos (n.p.: Little, Brown and Company, 1936; reprint, New York: Theatre Arts Books, 1968), 172 (page citation is to the reprint edition).

31. Fleming, *Arts and Ideas*, 697.

32. See Carlson, *German Stage*, 214-15.

33. Edward Gordon Craig, "The Artists of the Theatre of the Future," *The Mask* 1, 3, and 4 (May-June 1908): 58.

34. Carlson, *Theories of the Theatre*, 260.

35. David Magarshack's *Chekhov the Dramatist* (New York: Hill and Wang, 1960) is a valuable book for its thorough discussion of Chekhov's plays of direct and indirect action.

36. Nemirovich-Danchenko, *My Life in the Russian Theatre*, 160.

37. Henri Troyat, *Chekhov*, trans. Michael Henry Heim (France: Librairie Flammarion, 1984; reprint, New York: E. P. Dutton, 1986), 215 (page citation is to the reprint edition).

38. Anton Chekhov, *The Seagull*, trans. Michael Henry Heim (Woodstock, Ill.: The Dramatic Publishing Company, 1992), 22.

39. Michael Henry Heim, trans., *Anton Chekhov's Life and Thought: Selected Letters and Commentary* (n.p.: Harper and Row, 1973; reprint, Berkeley and Los Angeles: University of California Press, 1975), 277 (page citation is to the reprint edition).

40. David Magarshack, *Stanislavsky: A Life* (London: Macgibbon and Kee, 1950; reprint, Westport, Conn.: Greenwood Press, 1975), 183 (page citation is to the reprint edition).

41. S. D. Balukhaty, intro. and ed., *The Sea Gull Produced by Stanislavsky* (London: Dennis Dobson, 1952), 123.

42. Mikhail Chekhov, "Zhizn' i vstrechi" (Life and encounters), unpublished trans. Tony Hartman, *Novyi zhurnal* 9 (1944): 27-28.

43. Christine Edwards, *The Stanislavsky Heritage: Its Contribution to the Russian and American Theatre* (New York: New York University Press, 1965), 108.

44. Sonia Moore, *The Stanislavsky System: The Professional Training of an Actor* (1960; revised reprint, New York: Viking Press, 1966), 35 (page citation is to the reprint edition).

45. Adolphe Appia, *Music and the Art of the Theatre*, trans. Robert W. Corrigan and Mary Douglas Dirks (Coral Gables, Fla.: University of Miami Press, 1962), 83.

46. Edward Gordon Craig, *On the Art of the Theatre* (New York: Theatre Arts Books, 1956), 22.

47. Aronson, "Postmodern Design," 4.

48. Carl G. Jung, "Approaching the Unconscious," in *Man and His Symbols* (Garden City, N.Y.: Doubleday and Company, 1964), 20-21.

49. Craig, *On the Art of the Theatre*, 97.

50. Appia, *Music and the Art of the Theatre*, 10.

51. Stanislavsky, *My Life in Art*, 437.

52. Edward Braun, trans. and ed., *Meyerhold on Theatre* (New York: Hill and Wang, 1969), 25.

53. Vsevolod Meyerhold, "Inaugural Speech to the Company of the R.S.F.S.R.," in *Meyerhold on Theatre*, 170.

54. See *Meyerhold on Theatre*, 66.

55. See Norris Houghton, *Moscow Rehearsals: An Account of Methods of Production in the Soviet Theatre* (New York: Harcourt, Brace and Company, 1936; reprint, New York: Octagon Books, 1975), 100, for Meyerhold's use of *"jeu"* and *"jeux de théâtre"* (page citation is to the reprint edition). Houghton quotes Meyerhold's theory:

Two things are essential for a play's production.... First, we must find the thought of the author; then we must reveal that thought in a theatrical form. This form I call a *jeu de théâtre* and around it I shall build the performance.... In these three plays of Chekhov I have found that there are thirty-eight times when characters either faint, say they are going to faint, turn pale, clutch their hearts, or call for a glass of water; so I am going to take this idea of fainting and use it as a sort of leit-motif for the performance. Everything will contribute to this *jeu*.

56. Braun, *Meyerhold on Theatre*, 43.

57. Vsevolod Meyerhold, V. Bebutov, and Ivan Aksenov, *Amplua Aktëra* (Moscow: GVYTM, 1922), 2, quoted in Nikolai A. Gorchakov, *The Theatre in Soviet Russia*, trans. Edgar Lehrman (New York: Columbia University Press, 1957; reprint, Freeport, New York: Books for Libraries Press, 1972), 69 (page citation is to the reprint edition).

58. Vsevolod Meyerhold, "Balagan," *Liubov' k trëm apel'sinam*, no. 2 (1914), 28-29, quoted ibid.

59. Vsevolod Meyerhold, "Novye puti," *Rampa i zhizn'* (1911), quoted in Gorchakov, *Theatre in Soviet Russia*, 69.

60. Gorchakov, *Theatre in Soviet Russia*, 69.

61. Vsevolod Meyerhold, *O tèatr* (St. Petersburg: n.p., 1913), 149, quoted in James M. Symons, *Meyerhold's Theatre of the Grotesque: The Post-Revolutionary Productions, 1920-1932* (Coral Gables, Fla.: University of Miami Press, 1971), 120.

62. Symons, *Meyerhold's Theatre of the Grotesque*, 116.

63. Ibid., 111.

64. Braun, *Meyerhold on Theatre*, 49.

65. "Meyerhold o svoyom *Lese*," in *Novy Zritel* no. 7 (Moscow, 1924): 6, quoted ibid., 190.

66. Braun, *Meyerhold on Theatre*, 52-53.

67. Meyerhold's dynamic method of movement, "biomechanics," was not like the static practices of his symbolic period. Instead, this was a form of theatre that was less dependent on inspiration and mysticism and more interested in the effects of the mechanics of the human body. In his article, "Meyerhold's Production of *The Magnificent Cuckold*," Nick Worrall adds: "His experiments with new techniques of acting...can be seen to relate to the Futurist emphasis on a technology of artistic 'production' harnessed to the verb as 'engine.'...The 'engine' analogy can be traced through the theories of 'motor' reflexology in William James and Pavlov." (Nick Worrall, "Meyerhold's Production of *The Magnificent Cuckold*," *The Drama Review* 17, no. 1 (1973): 15.

68. Symons, *Meyerhold's Theatre of the Grotesque*, 114.

69. Gorchakov, *Theatre in Soviet Russia*, 207.

70. "Meyerhold Speaks," in *Pages from Tarusa: New Voices in Russian Writing*, ed. Andrew Field (Boston: Little, Brown and Company, 1964), 317.

71. Symons, *Meyerhold's Theatre of the Grotesque*, 155.

72. See ibid., 106.

73. "Meyerhold Speaks," 317.

74. See Symons, *Meyerhold's Theatre of the Grotesque*, 154.

75. Gorchakov, *Theatre in Soviet Russia*, 214.

76. Alexy A. Gvozdyev, *Teatr imeni Vsevolod Meyerhold, 1920-1926* (Leningrad: Akademiya, 1927), 52, quoted in Symons, *Meyerhold's Theatre of the Grotesque*, 159.

77. P. A. Markov, "The First Studio: Sullerzhitsky, Vakhtangov, Chekhov," trans. Mark Schmidt (Group Theatre, 1934), 13, Billy Rose Theatre Collection, New York Library of Performing Arts.

78. Ibid., 22.

79. Ibid., 30.

80. Ibid., 48.

81. Ibid., 46.

82. Ibid., 51.

83. Ibid., 49-50.

84. See Gorchakov, *Theatre of Soviet Russia*, 436.

85. Markov, "The First Studio," 51-52.

86. See Nancy Kindelan, "A Solution for Children's Theatre: Michael Chekhov's 'Psychology of Style,'" *Children's Theatre Review* 34, no. 2 (1985): 7-12, and "Beyond Realism: Michael Chekhov's Contribution to Style," *Theatre IN Sight* 2, no. 1 (1990): 29-32.

87. Markov, "The First Studio," 68-72.

88. Kindelan, "A Solution for Children's Theatre," 9.

89. Markov, "The First Studio," 68.

90. Beatrice Straight and Deirdre Hurst Du Prey, interview by author, tape recording, New York, N.Y., November 1976.

91. Michael Chekhov, "To the Actor" (unpublished 1942 version), 189-90, Michael Chekhov Papers, Deirdre Hurst du Prey Collection, Westbury, New York.

92. Ibid., 286.

93. Ibid., 192.

94. John Willett, trans. and ed., *Brecht on Theatre: The Development of an Aesthetic* (New York: Hill and Wang, 1964,), 143-44.

95. Ibid., 42.

96. Carlson, *Theories of the Theatre*, 384.

97. Willett, *Brecht on Theatre*, 96-97.

98. Ibid., 58.

99. "Dialogue: Berliner Ensemble," *The Drama Review* 12, no. 1 (1967): 115.

100. Carl Weber, "Brecht as Director," *The Drama Review* 12, no. 1 (1967): 105.

101. "Dialogue: Berliner Ensemble," 115.

102. Ibid., 116.

103. Ibid., 113.

104. Willett, 95.

105. Weber, "Brecht as Director," 104.

106. "Dialogue: Berliner Ensemble," 117.

107. Richard Hornby, *Script into Performance: A Structuralist Approach* (Austin: University of Texas Press, 1977; New York: Paragon House Publishers, 1987), 50 (page citation is to the paperback edition).

108. Weber, "Brecht as Director," 104.

109. Ibid., 103.

110. Ibid., 104.

111. Antonin Artaud, *The Theatre and Its Double*, trans. Mary Caroline Richards (New York: Grove Press, 1958), 70.

112. Ibid.

113. Ibid., 54.

114. Ibid., 75.

115. Ibid., 31-32.

116. Ibid., 54.

117. Ibid., 27.

118. Ibid., 24.

119. Ibid., 37.

120. Tyrone Guthrie, "Directing a Play" in *The Director in a Changing Theatre: Essays on Theory and Practice, with New Plays for Performance*, ed. J. Robert Wills (Palo Alto: Mayfield, 1976), 89.

121. Peter Brook, *The Shifting Point 1946-1987* (New York: Harper and Row, 1987, Perennial Library, 1989), 3 (page citation is to the paperback edition).

122. Peter Brook, *The Empty Space* (New York: Avon, 1968; reprint edition, Discus, 1969), 108 (page citation is to the reprint edition).

123. Brook, *Shifting Point*, 43.

124. Ibid., 236.

CHAPTER 3

1. Lester Polakov, interview by author, tape recording, New York, N.Y., 29 October 1990. As with each interview in this chapter, subsequent quotations in the text refer to the original citation. Lester Polakov is a visual artist, teacher, and scenic designer who resides in New York City.

2. Richard Jenkins, interview by author, tape recording, Providence, R.I., 15 November 1992. Richard Jenkins is an actor and former Artistic Director of the Trinity Repertory Theatre, Providence.

3. Zelda Fichandler, interview by author, tape recording, New York, N.Y., 14 November 1990. Zelda Fichandler is one of the founding Artistic Directors of the Arena Stage, Washington, D.C., and is currently the Artistic Director of the graduate acting program at New York University in New York City.

4. Thomas Skelton, telephone interview by author, tape recording, Boston, Mass., 6 October 1990. The late Thomas Skelton was a lighting designer, as well as a professor of design at the Yale School of Drama, New Haven, Conn.

5. Shirley Knight, telephone interview by author, tape recording, Boston, Mass., 9 February 1991. Shirley Knight performs in regional theatre, film, and television.

6. Mark Lamos, interview by author, tape recording, Hartford, Conn., 31 August 1991. Mark Lamos is an actor and currently the Artistic Director for the Hartford Stage Company in Hartford.

7. Robert Morgan, interview by author, tape recording, Boston, Mass., 19 September 1990. Robert Morgan is a costume designer and past Director of the Theatre Division, School for the Arts at Boston University.

8. Robert Brustein, interview by author, tape recording, Cambridge, Mass., 8 November 1990. Robert Brustein is currently the Artistic Director at the American Repertory Theatre in Cambridge.

9. Tori Haring-Smith, interview by author, tape recording, Providence, R.I., 11 December 1992. Tori-Haring Smith is the Dramaturg at the Trinity Repertory Theatre and a professor at Brown University in Providence.

10. Ming Cho Lee, interview by author, tape recording, New York, N.Y., 30 October 1990. Ming Cho Lee is a scenic designer and professor of design at Yale School of Drama, New Haven, Conn.

11. Arden Fingerhut, interview by author, tape recording, Williamstown, Mass., 11 October 1990. The late Arden Fingerhut was a lighting designer as well as the Chair of the theatre program at Williams College in Williamstown.

12. Olympia Dukakis, interview by author, tape recording, Providence, R.I., 3 January 1992. Olympia Dukakis is a Broadway and regional theatre actress who also works in film and television.

13. Jon Jory, interview by author, tape recording, Louisville, Ky., 16 March 1992. Jon Jory is the Artistic Director at the Actors Theatre of Louisville.

14. Douglas Wager, interview by author, tape recording, Washington, D.C., 10 June 1991. Douglas Wager is an Artistic Director at the Arena Stage in Washington.

15. Jane Greenwood, interview by author, tape recording, New York, N.Y., 20 January 1991. Jane Greenwood is a costume designer and a professor of design at Yale School of Drama, New Haven, Conn.

CHAPTER 4

1. Arthur Bartow, *The Director's Voice* (New York: Theatre Communications Group, 1988), 117.

2. Ibid., 116.

3. John Dewey, *How We Think: A Restatement of the Relation of Reflective Thinking to the Educative Process* (Boston, Mass.: D. C. Heath, 1933), 96.

4. Fred Alan Wolf, *Taking the Quantum Leap: The New Physics for Nonscientists* (San Francisco: Harper and Row, 1981), 79-85.

5. Amit Goswami, "Creativity and the Quantum Theory," *The Journal of Creative Behavior* 22, no.1 (1988): 17-18.

6. Wolf, *Taking the Quantum Leap*, 169-75.

7. Alistair Martin-Smith, "Quantum Drama: Beyond Time and Space" (paper presented at the Ontario Institute for Studies in Education, International Drama Education Research Symposium, Toronto, Canada, May 1989), 11.

8. Wolf, *Taking the Quantum Leap*, 128.

9. Ibid., 123.

10. Ibid., 131.

11. Ibid., 139.

12. Ibid., 184.

13. Max Jammer, *The Philosophy of Quantum Mechanics: The Interpretations of Quantum Mechanics in Historical Perspective* (New York: John Wiley and Sons, 1974), 44.

14. Wolf, *Taking the Quantum Leap*, 184-86.

15. Susanne K. Langer, *Feeling and Form* (New York: Charles Scribner's Sons, 1953), 240-21.

16. Ibid., 314.

17. Ibid., 307.

18. Ibid., 315.

19. Harry S. Broudy, *The Role of Imagery in Learning* (Los Angeles, Calif.: Getty Center for Education in the Arts, 1987), 21.

20. Langer, *Feeling and Form*, 28.

21. Ibid., 253.

22. Ibid., 254.

23. Broudy, *Role of Imagery in Learning*, 49.

24. Anton Chekhov, *The Seagull*, trans. Michael Henry Heim (Woodstock, Ill.: Dramatic Publishing Company, 1992), 5. Subsequent page references will be made in the text.

25. Timo Tiusanen, *O'Neill's Scenic Images* (Princeton: Princeton University Press, 1968), 12.

26. Langer, *Feeling and Form*, 313.

27. Henrik Ibsen, *A Doll House*, trans. Rolf Fjelde, in *Henrik Ibsen: The Complete Major Prose Plays* (New York: New American Library, 1978), 150.

28. Tiusanen, *O'Neill's Scenic Images*, 16.

29. Ibid., 16.

30. Francis Fergusson, *The Idea of a Theater* (Princeton: Princeton University Press, 1949; paperback edition, 1968), 230 (page citation is to the paperback edition).

31. Robert Morgan, interview by author, tape recording, Boston, Mass., 19 September 1990.

32. Zelda Fichandler, interview by author, tape recording, New York, N.Y., 14 November 1990.

33. Jay L. Halio, *Understanding Shakespeare's Plays in Performance* (New York: St. Martin's Press, 1988), 81.

34. Gerald F. Else, *Aristotle's Poetics: The Argument* (Cambridge, Mass.: Harvard University Press, 1963), 322.

35. All references are to book and section in *Aristotle's Poetics*, trans. S. H. Butcher (New York: Hill and Wang, 1961).

36. Marvin Carlson, *Theories of the Theatre: A Historical and Critical Survey, from the Greeks to the Present* (Ithaca: Cornell University Press, 1984), 17.

37. Jane Greenwood, interview by author, tape recording, New York, N.Y., 20 January 1991.

38. Zelda Fichandler, interview, 1990.

39. Robert Morgan, interview, 1990.

40. Jon Jory, interview by author, tape recording, Louisville, Ky., 16 March 1992.

41. *Aristotle's Poetics*, 28.

42. Richard Hornby, *Script into Performance: A Structuralist Approach* (Austin: University of Texas, 1977; New York: Paragon House Publishers, 1987), 10 (page citation is to the paperback edition).

43. Ibid., 27-32.

44. Ibid., 110.

45. Ibid., 32.

46. Ibid., 24.

47. Ibid., 44.

48. Ibid., 25.

49. Ibid., 27.

50. Lester Polakov, interview by author, tape recording, New York, N.Y., 29 October 1990.

51. Robert Morgan, interview, 1990.

52. Thomas Skelton, telephone interview with author, tape recording, 6 October 1990.

53. Arthur Bartow, *Director's Voice*, 115.

54. Hornby, *Script into Performance*, 120.

55. Ibid., 15-16.

56. Ibid., 28.

57. Ibid., 11.

58. Ibid., 117.

59. Ibid., 29.

60. Ibid., 20-21.

61. See Robert Brustein, *Reimagining American Theatre* (New York: Hill and Wang, 1991), 115-21.

62. Hornby, *Script into Performance*, 38.

63. Gaetano Kanizsa, "Gestalt Psychology: What It Is Not," in *Organization in Vision: Essays on Gestalt Perception* (New York: Praeger, 1979), 56.

64. Hornby, *Script into Performance*, 38-39.

65. Howard Gardner, *The Mind's New Science: A History of the Cognitive Revolution* (New York: Basic Books, 1985), 113.

66. Noel McInnis, "Gestalt Ecology: How Do We Create Our Space?" in *Emergent Man: His Chances, Problems and Potentials*, ed. Julius Stulman and Ervin Laszlo (New York: Gordon and Breach, 1973), 76.

67. Ibid., 77.

68. Brustein, *Reimagining American Theatre*, 288.

69. Ibid., 281.
70. Ibid., 292.
71. Ibid., 284.

CHAPTER 5

1. Ronald Bryden, "Chekhov: Secret of *The Seagull*" (n.p., n.d.), 15, Anton Chekhov Clipping File, Billy Rose Theatre Collection, New York Public Library of Performing Arts.

2. Olympia Dukakis, interview by author, tape recording, Providence, R.I., 4 December 1991.

3. Richard Jenkins, interview by author, tape recording, Providence, R.I., 15 November 1992.

4. Tori Haring-Smith, interview by author, tape recording, Providence, R.I., 11 December 1992.

5. Douglas Wager, interview by author, tape recording, Washington, D.C., 10 June 1991.

6. Michael Henry Heim, trans., *Anton Chekhov's Life and Thought: Selected Letters and Commentary*, (n.p.: Harper and Row, 1973; reprint, Berkeley and Los Angeles: University of California Press, 1975), 277 (page citation is to the reprint edition).

7. Quoted in John Lahr, "Chekhov and Impressionism," 2, Anton Chekhov File, Billy Rose Theatre Collection, New York Public Library of Performing Arts.

8. Ronald Bryden, "Chekhov: Secret of *The Seagull*," 15.

9. Quoted in Henri Troyat, *Chekhov*, trans. Michael Henry Heim (New York: E. P. Dutton, 1986), 78.

10. Anton Chekhov, *The Seagull*, trans. Michael Henry Heim (Woodstock, Ill.: Dramatic Publishing Company, 1992), 8-9. Subsequent page references will be made in the text.

11. *Anton Chekhov's Life and Thought*, 117. (Letter to Alexei Suvorin.)

12. Clarification of the source of this line is revealed in Heim's translation of *The Seagull*. See Charles Gounod, *Faust: Opera in Four Acts* by Michel Carre and Jules Barbier, English version by Ruth and Thomas Martin, *G. Schirmer's Collection of Opera Librettos* (New York: G. Schirmer, 1966), 7.

13. John Lahr, "Chekhov and Impressionism," 3.

14. Thomas G. Winner, "Chekhov's *Seagull* and Shakespeare's *Hamlet:* A Study of a Dramatic Device," *The American Slavic and East European Review* 15, no. 1 (1956): 111.

15. Thomas G. Winner, *Chekhov and His Prose* (New York: Holt, Rinehart and Winston, 1966), 116-17.

16. The line "She loves me, she loves me not" is found in *The Seagull* (9) and is said by Treplev to Sorin in reference to his mother's love for him. In Gounod's *Faust*, Marguerite repeats a similar line with one minor change—the "she" is replaced by "he." In the opera, the recitation ends on a more optimistic note, whereas Treplev ends with "she loves me not." This inversion foreshadows Treplev's failure. The whimsical and capricious nature behind Treplev's action also satirizes his mother fixation. See Gounod, *Faust*, 7-14.

17. For further commentary on Chekhov's use of romanticism, landscapes (nature), music, and the supernatural, see Joseph L. Conrad, "Vestiges of Romantic Gardens and Folklore Devils in Chekhov's 'Verochka,' 'The Kiss,' and 'The Black Monk,'" in *Critical Essays on Anton Chekhov*, ed. Thomas A. Eekman (Boston: G. K. Hall, 1989), 78-91.

18. Laurence Senelick, "Chekhov's Drama, Maeterlinck, and the Russian Symbolists," in *Chekhov's Great Plays: A Critical Anthology*, ed. Jean-Pierre Barricelli (New York: New York University Press, 1981), 164-65.

19. Robert Louis Jackson, *Chekhov: A Collection of Critical Essays* (Englewood Cliffs, N. J.: Prentice-Hall, 1967), 12.

20. Victor Emeljanow, *Chekhov: The Critical Heritage* (London: Routledge, 1981), 82.

21. Lev Shestov, "Creation from Nothing," in *Essays in Russian Literature*, ed. Spencer E. Roberts (Athens, Ohio: Ohio University Press, 1968), 222.

22. Donald Rayfield, *Chekhov: The Evolution of His Art* (New York: Harper and Row, Barnes and Noble Import Division, 1975), 204.

23. "Anton Chekhov's *The Seagull*: First Rehearsal Remarks by Douglas C. Wager—April 9, 1991," *On Stage at Arena Stage* 2 (summer 1991): 1, 5.

24. Wager, interview, 1991. Subsequent quotations refer to this citation.

25. Quoted in Pauline Bentley, "Chekhov: Contract with Conscience," in *The UNESCO Courier*, no. 1 (1960): 11, Anton Chekhov Clipping File, Billy Rose Theatre Collection, New York Public Library of Performing Arts.

26. Ibid., 5.

27. Troyat, *Chekhov*, 62.

28. See David Magarshack, *Chekhov the Dramatist* (New York: Hill and Wang, 1960), 14.

29. Troyat, *Chekhov*, 178.

30. *Anton Chekhov's Life and Thought*, 243.

31. Ibid., 285.

CHAPTER 6

1. Zelda Fichandler, interview by author, tape recording, New York, N.Y., 14 November 1990.

2. Richard Jenkins, interview by author, tape recording, Providence, R.I., 15 November 1992.

3. Anne Bogart, Conference Participant, Tisch School of the Arts, Design Symposium, New York University, comments at N.Y.U., New York, N.Y., 19-20 January 1991.

4. Robert Brustein, *Reimagining American Theatre* (New York: Hill and Wang, 1991), 115.

5. See Michel Foucault, *The Order of Things: An Archaeology of the Human Sciences* (New York: Random House, Pantheon Books, 1970), 304. There are numerous recent publications that illuminate the issue of auteuring. The Stratos E. Constantinidis article that I cite in this chapter is very helpful. In addition, I would suggest Roland Barthes, *Image, Music, Text*, trans. Stephen Heath (New York: Farrar, Straus and Giroux, Noonday Press, 1977); Michel Foucault, "What Is an Author?" in

Textual Strategies: Perspectives in Post-Structuralist Criticism, ed. J. V. Harari (Ithaca: Cornell University Press, 1979), 141-60.

6. Stratos E. Constantinidis, "Is Theatre under Deconstruction? A Retroactive Manifesto in a Language I Do Not Own," *Journal of Dramatic Theory and Criticism* 4 (Fall 1989): 41.

7. Ibid., 42-43.

8. Katherine Arens, "Robert Wilson: Is Postmodern Performance Possible?" *Theatre Journal* 43, no. 1 (1991): 15.

9. Bogart, Design Symposium.

10. Both Anne Bogart and Martha Clarke were participants in the 1991 Design Symposium, Tisch School of the Arts.

11. Brustein, *Reimagining American Theatre*, 120.

12. See Chapter 4.

13. Brustein, *Reimagining American Theatre*, 116.

Selected Bibliography

Anton Chekhov Clipping File. Articles. Billy Rose Theatre Collection, New York Public Library of Performing Arts.

Anton Chekhov's Life and Thought: Selected Letters and Commentary. Edited by Michael Henry Heim in collaboration with Simon Karlinsky. N.p.: Harper and Row, 1973. Reprint, Berkeley and Los Angeles: University of California Press, 1975.

Appia, Adolphe. *Music and the Art of the Theatre*. Translated by Robert W. Corrigan and Mary Douglas Dirks. Coral Gables, Fla.: University of Miami Press, 1962.

Arens, Katherine. "Robert Wilson: Is Postmodern Performance Possible?" *Theatre Journal* 43, no. 1 (1991): 15.

Aristotle. *Aristotle's Poetics*. Translated by S. H. Butcher. New York: Hill and Wang, 1961.

Aronson, Arnold. "Postmodern Design." *Theatre Journal* 43, no. 1 (1991): 2.

Artaud, Antonin. *The Theatre and Its Double*. Translated by Mary Caroline Richards. New York: Grove Press, 1958.

Balukhaty, S. D., intro. and ed. *The Sea Gull Produced by Stanislavsky*. London: Dennis Dobson, 1952.

Barnay, Ludwig. *Erinnerungen*, 276. Vol. 1. Berlin: n.p., 1903. Quoted in John Osborne, *The Meiningen Court Theatre, 1866-1890* (Cambridge, England: Cambridge University Press, 1988), 163.

Barry, Jackson G. *Dramatic Structure: The Shaping of Experience*. Berkeley and Los Angeles: University of California Press, 1970.

Barthes, Roland. *Image, Music, Text*. Translated by Stephen Heath. New York: Farrar, Straus and Giroux, Noonday Press, 1977.

Bartow, Arthur. *The Director's Voice*. New York: Theatre Communications Group, 1988.

Beckerman, Bernard. *Dynamics of Drama: Theory and Method of Analysis*. New York: Knopf, 1970.

Bergson, Henri. *Creative Evolution*. Translated by Arthur Mitchell. New York: Random House, 1944.

Brecht on Theatre: The Development of an Aesthetic. Translated and edited by John Willett. New York: Hill and Wang, 1964.

Brook, Peter. *The Empty Space.* New York: Avon, 1968. Reprint, Discus, 1969.

————. *The Shifting Point 1946-1987.* New York: Harper and Row, 1987, Perennial Library, 1989.

Broudy, Harry S. *The Role of Imagery in Learning.* Los Angeles, Calif.: The Getty Center for Education in the Arts, 1987.

Brustein, Robert. *Reimagining American Theatre.* New York: Hill and Wang, 1991.

Carlson, Marvin. *The German Stage in the Nineteenth Century.* Metuchen, N.J.: Scarecrow Press, 1972.

————. *Theories of the Theatre: A Historical and Critical Survey, from the Greeks to the Present.* Ithaca: Cornell University Press, 1984.

Chekhov, Anton. *The Seagull.* Translated by Michael Henry Heim. Woodstock, Ill.: Dramatic Publishing Company, 1992.

Chekhov, Mikhail. "Zhizn' i vstrechi" (Life and encounters). Unpublished translation by Tony Hartman. *Novyi zhurnal* 9 (1944): 27-28.

Chekhov Papers. Deirdre Hurst du Prey Collection. Westbury, New York.

Conrad, Joseph L. "Vestiges of Romantic Gardens and Folklore Devils in Chekhov's 'Verochka,' 'The Kiss,' and 'The Black Monk.'" In *Critical Essays on Anton Chekhov,* edited by Thomas A. Eekman. Boston: G. K. Hall, 1989.

Constantinidis, Stratos E. "Is Theatre under Deconstruction? A Retroactive Manifesto in a Language I Do Not Own." *Journal of Dramatic Theory and Criticism* 4 (Fall 1989): 41.

Craig, Edward Gordon. "The Artists of the Theatre of the Future." *The Mask* 1, 3 & 4 (May-June 1908): 58.

————. *On the Art of the Theatre.* New York: Theatre Arts Books, 1956.

Dewey, John. *How We Think: A Restatement of the Relation of Reflective Thinking to the Educative Process.* Boston, Mass.: D. C. Heath, 1933.

"Dialogue: Berliner Ensemble," *The Drama Review* 12, no. 1 (1967): 115.

Driver, Thomas F. *Romantic Quest and Modern Query: A History of the Modern Theatre.* New York: Dell Publishing, A Delta Book, 1970.

Edwards, Christine. *The Stanislavsky Heritage: Its Contribution to the Russian and American Theatre.* New York: New York University Press, 1965.

Else, Gerald F. *Aristotle's Poetics: The Argument.* Cambridge, Mass.: Harvard University Press, 1963.

Emeljanow, Victor. *Chekhov: The Critical Heritage.* London: Routledge, 1981.

Esslin, Martin. "Modernity and Drama." In *Modernism: Challenges and Perspectives,* edited by Monique Chefdor, Ricardo Quinones, and Albert Wachtel. Urbana: University of Illinois Press, 1986.

Fergusson, Francis. *The Idea of a Theater.* Princeton: Princeton University Press, 1949; paperback edition, 1968.

Fleming, William. *Arts and Ideas.* New York: Holt, Rinehart, Winston, 1963.

Foucault, Michel. *The Order of Things: An Archaeology of the Human Sciences.* New York: Random House, Pantheon Books, 1970.

————. "What Is an Author?" In *Textual Strategies: Perspectives in Post-Structuralist Criticism,* edited by J. V. Harari. Ithaca: Cornell University Press, 1979.

Gaggi, Silvio. *Modern/Postmodern: A Study in Twentieth-Century Arts and Ideas.* Philadelphia: University of Pennsylvania Press, 1989.

Gardner, Howard. *The Mind's New Science: A History of the Cognitive Revolution.* New York: Basic Books, 1985.

Gorchakov, Nikolai A. *The Theatre in Soviet Russia.* Translated by Edgar Lehrman. New York: Columbia University Press, 1957; Freeport, New York: Books for Libraries Press, 1972.

Goswami, Amit. "Creativity and the Quantum Theory." *The Journal of Creative Behavior* 22, no. 1 (1988): 17-18.

Gounod, Charles. *Faust: Opera in Four Acts* by Michel Carre and Jules Barbier. English version by Ruth and Thomas Martin. G. *Schirmer's Collection of Opera Librettos.* New York: G. Schirmer, 1966.

Guthrie, Tyrone. "Directing a play." In *The Director in a Changing Theatre: Essays on Theory and Practice, with New Plays for Performance,* edited by J. Robert Wills. Palo Alto: Mayfield, 1976.

Gvozdyev, Alexy A. *Teatr imeni Vsevolod Meyerhold, 1920-1926,* 52. Leningrad: Akademiya, 1927. Quoted in Symons, *Meyerhold's Theatre of the Grotesque: The Post-Revolutionary Productions, 1920-1932.* Coral Gables, Fla.: University of Miami Press, 1971, 159.

Halio, Jay L. *Understanding Shakespeare's Plays in Performance.* New York: St. Martin's Press, 1988.

Hornby, Richard. *Script into Performance: A Structuralist Approach.* Austin: University of Texas Press, 1977. Paperback edition, New York: Paragon House Publishers, 1987.

Houghton, Norris. *Moscow Rehearsals: An Account of Methods of Production in the Soviet Theatre.* New York: Harcourt, Brace and Company, 1936. Reprint, New York: Octagon Books, 1975.

Ibsen, Henrik. *A Doll House.* In *Henrik Ibsen: The Complete Major Prose Plays,* translated by Rolf Fjelde. New York: New American Library, 1978.

Jackson, Robert Louis. *Chekhov: A Collection of Critical Essays.* Englewood Cliffs, N. J.: Prentice-Hall, 1967.

Jameson, Fredric. "Postmodernism and Consumer Society." In *Postmodernism and Its Discontents: Theories, Practices,* edited by E. Ann Kaplan. London: Verso, 1988.

Jammer, Max. *The Philosophy of Quantum Mechanics: The Interpretations of Quantum Mechanics in Historical Perspective.* New York: John Wiley and Sons, 1974.

Jung, Carl G. "Approaching the Unconscious." In *Man and His Symbols.* Garden City, N. Y.: Doubleday and Company, 1964.

Kanizsa, Gaetano. "Gestalt Psychology: What It Is Not." In *Organization in Vision: Essays on Gestalt Perception.* New York: Praeger, 1979.

Kindelan, Nancy. "Beyond Realism: Michael Chekhov's Contribution to Style." *Theatre IN Sight* 2, no. 1 (1990): 29-32.

———. "Imaging *The Seagull*'s Faustian Leitmotif." *New England Theatre Journal* 4 (Spring 1993): 39-48.

———. "Seeing *The Seagull* Again." *New England Theatre Journal* 4 (Spring 1993): 128-31.

———. "A Solution for Children's Theatre: Michael Chekhov's 'Psychology of Style.'" *Children's Theatre Review* 34, no. 2 (1985): 7-12.

Langer, Susanne K. *Feeling and Form.* New York: Charles Scribner's Sons, 1953.

Magarshack, David. *Chekhov the Dramatist.* New York: Hill and Wang, 1960.

――――. *Stanislavsky: A Life.* London: Macgibbon and Kee, 1950. Reprint, Westport, Conn.: Greenwood Press, 1975.

Markov, P. A. "The First Studio: Sullerzhitsky, Vakhtangov, Chekhov." Translated by Mark Schmidt. Group Theatre, 1934, 13. Billy Rose Theatre Collection, New York Library of Performing Arts.

Martin-Smith, Alistair. "Quantum Drama: Beyond Time and Space." Paper presented at the Ontario Institute for Studies in Education, International Drama Education Research Symposium, Toronto, Canada, May 1989.

McInnis, Noel. "Gestalt Ecology: How Do We Create Our Space?" In *Emergent Man: His Chances, Problems and Potentials,* edited by Julius Stulman and Ervin Laszlo. New York: Gordon and Breach, 1973.

Meyerhold, Vsevolod. "Balagan." *Liubov' k trëm apel'sinam* no. 2 (1914): 28-29. Quoted in Nikolai A. Gorchakov, *The Theatre in Soviet Russia,* translated by Edgar Lehrman, 69. New York: Columbia University Press, 1957.

――――. "Meyerhold o svoyom *Lese." Novy Zritel* no. 7 (Moscow, 1924): 6. Quoted in *Meyerhold on Theatre,* translated by Edward Braun, 190. New York: Hill and Wang, 1969.

――――. *Meyerhold on Theatre.* Translated and edited by Edward Braun. New York: Hill and Wang, 1969.

――――. "Meyerhold Speaks." In *Pages from Tarusa: New Voices in Russian Writing,* edited by Andrew Field. Boston: Little, Brown and Company, 1964.

――――. "Novye puti." *Rampa i zhizn'* (1911). Quoted in Nikolai A. Gorchakov, *The Theatre in Soviet Russia,* translated by Edgar Lehrman, 69. New York: Columbia University Press, 1957.

――――. *O tèatr,* 149. St. Petersburg: N.p.: 1913. Quoted in James M. Symons, *Meyerhold's Theatre of the Grotesque: The Post-Revolutionary Productions, 1920-1932.* Coral Gables, Fla.: University of Miami Press, 1971, 120.

Meyerhold, Vsevolod, V. Bebutov, and Ivan Aksenov. *Amplua Aktëra,* 2. Moscow: GVYTM, 1922. Quoted in Nikolai A. Gorchakov, *The Theatre in Soviet Russia,* translated by Edgar Lehrman, 69. New York: Columbia University Press, 1957.

Moore, Sonia. *The Stanislavsky System: The Professional Training of an Actor.* 1960. Revised reprint, New York: Viking Press, 1966.

Nemirovich-Danchenko, Vladimir. *My Life in the Russian Theatre.* Translated by John Cournos. N.p.: Little, Brown and Company, 1936. Reprint, New York: Theatre Arts Books, 1968.

Osborne, John. *The Meiningen Court Theatre, 1866-1890.* Cambridge, England: Cambridge University Press, 1988.

Rayfield, Donald. *Chekhov: The Evolution of His Art.* New York: Harper and Row, Barnes and Noble Import Division, 1975.

Saint-Denis, Michel. *Theatre: The Rediscovery of Style.* New York: Theatre Arts Books, 1960.

Sayler, Oliver M. *The Russian Theatre.* New York: Brentano's, 1922.

Senelick, Laurence. "Chekhov's Drama, Maeterlinck, and the Russian Symbolists." In *Chekhov's Great Plays: A Critical Anthology,* edited by Jean-Pierre Baricelli. New York: New York University Press, 1981.

Shestov, Lev. "Creation from Nothing." In *Essays in Russian Literature,* edited by Spencer E. Roberts. Athens, Ohio: Ohio University Press, 1968.

Stanislavsky, Constantin. *An Actor Prepares.* Translated by Elizabeth Reynolds Hapgood. New York: Theatre Arts Books, 1948.

———. *My Life in Art.* Translated by J. J. Robbins. N.p.: Little, Brown and Company, 1924.

Styan. J. L. *The Elements of Drama.* London: Cambridge University Press, 1960.

———. *Drama, Stage and Audience.* London: Cambridge University Press, 1975.

Symons, James M. *Meyerhold's Theatre of the Grotesque: The Post-Revolutionary Productions, 1920-1932.* Coral Gables, Fla.: University of Miami Press, 1971.

Tiusanen, Timo. *O'Neill's Scenic Images.* Princeton: Princeton University Press, 1968.

Trachtenberg, Stanley, ed. *The Postmodern Moment: A Handbook of Contemporary Innovation in the Arts.* Westport, Conn.: Greenwood Press, 1985.

Troyat, Henri. *Chekhov.* Translated by Michael Henry Heim. France: Librairie Flammarion, 1984. Reprint, New York: E. P. Dutton, 1986.

Wager, Douglas C. "Anton Chekhov's *The Seagull:* First Rehearsal Remarks by Douglas C. Wager—April 9, 1991." *On Stage at Arena Stage* 2 (Summer 1991): 1, 5.

Waxman, Samuel Montefiore. *Antoine and the Théâtre-Libre.* 1926. Reprint, New York: Benjamin Blom, 1964.

Weber, Carl. "Brecht as Director." *The Drama Review* 12, no. 1 (1967): 105.

Winner, Thomas G. *Chekhov and His Prose.* New York: Holt, Rinehart and Winston, 1966.

———. "Chekhov's *Seagull* and Shakespeare's *Hamlet:* A Study of a Dramatic Device." *The American Slavic and East European Review* 15, no. 1 (1956): 111.

Wolf, Fred Alan. *Taking the Quantum Leap: The New Physics for Nonscientists.* San Francisco: Harper and Row, 1981.

Worrall, Nick. "Meyerhold's Production of *The Magnificent Cuckold.*" *The Drama Review* 17, no. 1 (1973): 15.

Zola, Emile. *La Fortune des Rougon.* Vol. 1, *Les Rougon-Macquart,* 3, edited by Henri Mitterand. Paris: Editions Fasquelle et Gallimard, Bibliothèque de la Pléiade, 1960-67. Quoted in William J. Berg and Laurey K. Martin, *Emile Zola Revisited,* 10. New York: Twayne Publishers, 1992.

Index

About the Author

Nancy Kindelan is Associate Professor of Theatre at Northeastern University. She directs in academic and professional theatres throughout the New England area. Her scholarship has appeared in the *Journal of Dramatic Theory and Criticism, New England Theatre Journal*, and *American Theatre Companies,* as well as other publications.

ISBN 0-313-29736-3

90000>

EAN

9 780313 297366

HARDCOVER BAR CODE